FIERCE OPTIMISM

FIERCE OPTIMISM

Seven Secrets for Playing
Nice and Winning Big

LEEZA GIBBONS

DEY ST.
AN IMPRINT OF WILLIAM MORROW PUBLISHERS

DEY ST.

HarperCollins
PUBLISHERS
Since 1817

FIERCE OPTIMISM. Copyright © 2016 by Shooting Star, Inc. All rights reserved. Printed in the United States of America. No part of this book may be used or reproduced in any manner whatsoever without written permission except in the case of brief quotations embodied in critical articles and reviews. For information address HarperCollins Publishers, 195 Broadway, New York, NY 10007.

HarperCollins books may be purchased for educational, business, or sales promotional use. For information please e-mail the Special Markets Department at SPsales@harpercollins.com.

A hardcover edition of this book was published in 2016 by Dey Street Books, an imprint of William Morrow Publishers.

FIRST DEY STREET BOOKS PAPERBACK EDITION PUBLISHED 2017.

Library of Congress Cataloging-in-Publication Data has been applied for.

ISBN 978-0-06-243253-7

17 18 19 20 21 DIX/RRD 10 9 8 7 6 5 4 3 2 1

To Steven,
whose optimistic heart saw mine and gave it a home.

To my children,
who are my reason for seeing everything
sunny-side up.

To my father,
whose positive lens through which he views life
has never been out of focus.

And

to all those who believe in the strength of nice
and that the pursuit of optimism is always worth the effort.

CONTENTS

INTRODUCTION

We are in an unsettling time right now. Most of us are feeling uncertain about our futures—politically, financially, environmentally—and maybe even downright worried. The loudest, brashest voices have become the fearmongers who are using their bully pulpits to convince others that it's a mean world, and only those who are willing to respond in kind will win. We have seen a growing trend in our culture toward a way of thinking that not only tolerates but also promotes this kind of negative, mean-spirited behavior, which could turn the most hopeful among us into naysayers.

And so I can understand why you might look at me with a raised eyebrow and think: *Really? You're going to write a book about optimism, now?!* Yes, now. In fact, there has never been a better time. This is not the moment to allow the floodwaters of negativity to wash us away from the place of hope, and faith, and high ideals for ourselves and others. Rather, it's time for us to band together *against* negativity and fear. What could be a better rallying cry than Fierce Optimism? But let me be clear. I'm not talking about wishful thinking, or even the power of positive thinking. I'm talking about an idea that most content, successful people already know: optimism is a proven strategy for success that is scientifically quantifiable and easily applicable in both your professional and personal lives. It works.

After more than thirty years in Hollywood, I've seen a lot, and I've developed some survival tactics. At the top of the list is my optimism, which has been crucial for creating the life of my dreams and getting me closer to being the person I want to be. And if it can work for me, here, it can work for you, there, no matter what you're dealing with or how you've been getting by up until now. Let me share with you how I came by my ferocity, and my optimism, as well as the other strategies that have served me well.

My life comes with some great perks. One of the cool things about my job is that I've been asked to appear on many game and competition shows over the years, from *Hollywood Squares* and *Pyramid* to *Don't Forget the Lyrics* and *Dancing with the Stars*. Being a "Go big or go home" kinda girl, and a perennial optimist who always expects the best, I'm usually all in. But when I was contacted about competing on *Celebrity Apprentice,* I thought: *Seriously? Me? Take on a team of celebrities hardwired for drama? I'm way too boring to be on that show.*

It's true. I have a master's in drama avoidance. But I'm also as competitive as Donald Trump himself. The difference is, I don't think Trump has ever met a controversy or conflict he didn't like. That is the environment in which he thrives, and for him it seems the higher the stakes, the more thrilling the gamble. I may be much more understated than he is (well, seriously, who isn't?), but we share some of the same beliefs and have many similar ways of doing things.

Actually, I think there's a lot we can all learn from Trump. Early in his campaign, his team had a board at the front of the room where they managed his candidacy, which said, "Let Trump be Trump." There it is, a useful message for all of us: we do best when we are one hundred percent exactly who we are. That's where your strength and your power are, as well as your best chance to win. Trump owns this, and then some. In an interview with the *Wall Street Journal* he said, "People think of me as not necessarily being nice but being competent. In a CNN poll, I was last in niceness. Enough with the niceness!"

Obviously, that works for him, but for me, nice is a part of who I am. It's how I was brought up. Mr. Trump even said it was how I won *Celebrity Apprentice,* by leading "with kindness." Again, we all win not by copying others but by simply being ourselves. This is a lesson I've been mastering over many years now. But it *still* took all of my optimism to face down my fears and to agree to test out this theory on Trump's show.

I was immediately tempted to rise to the *Celebrity Apprentice* test, because that's how I've always lived my life, but this was Donald Trump's boardroom, a venue so threatening, even the meanest girls and toughest guys had been reduced to tears, pouting, backstabbing, and tantrums. I knew I could do the work, but could I still be me while taking the heat? Could

I play it my way—nice and easy—with my positivity dialed up to the max? Did I even want to? They needed an answer in a few days; the cast was all set except for this one last slot. If I said yes, I'd be on a plane in forty-eight hours, headed from Los Angeles to Trump Tower in New York.

My husband, Steven, is not only the love of my life, but he also runs our business. He was the one who'd originally fielded the call inquiring if I'd be interested in competing on the show. Having had more than twenty years of experience managing talent (from Charlie Sheen to Arsenio Hall), he knows what works, and has guided game-changing decisions for many stars. As my business partner, my husband, and best friend, I value his opinion. From the get-go, Steven was convinced I should do it, and that I could win. Even my kids encouraged me to go for it.

"I don't know, honey," I said skeptically to Steven. "What if I break down?"

"You won't."

Steven knows me well enough to give me the space I need for my self-doubt. I usually talk myself out of it in a few minutes. After a brief, strategic pause, he played the best card in his hand.

"You know, sweetheart, this can be a real game changer for your charity," he said. "That's more than enough incentive to get you to the winner's circle."

Bam! There it was. *I hate it when he does that.*

I was backed up against my own passion and staring right at my purpose.

But if there's one thing I've learned about getting ahead, it's this: you won't get anywhere without doing your homework, and then preparing yourself some more.

I told everyone to put a pin in their persuasive pushing, while I tried to binge-watch a season's worth of episodes on YouTube. I've always been a fan of the show, but I'd never watched it as someone who might have to walk into that lion's den.

My first thought: *OMG.*

Not only did I not have enough sexy outfits to rock the boardroom with the other women, I didn't think I could possibly trash-talk my way through thirteen episodes. By the time I clicked through to view the finale, I was out of breath and out of time. I had to make a decision, now. Then, on that final show, I watched the heartwarming features describing the celebrity contestants' nonprofit affiliations and the major money the winner could earn to make a difference. That was the most conclusive incentive for me, ever. I was in.

By the time I'd agreed, I was ready to win. After all, I already ran my own business, which was full of entrepreneurial risks. I'd created budgets, developed and sold products, written and produced radio and TV shows, and managed a staff of hundreds. I was accustomed to being in front of a camera on live shows with large audiences. *Yep, I can take this on,* I thought with increasing confidence.

Aside from my family, though, no one else seemed to think I had a prayer. Before we'd shot a single task, on the first day of our press tour, one of the journalists gave me a skeptical look and a warning.

"The other contestants have you pegged as the first one out," she said. "They think you're going home the first week."

"Why?" I said, genuinely dumbfounded.

"Because nice girls don't go very far in this game," she said. "Look, it's already started. Put your guard up."

"Meaning what?" I asked.

"Just watch your back," she said. "The game has already begun."

I hadn't even met the other contestants yet, and they'd already counted me out.

That was exactly the challenge I needed, and it forced me to ask myself a serious question: *How nice can I be and still come out ahead?*

This thought was immediately followed by a sense of deep certainty, the kind that comes from having fought long and hard to find my place in the world. *What else can I do? Trying to be nice is what I know. It's my true north, my personal operating system. It's not like I'm going to turn into somebody else to win a title on a TV show.*

I plunged forward, now determined not only to win, but also to do so with a strategy no more complicated than simply being myself. I surveyed the qualities I'd always relied on in my nearly four-decade career in one of the most competitive fields imaginable, as well as my experience running a production company and a nonprofit organization devoted to supporting family caregivers of those with chronic illness and disease. I came up with seven strategies that had always served me well: self-worth, focus, resilience, empathy, loyalty, forgiveness, and most important, optimism. Once I had my arsenal of positivity in place, I was determined to stay in my lane and draw on these strengths, no matter what kind of negativity and aggression came my way. It wasn't easy. That's for sure.

You can decide for yourself whether you think I'm full of it or not. But I hope my business credentials speak for themselves. I traveled around the world on assignment during my sixteen years as a host and reporter on *Entertainment Tonight*. For seven years I kept it cool in front of the camera during every kind of technology and wardrobe malfunction imaginable while hosting my own show. I've been lucky enough to receive recognition that means a lot to me, including an Emmy, a star on the Hollywood Walk of Fame, and credit as a *New York Times* bestselling author. I'm the CEO of my own company, which includes production, product development, and marketing arms, along with doing the thing I love best, storytelling, through hosting, appearances, and speeches. When I created Leeza's Care Connection to support family caregivers I was called a social entrepreneur. (My mother would be so proud that I'm finally "tooting my own horn"!) But I think I was just being a daughter honoring my promise to my mom to try to make a difference. I've gone through divorces and raised incredible kids. All of which has made me strong. I'm not a pushover, and I'm not afraid of a challenge. Okay, fair enough, but *Celebrity Apprentice* was definitely among the toughest trials of my life. It was also among the most important. As I dug deep to face each task, trying to resist the manipulation, backbiting, and sheer nastiness that sometimes seem to erupt out of nowhere on the show, I began to reassess what it really means to be nice, and what it really takes to be optimistic.

Here's what I know: positivity as a worldview can be employed strategically and effectively. If that's true, then why is it that in business it can be viewed as a character flaw, or something that makes you an ineffectual weakling? And in our personal lives, why can it easily be dismissed as pie-in-the-sky, delusional thinking?

Nice is not your mother's four-letter word. I'm talking about the *new* nice. The real definition of personal and professional success is to be kind and generous to everyone who crosses your path while standing your ground and being impeccable with your integrity. Niceness requires much more than smiling and allowing others to talk first. It demands more than keeping your cool and being generous with praise. It's more than making other people feel good and saying please and thank you. I believe in all of those things, sure. But more than that, I believe *nice* is such an important tool for business and life that it needs to be given a better seat at the power table. As does optimism. I think these two qualities go hand in hand, and some of our most powerful competitors already know it. Many of the biggest success stories out there have these underrated elements at their core. So why don't we all accept that being a good person doesn't mean being bad at business, or boundaries, or any of life's most challenging (and rewarding) areas?

After I won *Celebrity Apprentice,* I got lots of notes, posts, and emails, everything from those who said they'd known from the first week that I'd win, to others who were as incredulous as

Trump himself that I'd actually pulled it off. I was enormously gratified by the support and encouragement from the many who said, "You kept it classy. You played it just the way I would have." Or, "My daughter is twelve and watched every episode. Finally, I could show her a female role model in business who doesn't scream and yell and play dirty."

As lovely as that was to hear, it broke my heart to realize a female success story with integrity was a headline. (By the way, I believe there were other women—and men—on the show who stood for that, too. This isn't a way of succeeding that I pulled out of a hat. I've known plenty of men and women who have inspired me, and who have become wildly successful without sabotaging anyone else. Isn't it about outdistancing, outperforming, and outdelivering? Isn't that what gets the gold? Unfortunately, not according to many people these days. In fact, I'd come to realize, the notion of "outclassing your competition," or simply trying harder, had at some point been relegated to the list of things as anachronistic and outdated as a Rolodex.

But I knew from personal experience that, in business and in life, nice girls really can finish first. Many thought I'd just had a chance to prove it in an international forum on *Celebrity Apprentice*. All I know is I maintained my positivity and belief in myself in the face of some intense competition (and drama) from my opponents. So now what? I decided to own it and embrace a new cause: The New Nice fueled by Fierce Optimism. If nice needs a rehab, which it clearly does, I'm your girl!

Look, I'm a reporter by training. I've had a bird's-eye view of many trends and fads and movements over the years. And from where I stand, there is much evidence to show that, on a parallel track to the mean-spirited crossfires we see on TV, and the venom of those whose keyboard courage makes them feel entitled to bully and bash others on social media, is a steady stream of people who are civil, tolerant, polite, compassionate, and caring. Instead of sinking to the depths of bad behavior, they're continually elevating those around them with their positivity and optimism. And guess what? It's paying off. Ask Spanx founder Sara Blakely, whose optimism built a billion-dollar company. Or Amy Schumer, who was optimistic enough about her ability to create the career she now has that she dared to walk away from high-paying opportunities until her personal stock rose, never doubting that it would.

I'm not exactly sure when it began to happen, but optimism is undergoing a makeover, and it's on the way to a new, powerful persona. More than just hoping for the best, or seeing the glass half-full through rose-colored glasses, it's now time to own the glass and recognize the rise of Fierce Optimism as a major player. The kind that fuels the bottom line in business and claims the top spot in your family. Give yourself permission to believe in possibilities. It truly is the cornerstone of success. And it's a powerful antidote to those who are trying to push us in the direction of negativity and fear. We all get to choose. What side do you want to be on?

I didn't create this movement. I'm not the Pied Piper of Positivity. But I heard it when Donald Trump said, "Leeza, you led with kindness. I don't see these people in New York.

I see brutal, brutal killers. I don't meet people like you." I figured it was time for me to take on the mantle of niceness and optimism. I do this to pay respect to my parents, who taught me; to celebrate my mentors, who lit my path; and to do my part to represent the old-fashioned values that have helped me (and so many others) build a career that lasts. Consider this a throwback guide, if you will. A look back at the things that have allowed me to look ahead.

I loved Sheryl Sandberg's book *Lean In,* which created a furor by laying out some hard truths about why women don't hold more leadership roles and giving them advice about how to take more power. Now, I think we have to do more than that. We have to lean in, raise our hand, stand our ground, and claim our optimism as a strong, effective strategy for winning. It's what my mom called "I will" being stronger than IQ.

Maybe you're rolling your eyes right now. And I get it. I really do. I mean, seriously, who writes a book about being nice and optimistic, especially now? How optimistic can you really be? I'm sure there are plenty of people in my professional— and personal—life who would love to be the first to recount a time when I was negative, or bitter, or just plain bitchy, like everybody else. Or those who think I'm just naïve and don't see things realistically, particularly given the stressors many of us are currently facing. Just like in real life, in Hollywood there's no magic wand or CGI special effect to make heartache or disappointment go away. I had to develop real coping mechanisms to deal with the challenges I faced, and these tools can be useful in any and all walks of life. Having done a lot of living so far, I've come out on the other end with the hopeful (if not revolutionary) assessment that we're more similar than we are different, and that we can all learn from each other and help each other along the way.

I know that, by holding my story up as an example, I'm opening myself up for people to judge my life and my behavior. But the thing is, people are going to do that anyway! So I offer it up to you. I've learned most of these strategies the hard way. Sometimes I got it wrong, and I really fell on my face. But I kept getting up, and eventually I got myself to the life of my dreams. I know in every fiber of my being, you can, too. My goal was to get real in this book, to confess to moments where I don't come off so great, or I could have obviously done better, or I was afraid, because I truly believe we have to let our mistakes teach us, and sincerely forgive ourselves, in order to move on. By reporting back from the front lines with what I learned about doing better, I'm hoping you can see areas in your own growth where you might have played it differently or you might play it differently yet. Not to sound like a political candidate, but in the past year we've lived through some dark times in this country and in the world at large. We have felt vulnerable, and uncertain, and sometimes afraid. That's all the more reason why we should come together and support each other to find our strengths. And let optimism be the great unifier.

If you're reading this you probably already know a thing or two about optimism, and I hope this will be a pat on the back. If not, and you want to sustain success, walk through these pages and see what I mean.

We only become powerful by giving ourselves over to the journey of our lives, and then looking back at our path with honesty and forgiveness. My quest here was to examine my life, loves, losses, parenting experiences, and more to see what worked, and what could have maybe gone a little better. I love my life, which includes my work and family, and I've arrived at this place—and done okay for myself—by being nice and by looking on the bright side. That's where real strength lives. That's what has worked for me, and it can work for you, too. Read on.

CHAPTER ONE

Sorry Is As Sorry Does (Self-Worth)

I f I could come back as anyone, it would be Beyoncé.

Along with the births of my children, getting my star on the Hollywood Walk of Fame, and my wedding to the love of my life, Steven, one of my all-time best moments was when the queen of pop complimented my purposely over-the-top hairdo backstage at an event by saying, "Your hair is fierce."

As much as I've made my career on being the sweet southern girl next door, known for heartfelt interviews with celebrities, cultural icons, and regular folks with important stories to tell, my closest friends have also described me as a wannabe drag queen. Okay, I can own that! There is a part of me that's always wanted to be unapologetically larger than life, to make a statement, and to take up space.

Not that I've acted on these desires. After all, I'm not

Beyoncé, now am I? And I maintain that competing on *Dancing with the Stars* was the biggest professional challenge of my life. Dance Floor Diva I am not. In fact, in the forty years I've been at it, I've never been any good at pulling off any kind of diva act. Instead, I've kept returning to the things that worked for me: preparation, accountability, highlighters, file folders, coffee, Altoids, and always expecting the best from others and from myself.

Oh, and a new take on self-confidence that doesn't look anything like those old, outdated ideals we once had, where those on top were bullies who clung to a claim of their own infallibility even when the evidence was clearly against them. I've seen a lot of people lately—some famous, and some not—playing it in a humbler, kinder (or quieter) way and succeeding big.

Sometimes failing gracefully is actually where the power resides. I was so impressed by the guts it took for Blake Lively to close her online venture, Preserve. Rather than denying that her company wasn't working, she took a deep breath, honestly assessed the situation, and acknowledged that folding was the best way to ensure future success by controlling how she eventually reenters the marketplace. As she showed, there is strength in saying, "This isn't working." That's when you pivot, learn a new approach, and come back better. It's not dissimilar from choosing to leave a marriage or a toxic friendship.

Please don't confuse this technique with quitting. It's about acknowledging something is wrong that can't be fixed and owning what comes next. The potential power of such moments is so strong that if played well enough, they will give you the energy and motivation to create a much better outcome than if you'd denied reality and stayed the course. That's having a healthy sense of your own self-worth!

What's tricky, though, is that it's often easier to cultivate and maintain self-worth in the areas where we're already strong, and tougher for us when we're dealing with matters that are more challenging. This was definitely the case for me. But that's why we get up every day and keep on trying, again and again.

I'm lucky. I was raised to know my strengths—and my self-worth—and to focus on developing what I was good at until I could be great, rather than trying to be someone I'm not. My parents, the ultimate optimism role models, gave me such a great, positive foundation in life, which equaled a confidence that everything would be okay, no matter what happened. My mother never hesitated to tell me, "Don't be too big for your britches," while at the same time reminding me, "It's a poor frog who doesn't praise his own pond."

I got off track plenty of times along the way, but even through a series of moves from my home state of South Carolina to Dallas, New York City, and Los Angeles, in search of career success and personal fulfillment, I never lost my sense of who I was and what mattered to me. (I never lost my glossy pink nails and lips, for that matter; some things are nonnegotiable.) I may have been secure enough about making it someday, but I just couldn't get there fast enough. When I was starting out, I'd often worry that I wasn't achieving, learning, or growing enough. I mean, I'm the girl who raced through college, skipping graduation so I could just get on with it. Although "it" has always seemed just out of reach, my strong sense of self-worth meant that if I did the work, set my goals, and buckled myself in, I had a pretty good shot at making things happen. See, I've always run on optimism, no matter how much I've had to prove myself or how many setbacks I've faced. Not so much as a strategy, but more as a worldview that I've held from the get-go.

Embarrassed about my ambitions or dreams? Not me. I never apologized for the lengths I had to go to make them happen. When my inspiration, Barbara Walters, made headlines in 1976 for being the first female anchor on network nightly news (making more money than the men!) I said, "That's for me! I'm gonna make a million dollars in the broadcast business, too." At the time I was a freshman journalism major at the University of South Carolina, and my classmates were quick to shut me down.

"Listen to yourself," they said with the southern accents we all had. "You're from Irmo, South Carolina. What's gotten into you? You can't do that."

I didn't make any excuses for aiming high, and I didn't let their negativity deflate my sense of self-worth. I just kept moving forward without apology or hesitation.

Can we please all just take the memo to stop apologizing for daring to ask a question, disagree, or even just breathe the oxygen! Look at comedian Amy Schumer's "I'm Sorry" skit, which struck such a nerve that it went viral in a nanosecond. Along with the rest of the world, I love Amy because of her no-excuses approach. She's created a version of herself that she is totally comfortable with, and everybody else can just deal.

I think her skit about apologizing would have worked coming from anyone, but maybe it's even more powerful because it's a commentary by someone for whom the message is antithetical. I mean it's not a new assessment, is it? It's familiar, this all-too-true depiction of the lengths to which women feel the need to apologize for, well, everything, including the space they take up in the world. The sketch earned (uneasy, knowing) laughs and inspired write-ups in the *New York Times* and the *Huffington Post*. And I get why. I do. It's all about who we are and how others see us.

Something amazing happens when people are given the opportunity to own their life without apologizing for who they are and how they do things. In my years spent interviewing people, often about the most sensitive subjects, I've found that we all have a fundamental need just to be seen, to know we have value, as a way to reinforce our self-worth. I've tried to honor that with everyone I've sat down with in front of a camera, as well as with my coworkers and kids, and others whose lives have crossed my path. Because I've seen this fundamental human truth in action so many times, I want to encourage you to own it, too. You really can play it your way and win at work and life. No excuses. No apologies. To ourselves, or anyone else. Amy Schumer–style.

Amy is like, "This is who I am, take it or leave it." She loves her body, her friends, and her job, and she's channeled this confidence into hot-ticket status. Even before she was über-hot, she played like she was. Several years ago, she accepted a million-dollar book deal, only to walk away, saying she thought she could earn more down the road. And yes, a million cool ones is good, but eight million a few years later is even better. How's that for some fierce optimism *and* some unapologetic self-worth? She knew her value. She stood her ground. She got paid. Big-time.

I know boldness like that doesn't come naturally to all of us, but it can definitely be acquired. The first step to getting where you want is deciding that you can no longer stay where you are. I think most people who have been on the journey more than a minute get to that pivot point pretty soon. The problem is, the path we choose for ourselves is often confusing and full of challenges, and doesn't unfold as we expected. And so we give up, we settle, we become pessimistic. We start disappearing from our own lives for no other reason than it's convenient to fall in line with the direction we're given. We see others playing small, apologizing for their opinions, or being nasty to their colleagues, and we feel tempted to mimic that behavior. That's just what can happen when we spend time with people who are curmudgeonly, negative, rude, or abrasive. But when the example set for you is this shabby, maybe you have to break up with yourself and learn how to rebuild from the ground up.

Okay, even if you're up for the challenge, where do you start? I know it might seem hard, but the strategies for reclaiming your authentic self aren't classified info. We all have access to tools that can help us to be who we want to be, taking responsibility for our choices and having pride in everything we've gone through along the way. I've been lucky to have known some of this from the start, but there are plenty of lessons I definitely had to learn on the fly. Let me share some of them with you now.

"NO, I WILL *NOT* SHOW YOU MINE"

I've learned that most everything in life is a negotiation. I'm a middle child, between my big brother, Carlos, and little sister, Cammy, so working things out just comes with the territory. My parents always said I was a natural negotiator, but they never knew about this: my first negotiation was pretty high stakes, even if the setting was the South Carolina woods, not a big-city boardroom.

I was ten or eleven at the time, and I was staying with my mom's sister, my aunt Wayne. (Yes, that's really her name; you gotta give my family points for originality.) I often stayed with her when my parents traveled for my dad's job as head of the state's education association. I loved visiting my aunt Wayne because she and my uncle Jimmy ran a general store and no matter what kind of candy I wanted, or how much candy I wanted, Aunt Wayne would always ring it up as costing a nickel. I'd walk out of there with a big bag, all my own, knowing that I was the most special kid on earth. Just to put a cherry (and sprinkles) on top of how much I loved it there, the most magical person on earth, my granny, lived with my aunt Wayne. I stayed with them in Summerton, South Carolina, a lot, enough that I was close to my cousins and their friends, and we were always running off together on one adventure or another.

On this particular occasion, the local boys were building a fort in the woods behind Aunt Wayne's house and they invited me to check it out. I was a bit of a tomboy myself and figured I could build a better secret hideaway than most of those boys, but I was intrigued. It wasn't much of a fort, truth be told, just some old lumber they'd found, balanced between a couple of trees, but they were as proud of themselves as could be, showing me all of the fort's special features.

One of the older boys, a fat, awkward kid with pimples and high-tops, suddenly turned and gave me the once-over.

"Hey, Leeza, we'll take down our pants and show you ours if you'll show us yours," he said. And then, seeing I was blank-faced, he added, "We'll give you twenty-five cents."

"What?" I asked, too stunned to say more.

"Yeah," he said, unbuckling his pants. "We'll give you twenty-five cents. For a look."

Then they stared me down, waiting to see what I'd do.

"Oh, give her fifty cents," said the leader's sidekick.

I snapped out of my shocked inertia, returning to the world around me, the hot, humid air against my skin, gnats buzzing around my eyes and these boys with their hands on their zippers.

"No," I said. "I will *not* show you mine, and I'm gonna go tell Granny."

That was a bigger threat than calling the cops, and they knew it.

"Forget it," the leader said, trying to backpedal his way out of any trouble.

With that, I turned and ran through the woods, making a beeline right for Aunt Wayne's house, but I never did tell Granny or anyone else. In fact, I never spoke of that moment, until now. But it stayed with me, and not in the way you might think. It wasn't that it was a traumatic experience—I knew the boys didn't mean me any harm, and I wasn't really scared—but it became an important lesson for me. Right then and there, I knew I had the power to say no, and with that knowledge came an understanding of the great force contained in that one little word.

I also knew I could probably have gotten their price up higher. I mean, after all, they doubled their offer without any prompting from me! That's a lesson I've gone on to use a lot in negotiating throughout my broadcast career! Keep your mouth shut until you see where they're going to go next.

I wasn't about to show those boys anything, and ironically, I felt more of a sense of personal power than anything else when it was over. But, still, it was a valuable moment in my life. In a very real sense, that was the first business proposition I ever had to face, and it really did teach me that the power you possess in any negotiation is the power to say no; but you can't do it if you don't value yourself. It's a lesson that stuck with me, and came in handy many times over the years, as you'll see in the pages of this book. All thanks to the MBA I received in the woods behind my aunt Wayne's house.

Years later, as I stepped into the professional world, I did well by my "ruffle the feathers, but don't turn over the applecart" mentality from the South. (Southerners use niceness as though we invented it. My mother used to say, "Honey, you can step all over him without ever messing up the shine on his shoes.")

PUT ME IN, COACH

I didn't choose the entertainment business. I guess you could say it chose me. It helped that I had the self-worth to believe in my vision even when almost no one else did.

My first job after I graduated from the University of South Carolina's journalism program was as a news reporter for WSPA in Greenville-Spartanburg, South Carolina. My mom always thought knowing how to work your southern charm was a birthright, and I saw how correct she was when I started working at Channel 7. I had become friends with our intern, Annie, when we were downtown on a shoot with one of our news photographers, Maxie Ruth, an African American veteran of the station, who was ex-military and a former police officer. No one messed with Maxie. He intimidated many on our staff because he was plugged into the tristate area we covered and had all of the contacts. But Grits Girls know how to work it, and so I knew I had to get in good with Maxie.

He called Annie and me his "blond-headed babies" and on this hot day in downtown Greenville-Spartanburg, he wasn't happy with me. I was dressed all cute, like Reporter Barbie, in a pair of pink patent leather Candies shoes, those slides that had a stiff wood platform and no back to them.

"Get those G-D shoes off and pick up the tripod," Maxie said with a disapproving look as I struggled to keep up in my platforms.

Without hesitation, I whipped 'em off, handed them to Annie, and grabbed the tripod so we could keep going. I wasn't necessarily embarrassed, but I got the message: Don't hold up production for anything as silly as shoes. And pitch in to carry your weight. Once the action slowed down, I thanked Maxie for teaching me the unspoken rules of how to behave in the field and, after that, I sought his advice on everything! Annie later told me that, having watched me value what Maxie had to offer and charm him into sharing it with me, she knew I could do the same in Trump's boardroom on *Celebrity Apprentice.*

After my victory, she said, "I knew you were raised by a strong southern woman to be a churchgoin', family-lovin', football-cheerin', sorority-smile-wearin' good girl. Southern women can cut off their nuts and make 'em think you did 'em a favor!"

Well, my mom and Maxie taught me a lot, but none of their wisdom could save me in the studio at WSPA. I hosted what they called cut-ins, which were these five-minute news segments we had to write, produce, and edit ourselves—like a one-man band of journalism. I went on air to anchor and intro the stories at the top of the hour.

I was hardworking and capable, but this part of my job was an epic fail. Back then I was issued a Canon Scoopic film camera, which meant we actually had to use a magnet to erase any audio we didn't want to include in the piece. There was no undo or back button or any other way to reclaim the deleted section. I routinely erased the wrong audio when I was editing my film strip, which meant the sound bites from the people I'd interviewed made no sense. On top of that, I *really* didn't have it together on the air and would frequently dump out of the segment two minutes early, while a frantic stage manager stood just beyond the camera's lens, motioning for me to stretch out the material. I never improvised or even looked up at the camera. Struck numb with panic, I just shuffled the papers on my desk while the music ran in a constant loop until we could rejoin the national programming at the top of the hour. It's amazing that our news director, Harvey Cox, allowed me to come back after the first of these disasters.

Working for *Eyewitness News* was a great gig, though. As the new "girl reporter," I covered all kinds of drama, from loose mountain lions to burst water mains. I was fresh out of school, and this was not a bad trajectory for a new graduate. But I was never satisfied. I desperately wanted to be a success, to be *something*. Lily Tomlin joked, "All my life I've wanted to be somebody. I guess I should have been more specific." Well, I knew what I wanted, and it was specific enough for me. I wanted more.

If you want to go further in the news business, you set your sights on bigger and better markets. Me? I wanted to go to Dallas and work at WFAA. Not only because it was the Big D, right at the height of Cowboy Chic, but especially because of the impressive reputation of the station's news director,

Marty Haag. For anyone working in that market, Marty stood for excellence in broadcast news. To work for him meant you were among the chosen ones. For me, he was like Santa Claus, the pope, and my fairy godfather all wrapped up into one; someone who could make me better than I was and launch me to the heights for which I was surely destined.

Somehow I conned Sydney Benton, the woman who managed Marty's schedule and pretty much ran the WFAA newsroom, into giving me an appointment. I tried on everything I owned in search of the right interview outfit. Serious but not stuffy. Feminine but not flirty. My selection was like something you might wear if you were in the Redneck Recovery program: a wide belt made of grosgrain ribbon to cinch the waist of my button-up-the-front skirt—with pockets—and a neck scarf that came to a point in the back.

My Aqua Net hairspray was working overtime as I threw my shoulders back and walked through Haag's door, my heart pounding so hard I was certain it was causing my little cameo necklace (a gift from my parents) to visibly shake.

"You've got gumption," the Wise One pronounced, sizing me up.

He was fatherly but not stern. Still, I could already tell from his tone of voice that I would not be a happy camper when it was time for me to exit his office.

"I've looked at your reel, and I think there is some promise there, but you're not ready for Dallas," he said. "I'd like to send you to our sister station in Beaumont. Do you know where that is?"

"Sure," I lied.

The truth was, it didn't matter where it was. If Marty Haag wanted me to go there, I was already on my way.

"We're going to premiere *PM Magazine* there," he said. "It will give you a chance to grow and learn while you get some experience."

I was then told that Beaumont was right *outside* Houston, and if I improved enough, I *might* make it to Dallas after all.

Sight unseen, no mention of salary, I knew this was the right move for me.

But Harvey Cox wasn't so sure.

I announced to Harvey that I'd be leaving his newsroom to take this new job. He looked back at me as if I'd just told him that he could no longer have his police scanner at home with him at night. See, Harvey Cox was hard-core. He wanted to be where the action was. Breaking news, baby. *Fuzz and Was,* we called it. Cop chases and murders. (Never mind that we had very few of these to cover at WSPA.)

Harvey called me into his office. His expression was serious, but what came next wasn't exactly the pep talk I'd anticipated. He had taken a chance on me by hiring me right out of college, and now he clearly thought I needed some wisdom about my career.

"No one's ever going to take you seriously if you go and report for this fluff magazine show," he said. "I mean you can be a hard-core journalist."

Obviously, he'd decided not to mention the hard-hitting series I'd done called "Running for Your Life" during ratings sweeps, which had featured me in a tight T-shirt and shorts, jogging behind the news van while cameras caught me with my hair (and other things) bouncing in perfect cadence, being the "hard-core journalist" I was. My Emmy must have gotten lost in the mail.

"You're leaving all this to go do that?" he continued. "You better think about it, Leeza. You could be ruining your career."

"I appreciate your concern," I said. "But I've got to give it a try."

It wasn't that I didn't hear him. After all, he was a veteran news producer and I was the girl who'd been dubbed an "anchorette wannabe." And yet, I had enough natural self-worth that I didn't believe him, not for a minute. It honestly never occurred to me that my new job—and by extension, my journalism career—wouldn't work out.

Whether I was faking it, or actually felt it, that's just who I was, and how I saw my future. Cocky? Maybe, but I've always kind of had this "Put me in, Coach" attitude throughout my entire career and my whole life, really. Now I can see how lucky I was to be hardwired with that kind of optimism and blind faith in my choices and myself. At the time, I didn't know anything about the arrogance of youth, but it was clearly working for me. Of course, a good attitude was no protection against messing up and falling down. If our mistakes are our teachers, I have a Ph.D. in life lessons, as you'll see throughout this book. But I never lost my sense of promise and possibility, and that was both a source of solace and a confidence booster for me. It still is.

I loaded up a U-Haul and made the move to Beaumont to start working for *PM Magazine* at the CBS affiliate, KFDM. Now, this was something totally different from straightforward news, and at the time it was fairly revolutionary. We were among the early shows to do the kind of lifestyle stories where reporters weren't behind a news desk or doing stand-ups reporting on the action. We were part of the action, living the stories we covered. Whether it was searching for gators in the swamps of Louisiana or driving cross-country in an eighteen-wheeler, we'd put ourselves in the scene, add music to the footage, and make everything seem like a mini-movie. Bingo. Here was the challenge I'd craved, a chance to live large, take chances, *and* be involved with everything from booking interviews to editing. It was the best kind of fun. And I was good at this kind of experiential, on-the-fly reporting. Hard news had been, well, hard. But I could jump out of a plane, stomp grapes, tap-dance, ride bulls, whatever. As long as the camera was on me, I was fearless.

I was also restless. I may have immediately taken to my new job, but I was still always pushing myself to do more, be better, have a greater impact at work and beyond. And I'd already learned one of the best tools for getting ahead. There was an anchorwoman named Annette, from WFAA, with this supercute, short blond hair, and she was always perfectly put together. She intimidated me because she seemed cool and unapproachable—everything I wasn't. One day I found myself in the women's room at the same time with her. Nervously, I watched her apply her lip gloss in the mirror. Then I realized this was my chance. If I was going to make it, I had to dare to learn from the pros. I rallied my nerve and smiled at her. Her reflection smiled back at me.

"What's your secret?" I asked. The question was open-ended, but she didn't hesitate with the answer she knew I needed to hear.

"You really have to know who you are," she said.

That was it. She put the wand applicator back in her lip gloss and threw the bag over her shoulder.

I nodded at her in agreement and smiled wider as she left. "Thanks," I said.

There it was. Simple yet satisfying. Besides, I was happy to leave well enough alone. There was no way I was going to ask a follow-up question. It didn't matter. I knew what she meant. I was twenty years old. I'd yet to face any of the major challenges of my life, the moments that would make me question my decisions and beliefs. But her words made sense to me at a fundamental level. I felt confident that I did in fact know exactly who I was.

Annette's basic advice guided me through the next thirteen months. I received positive feedback—more than just a pat on the head—but no promotion. Still, I always had Dallas in my sights. I consistently called Marty Haag to see if he was ready to wave his magic wand and move me to the big time. "Did you see that piece I did for the national reel?" I asked. "What did you think?"

And then, one year and one month after moving to Beaumont, I got the call that it was happening; I was being moved to Dallas to cohost Channel 8's version of the popular TV newsmagazine *PM Magazine*. Coach was putting me in the game. And I was ready to play.

MORE THAN JUST HOT

Big D, look at me! I'd made it to Dallas, but my role as a "natural negotiator" apparently didn't make it with me.

Here's what happened when I tried to get more money from my *PM Magazine* contract after I'd been with the show for about a year. When I saw my executive producer, standing there all cool and in charge at an office party, I thought this was my moment. Now I had an agent, but my dad had told me to always deliver bad news and ask for money in person. At this point, I felt I had proven myself and so, following Dad's advice, I approached the man holding the purse strings.

He responded to my request for more money and more exposure on the air with these humiliating words: "Well, I'd like to work with you on this, but first, I think there are some things you need to work on, like pushing back from the dinner table."

"What?" I asked.

Clearly, snappy comebacks weren't my thing early on, and I wasn't quite sure what he meant by that anyhow. And then I got it: *He's saying I'm fat.*

I didn't know whether to slap him or cry. Neither was a good option, so an incredulous stare was all I could muster. I suppose *fat* is a subjective term, but I've always been around the same size. Looking back, I may have been a couple of sizes bigger then than I am now. Maybe I was plumper than he thought I should be—and a little more zaftig than I really wanted to be—but it had never occurred to me, because I certainly didn't think I was fat. And besides, what if I had been? I mean, was that in any way affecting my ability to do the job?

I searched my mind for something to say, but I couldn't think of anything to come back at him with. Nothing. I had that awful, flushed feeling, with a big lump in my throat. *I need to leave before I burst into tears,* I thought.

I managed to get away from the scene and leave the party with as much dignity as possible, and I'm sure he didn't have any idea he'd just crushed me. When I got home, I stood before the full-length mirror and, for the first time, felt awful about my appearance. I ended up signing a new contract and I moved forward. I didn't become anorexic, or obsess on the need to lose weight for him or anyone else, but seriously, that hurt! Not surprisingly, the next season I was noticeably slimmer.

Nothing can chip away at your confidence quite like a career in the public eye, where your appearance is not only part of your job, it's part of business negotiations, too. Look, I'm well aware that a lot has changed since I started out in the early 1980s. My fave fierce ladies, Beyoncé and Amy Schumer, have set a lot of people straight and have rebooted unrealistic body image expectations in our culture. But no matter what sizes we come in, even today we still get paid less. Do we need to negotiate more forcefully on our own behalf, asking for what we want? Of course. Does this discrepency in pay have anything to do with the respective value of what women offer, versus the contribution of men? Not usually. You decide. When Sony's emails were hacked into in 2014, there it was, ripped from Sony's server. Jennifer Lawrence, who is so skinny her email handle at the time was "Peanutbutt," was making a lot less than "the boys" in their movie *American Hustle.* This not only led to vocal outrage; it also caused a public debate about how men and women are compensated. So it's not always just about the Skinny Minnies versus women of size. Jennifer Lawrence, who is one of the "nice" girls in the industry, was plenty strong to take this on respectfully.

And while we have more size acceptance in our culture, with personalities like Oprah, Carne Wilson, and Tyra Banks taking on the issue with grace and strength, we still can't quite seem to get the industry to accept the reality that women are more than a size, and we're capable of being more than just hot.

We're getting there, but these more progressive attitudes, as well as the more humane HR practices of recent years, were not around to protect me back when I was starting out. And we still have a ways to go.

When I got called out in Dallas for being too big for the big money I wanted, I had no idea that I would soon engage in standoffs with my Hollywood bosses, too. I should have taken a deep breath and prepared myself, because there would be plenty of image police in my future, and it was going to take a ferocious sense of my self-worth to stand up to them.

SORORITY GIRL, BIG CITY

Good thing I hadn't taken it too personally when our show producer criticized my body, because I was headed for even more scrutiny. It wasn't long before I jumped markets again, all the way to the Big Apple this time, for a cohosting job on the WCBS show *Two on the Town*. My producer, Andrea, would go on to become one of my most respected colleagues and greatest friends, but you wouldn't have known it from our first impressions of each other. I was all big, blond hair and glossy pink nails and lips. Andrea had sleek dark hair, wore very little makeup, and, like most of my new compatriots in the big city, was one of the PIBs: People in Black. She wore all black, *all the time*. It was Andrea's job to get me up to speed, and she later told me that she was far from certain she was up for the challenge. In fact, when I arrived in New York, she went to her boss, Bobbee Gablemann, and said: "This sorority girl look is more than I can handle."

Well, I *was* in the Tri Delta sorority back in South Carolina, but I didn't think we all had a *look*. Maybe I just liked the preppie style, and lots of hair spray, and a variety of hair adornments. And so what if I embraced bold statement jewelry before it was a trend?

It didn't matter because Andrea and Bobbee weren't about to give up on me. I was their pick the minute they saw my audition tape. They'd narrowed their search down to Maria Shriver and me. What was the swing vote? Clearly, Maria (my hero today) was more refined. She was just like she is now: smart and beautiful. But she apparently wasn't shameless. And I was. My demo reel included a scene of me jumping up on a table in a crowded restaurant and breaking into a jitterbug. That's what gave me the edge.

They'd thrown the dice on me. So now they were determined to make it work. They sent me to a stylist on the Upper East Side whom the station used for media makeovers. I rode my city bike with the fat wheels to my appointment. When I arrived, perhaps a little windblown, there were half a dozen PIB stylists waiting. They studied me like I was a science experiment, rolled their eyes slightly, and over several cups of coffee, went to work.

Right after I moved to New York, a Dallas publication ran a feature on my big-city career move that included mention of my pink lips, pink fingernails, and pink dress amid a sea of black. Okay, and, your problem with that is *what*? The list of problems was enormous, apparently, and the stylists' patience was not. I was a little overwhelmed. I'd never met anyone like these people, and now I was surrounded by a whole gaggle of them. They talked fast—and loud—and seemed quite sure they knew exactly what was best for me. They weren't mean about it, but they were firm on the fact that my look had to be toned down. A lot. My inherent self-worth had buoyed me when I'd been dealing with negativity from people I knew and understood because they were mostly like me, but now I was floundering in a world that was all new, and I'd be lying if

I said my self-confidence didn't take a hit. This was definitely in the *before* stage of my growth, and the lesson I was about to master is the kind I'm hoping you can avoid having to learn the hard way.

"GIVE HER THE WORKS"

Apparently the makeover was okay. I made my debut on the show, and the station wasn't deluged with complaints from people repulsed by my look. I didn't love the feeling of needing to be a new me to be appropriate for a new realm of TV, but I loved everything about my new job. As long as the camera tally light was on, I was up for anything: climbing the Brooklyn Bridge for our promo, piloting a helicopter over the East River, hang gliding, whatever Andrea and the other producers asked me to do.

And then, about a year into it, the opportunity suddenly ended (more about that in the next chapter). When I eventually regrouped a few months later, I'd landed at *Entertainment Tonight*, based in Los Angeles, where there were lots of pluses, including the relocation apartment the show gave me at the Oakwood apartment complex, complete with men dripping in gold chains by the pool and a fireplace with amber-colored plastic mock flames that turned on with the flip of a switch. Swanky, right?! But there were negatives, too, including the fact that my New York City makeover still wasn't quite glam enough for the Hollywood high life. My new producers immediately sent me to a then-well-known beauty wizard, Leslie Blanchard, with explicit instructions: "Give her the works."

Here we go again. I took a seat in a stylist's chair in front of a ginormous mirror, with a team of *fabulous* people. The message was crystal clear: *You don't look like anyone that could be on television here. We need to cut and darken your hair. We need to change your style and give you a total fashion makeover. Everything about you is wrong.*

Gulp. Even though I'd just arrived from Manhattan, where I'd actually been doing pretty well, I felt like I'd fallen straight off the okra truck and landed on a red carpet that was not ready for the likes of me. Self-worth dinged, I sank lower in the chair under the weight of the disapproving glares of the Hollywood hotshots around me. I didn't give any pushback, thinking: *They're right. I'm just a redneck, and I don't know how to dress, and so I'm going to let the professionals tell me how it's done.*

As I saw their handiwork take shape in the mirror, I began to think, *Wait, it took me a long time to grow out my hair! What are you doing?* The next thing I knew, I had coppery-brown hair in the newscaster bob of the day. I'd loved my blond highlights, ever since my friend Cathy Moore and I locked ourselves in her bathroom with a box of Frost & Tip. And my Farrah Fawcett–inspired wispy layers were kinda sexy, or so I'd thought. It was all gone.

So was my self-worth, which was being slaughtered. Mirror, mirror on the wall, meet the new Leeza with the short red hair and red matte lipstick to match. No peachy-pinky highlight on my lips to brighten my attitude. And no hiding my displeasure, either, even though I certainly wasn't going to complain. Instead, I stood up, smoothed my shirt, grabbed my purse, and announced we'd better wait until another day to tackle my wardrobe.

"You must be exhausted from all your hard work," I said as politely as I could. "Thank you."

I bolted, rather than say what I was really thinking. I knew the real me that had always worked on camera, and this wasn't her. I knew her *way* better than they did, but I didn't trust myself now that I was in the big leagues. I was also young, and maybe that's why, despite my confidence in my professional abilities, I hadn't yet developed the situational self-worth to believe in my own inner voice under every circumstance.

MAKE IT UP AS YOU GO ALONG

ET was unlike anything I'd ever done before. Heck, at that time, it was unlike anything *anyone* had ever done. A monster show that had to be fed several times a day, *ET* was the granddaddy of all the entertainment news magazines, and thirty-five years later, has spawned dozens of imitators. The production style was different, as was the whole rhythm of the show.

I arrived ready for action and took my place in what they called the "talent oasis," where the on-camera reporters all had cubicles. I listened in on the conversations of the veteran reporters, like Jeanne Wolf, as she tried to cajole publicists into giving her an exclusive with the celeb of the moment with all the passion of a scientist on the verge of discovering a cure for cancer. I loved hanging out in the edit bays. They cranked 'round the clock, and the segment directors orchestrated the elements of their pieces like conductors, fighting for seconds of airtime. I listened to what they wished they'd had from the field assets to make the story better and I listened even harder to the cursing and slamming of those photographers, produc- ers, or reporters who'd failed to get it. This was how I tried to figure out where the land mines were, professionally.

I kept diaries during these years, and I wish I'd recorded more specifics about the people or stories I was covering. In- stead, there was a lot of introspection. Looking back, it's te- dious and more than slightly annoying to read how much time I wasted questioning my growth ("I just don't feel I'm challeng- ing myself enough.") and my timetable for success, ("I think it's passing me by, and I feel out of control.") Puhleeeeez! It was all about what I didn't have when I could have been enjoying all I did have and all I was accomplishing. See, from my vantage point, other people really did have it all. The young Turks, who were always in the middle of the action at *ET,* got my atten- tion the most. Like writer Billy Olson, who held court, cracked jokes, and smoothed things over when no one else could. I'm certain Bill never wrote self-obsessing entries in a journal like I did. The powers that be employed Bill Olson when it mattered most. Like the time producers were watching the daily feed on the monitors in the newsroom when Mary Hart stepped onto the stage wearing a St. Pepper's Lonely Hearts Club band–type getup.

"Billy, get down there and make her take that horrific thing off," they shouted.

To negotiate the change, Billy said nothing about the jacket (which, in Mary's defense, was in style at the time). He went right to: "It just doesn't make your fabulous blue eyes sparkle. It kinda competes."

The jacket was off in under thirty seconds. I was taking notes and mentally recording all this stuff. What works, what doesn't. Who has enough trust to leverage change. Billy did. He and his cronies used to say: "Don't complain. Someday we're gonna look back on these as 'the good old days.' " We do.

At work, I was confident that I knew my stuff, and I wasn't hesitant to communicate what I thought to my producers or the crew when we were in the field. This was my ultimate comfort zone.

One of the early stories I went on for *ET* was an interview with actor Tab Hunter, who was filming a spaghetti western out in a canyon somewhere. Now, first of all, I had no idea who Tab Hunter was and I didn't know what a spaghetti western was, either, but I knew exactly what the story called for, and so as we arrived on set and scoped out the available locations for shooting our interview, I turned and confidently faced the crew.

"I want to do this as a walk-and-talk interview, here," I said, pointing to the backdrop I had in mind. "And, how 'bout if we do it on horseback?"

"Really?" asked the cameraman. "You don't want to set up

an interview with the lights and reflector, so we can get your reversals and everything?"

"I don't need reversals," I said, dismissing their suggestion that the segment should include footage of me listening to Tab answer my questions. "This story doesn't really need that."

"Okay," he said, hesitantly. "But how 'bout we just do it sitting on the ground here under this tree? I don't have the right gear to follow you guys on horseback, and I'm not getting in the saddle today."

I later found out he was a little surprised by this take-charge new reporter who was acting more like the director, and who didn't seem concerned about her lighting or want to count seconds on air. But, remember, I had been schooled in the Maxie Ruth style of reporting back in Spartanburg, and I knew to pitch in and pull my weight. To break away from the pack, I was always looking for "the thing" that could shake up the segment. I didn't have anything against the status quo of standard, packaged celebrity stories. I just preferred what I knew best: getting out there, having fun, and living the story, while waiting for a moment. I was looking for a way to stand out from the cookie-cutter mold of other reporters. Not that I really knew the formula enough to reject it. I just knew me. Earning the crew's respect was much more important to me than cutaways. A reputation is a forever thing, and I knew this was no time to diva out. I focused on creating pieces that were fun and un-expected. I was making it up as I went along. As I became more experienced I realized most of life is that way.

Luckily, the kind of intimate approach I felt most comfortable with worked for the show. In fact, it was the hallmark of the show at the time, and the celebrities I covered liked being invited outside their usual box. I laugh about that now because, of course, there is no box anymore; the lines are not only blurred, they've all but disappeared.

I didn't let much hold me back, but I did have that haircut hangover for months after starting at *ET,* and that made me feel like an imposter in my own life. Some days it seemed like everyone had a secret code that I hadn't deciphered about looking cool and being in charge. These funks usually didn't last long, and I made sure not to let on. *Take a deep breath, and just see it through* was my advice to myself, and it usually worked.

Then, something like this would occur, and I'd sink deeper. During my early days at *ET,* which we filmed at Merv Griffin's Trans-American Video (TAV) studios in Hollywood, the staff parked in a lot right next to the stage. Having just arrived from New York, I was still celebrating having a car, and I always got excited to head home in my little silver Porsche Targa 911. It was an impulsive indulgence I'd bought for myself when I signed the deal that took me to the west coast. My mom and I had driven out together, on a road trip that found us making the kind of memories I loved creating with her, like when she popped her head out of the car's bikini top to flirt with truck drivers we passed. She and Daddy were concerned that I'd spent too much on a "fancy" car. But I loved that car. For me it was a symbol that my hard work was paying off, and that I was finally making it in a city made for such a top down, full-speed-ahead set of wheels.

One day as I rummaged in my purse for my keys, I noticed an ugly scratch all along the driver's side of my prized possession. My heart sank. *Someone keyed my car. What's this about? I thought this was going to be the place where I was supposed to fit.* I was certain this was a deliberate act, that someone was leaving me a message. I tried to reassure myself that this was just how show business went sometimes. There was limited airtime, and when I'd been brought on board it was generally understood that I was being tested to possibly replace their current weekend anchor, Dixie Whatley.

Dixie would never do this, I thought, as I got in to drive home, feeling horrible that anyone would see me as an enemy. *She's been so nice. But have I been targeted?* My presence had obviously created some tension around the studio. *What am I thinking? Of course. These are Dixie Whatley people, and they support Dixie.*

I know it's pretty far-fetched. Could I be more paranoid? I have no idea what actually happened. Chances are the scratch may have just been (and probably was) a random act of vandalism. I ended up becoming friendly with Dixie. I didn't have it out for her in any way. She didn't have it out for me, either. She handled herself like a pro and never made me her enemy in the studio's game of musical chairs.

I learned how to double down on keeping my fear in check by looking closely at what was happening during this phase of my life. Technically, fear is just a reaction. It's how we feel when we're facing something we think is going to happen. I thought

Dixie would resent me, that the staff would have it out for me. Fear can get us all caught up in playing theoretical scenarios in our heads: *What if I don't know enough? What if I don't fit in?* We whip ourselves into a psychological frenzy with all of this anxiety.

None of this is solution driven. Many (if not most) of the things we hang on to that cause us to be afraid are things we really can't control, or things that never happen anyhow. The only thing to *really* worry about is not having the disposition or confidence to know that *if* and when the things you fear ever present themselves in real life, you'll know how to deal. The antidote for fear is action. When there is a real problem, challenge, or crisis, act in your own best interest. Until then, try to manage your anxiety and keep moving forward. Dixie and I have since reconnected and talked about the pressure of being "the new girl." She'd replaced *ET* anchor Marjorie Wallace when she first came to the show and also felt like an outsider for a while. Even though it can be a brutal business, and Dixie bore the brunt of lots of tough decisions made by our producers, she has managed to look back and reflect on that time realistically and with gratitude for the places it took her. Now she in a Boston-based artist, living life happily and passionately as a married woman who travels the world with her husband pursuing her first love: art.

One of my favorite series at *ET* was one I worked on with Billy Olson called "The Real Men of Rock." This was during the late '90s, and when we said *ET* gave you an all-access backstage pass, we meant it. Before social media, entertainment news was the only way you could get access to stars, and we were the big gun in town.

I learned who was real, and who was faking, by hanging backstage at concerts, and on sets and in the homes of the hottest stars. I couldn't have had a better lens on human behavior. From Eddie Van Halen's marriage tips for staying happy with (then wife) Valerie Bertinelli, to Rod Stewart's confession that his spiky hair resulted from being washed with soap and water, America ate it up. For me, it wasn't just about gathering sound bites to pacify the show's voracious need. It was a learning lab. From my conversations with celebrities in intimate settings, often during the height of their fame, I've come to believe that fame doesn't change a person. Fame just gets you to the essence of who you are supposed to be faster. If you were always going to be a great, decent, kind person, fame allows that to come out, sooner and stronger. If you were already a jerk, fame makes you a bigger one.

I had the good sense to keep my head down, keep moving, and earn my place at *ET* by showing them how hard I could work and just how much I could offer the show. Interviewing Boy George in bed at the Bel-Air Hotel, singing and dancing with Eddie Murphy at his recording studio, scuba diving with Mickey Mouse, or investigating Natalie Wood's mysterious death near Catalina Island, I tried to deliver my stories with an unscripted edge. Feedback was positive. "Because you were refreshing and good, people liked working with you, and the suits left you alone," Billy later told me. Still, I couldn't shake my fear that I wasn't enough. Maybe it was the echo of Harvey Cox's words in my head and my secret anxiety that he was right: I might never be taken seriously. That's what I wanted way more than the halo effect of the Hollywood lifestyle I'd suddenly achieved. It didn't help that my friends back home were quick to dismiss my job, saying I had stars in my eyes.

"Leeza's gone Hollywood," they said.

Their words conjured up Mom's warning not to get too "big for my britches." Then a story broke that seemed to prove to everyone it was true. The first time I went to Spago was with Ed Marinaro, the pro football player turned actor who was starring on *Hill Street Blues* at the time. When my picture was printed in the tabloids as Ed's new "gal pal," whatever that means, my hometown friends sang a chorus of "I told you so."

I worried about stuff like that. Being misrepresented, becoming an intellectual slug, not living a life of significance. If you're thinking, *Come on! Lighten up, Leeza!* you're not wrong. Of course, it was ironic I was feeling these fears *now,* at a time when I had been given the biggest opportunity I could have been offered, and I was getting high marks. The job turned out to be such fertile ground for the things I came to most love and value in my career.

At the time, though, celebrity was something I just didn't know or understand. Why were people taking my picture when I was just doing my job? Why were the powerhouse publicists such tyrants, barking out directives with such strict control over their star clients? Why were some celebrities so guarded while others acted like my best friend? These early years at *ET* really were like an on-the-job crash course in Hollywood basics for me, and I learned a lot about how wanting something you don't have, or fearing you're going to lose it all can make people crazy.

TESTOSTERONE WARS

"Now, Leeza, let's not turn this into a dick-swinging contest," one of my *ET* producers said to me during one of our daily production meetings.

The tension had been building between us for months, but I hadn't thought he'd go quite this far. His words hung in the air, the room completely silent, as more than a dozen staffers circled the big table, working together against our constant tight deadlines.

I stood up and gave him my biggest, sweetest smile.

"Well, I'd never turn this into a dick-swinging contest because, number one, I don't have a penis, and number two, even if I did, I would never pull it out and measure it against yours."

And with that, I turned on my heels and left the room. This kind of F-you was a detour from my normal tactics, but my "keep it cool" approach hadn't worked.

My then-assistant Jeff Collins later told me that as the door closed behind me, it was all everyone could do to keep a straight face. As soon as the producer left, everyone in the room applauded.

I didn't need to hear their applause to feel like I'd been in the right to take a stand and derail any chance for the tension to get worse. During these years, while I was working my butt off at *ET,* I'd also landed my own talk show, *Leeza,* as well as a radio show and a Top 40 countdown show, à la Casey Kasem, along with a production company deal at Paramount, Leeza Gibbons Enterprises. I was in overdrive, managing to run my business and mother the children I had between 1989 and 1997 without losing my sanity. Most days. Strategy? I really didn't have one. I just tried to balance my conflicting obligations by never thinking about all that was on my plate and simply doing my best at every task that came up during the day. I was so high up on the tightrope I didn't dare look down.

I worked on the *ET* stage in the mornings, and then walked next door on Stage 26, to host my talk show and record radio. Most afternoons I had playtime and nap tuck-in for the kids, then I did promos for the affiliates and took development meetings in the Leeza Gibbons Enterprises production suite, in the same Mae West Building as the *ET* offices. On top of all that were screenings, photo shoots, and appearances. It was soon all standard fare, and all exhausting. (I figured if my plate was full, that just meant get a bigger plate.)

It wasn't big enough, though, for this producer who kept messing with me because he could only get me for *ET* assignments when I was available, rather than any time he wanted to schedule me for something. In my view, he had a habit of giving me assignments that were inconvenient, or sometimes impossible for me, just to frustrate the process and make it seem like I wasn't a team player. Jabs were delivered in these pithy, often condescending memos that sometimes demanded last-minute schedule changes or travel plans.

I'd always tried to maintain my professionalism and positivity, but by the time of this production meeting, when he'd mentioned one of his typical schedule changes, I'd had enough. I kept my tone as conciliatory as possible, pleasantly explaining that I had permission from our Paramount bosses to host a pageant at the time he wanted me available. It would be impossible for me to travel due to the pageant rehearsal schedule. I couldn't take the assignment he was giving me, end of story. Why he felt perfectly comfortable talking down to me and throwing his weight around, because I was a woman, or just because, I don't know. Regardless, those were his limits. He had crossed mine at the mere mention of swinging dicks, and I couldn't let it stand.

These days we have powerful new advocates in the form of people like international lawyer and political scientist Anne-Marie Slaughter and Facebook CEO Sheryl Sandberg on the case for us. They, along with other modern-day feminists, are writing popular articles and books debunking myths long thrown at women about their business acumen, work-life balance, and need to "have it all." I've always said balance was bogus, but back in the 1990s I often felt like a lone wolf. Now,

thankfully, my own experiences are being echoed in many can-
did discussions of how our views of women and our roles in
the family, the business world, and our culture at large do and
don't differ from reality. I think it was a step toward syncing
up expectations and reality when Mark Zuckerberg took two
months off to help care for his newborn daughter.

While the heat is on, we are the only ones who can re-
fine and redefine our own terms at home and at work. I failed
every time I looked for the center of the seesaw. It's because, as
Anne-Marie Slaughter says, "Balance is a luxury very few will
ever attain." This is what Zuckerberg, Sandberg, Slaughter, and
others get right. They have rewritten the narrative for their own
lives, and it's affecting all of us. I believe you have to do your
own version of what they have done, get comfortable being in
the center spotlight of your life. But when you want to grab the
reins, expect pushback, and even embrace it. That means you're
right on course. So when I got resistance to standing up for myself and it was misconstrued as not being on "the team," I knew
this was bound to keep happening until I said, "No more."

Now, would a nice girl shut down a producer by exiting
a meeting after refusing to see who had the biggest balls? Of
course she would. You have to know your limits, especially if
you're nice, so people don't walk all over you. You have to focus
on where you want to go and not let others try to trip you up
on your path. We teach people how to treat us, and we get exactly what we're willing to put up with. I believe you've got to
raise your hand, speak your truth, and stand your ground. This

scenario I faced at *ET* combined all three. Success isn't always about taking action. Sometimes it's about waiting, sometimes it's about going along with what's expected of you, and sometimes it's about getting the last word in, closing the door, and walking away.

And then, no matter the outcome of the confrontation, you have to let it go. I never held that exchange against this executive. I didn't gloat. I continued to do my best work for him, and he taught me a lot. In the future I would find myself in full-on testosterone wars many more times in my career, most often with other women. In fact, this was the beginning of my building on my self-worth and optimism by developing a sense of what was true for me, and what I could accomplish through persistence and measured steadiness, which eventually helped me to win *Celebrity Apprentice*. And, yes, I am proud of the fact that I'd learned the art of the comeback by this point because it would surely come in handy in the years ahead, in front of the camera and not.

Business is sometimes complicated and almost always imperfect. So is life, for that matter. Those who do it well are comfortable with that. The optimist in business will modify her approach and redirect her path, as long as it's still on her journey. Learning how to be flexible is always the right choice. This is Darwinian. Sharpen your ability to focus on where you want to go, not so much on the detours along the way. If you don't, those who can, will outdistance you easily, even when they've got nothing on your skills.

YOU ARE IN CHARGE

I'm a big believer that you become like the five to ten people you're with the most. During my time at *ET,* I was mostly with my crew, and my team, whom I loved, and they were my home base. But I was also getting feedback on the world from celebrities, many of whom were at the top of their field: brilliant, confident, and gifted.

In the early years, I was so young that I had a lot to prove. Every assignment was a test for me to show whether or not I had the right stuff as a journalist. I got some insights when I was sent to interview Ted Koppel, who always handled interviews with intelligence and excellence. This man has done it all: as a war correspondent, political analyst, and anchor/reporter who has covered every important event and interviewed every significant newsmaker. I'd become a devotee during Koppel's twenty-five years anchoring ABC's *Nightline,* but this was not the time for me to come off as a sycophant sucking up to the master. Thinking it would help keep me from looking like an intimidated schoolgirl, I admitted to my nerves up front.

"I have to tell you, it's daunting to be interviewing you," I said.

Koppel was once a teacher and has mentored thousands of interns during his career. He instinctively offered me this: "Whether it's an author, or a relative, or a head of state, no matter who is in that other chair, always remember you are in charge," he said. "You are the one controlling the field and the energy. This is your forum. Always remember that, no matter who it is."

Lesson learned. Ever since then, I've always done just as he advised. Of course, being a "control enthusiast," as I am, I liked receiving permission to be in charge. I also immediately recognized that this was a really meaningful bit of knowledge to have in my back pocket, especially when I later found myself opposite someone like Bette Davis, who obviously didn't want to be sitting in the chair across from me. I don't think this advice only applies to journalists, either. Obviously there's much we can't control in life. But when we are going into a situation where we have a very specific outcome in mind—a business negotiation, a marriage proposal, a curfew dispute with a child—it helps to remember that it's your table, so set it appropriately.

As I aged and weathered more personal and professional setbacks, I found myself increasingly drawn to those people who had survived their own ordeals in life and emerged stronger and wiser. The two best examples of this that come to mind are Jane Fonda and Elizabeth Taylor, both of whom I got to work with several times during my career. Meeting these iconic women and seeing their vulnerabilities made them so much more relatable to me, even though they were larger-than-life legends. Watching them try to make sense of their own experiences galvanized me for the work I was doing on this front in my own, more ordinary life.

When I met Jane Fonda, it was immediately clear that she

was very powerful and she knew what she wanted. The student in me began taking notes as she came right in, gave input on how to set the lights, and then made suggestions about what we could shoot to best tell the story. She wasn't bossy. She just knew what was right for her.

I was interviewing her about a series of her videos on the power of walking, so we grabbed her dog and headed out in Santa Monica. She instructed the crew not to shoot her from the back. Now, this is the original fitness queen, Jane "Feel the Burn" Fonda, whose hips must have been all of, what, thirty-three inches? I made sure our team followed her directive. I also tied my sweater around my waist so I didn't feel so wide next to her. I had so much respect for her ability to know what she needed from an environment in order to feel safe and to be her best self while there.

But the queen of "know where you're going and look good when you get there" was Elizabeth Taylor. I was struck by a revelation she made during our interview on the set of her TV movie *Poker Alice*. She said she liked to receive gifts from the producers every day—a fourteen-karat gold whistle, a gold flashlight, a sterling silver this-or-that. *Huh?* She was Elizabeth Taylor. She could have bought herself all of these special items, and more, every day of her life. Then I learned from the production team that this was standard practice: the gifts were presented to her in front of the crew and received with much delight.

"These gifts," I asked her. "Do they help you turn in a better performance?"

"Oh God, yes," she said in her breathy, half-British, half-little-girl voice. "It makes me a very happy human being."

And then, when she described herself as a little girl inside, I realized that the gifts connected her to that inner child, who liked to be surprised. There was a part of her that needed to feel special, and when she did, she was better able to show up for her performance every day and really be at her best.

In order to stand up for yourself, and own your self-worth, you have to know yourself. It's what Elizabeth Taylor taught me, as well as so many others I interviewed over the years, not to mention the anchorwoman Annette, all the way back there in that ladies' room in Spartanburg, South Carolina. Know what you need, ask for it, and never apologize. Coco Chanel said it best: "The most courageous act is still to think for yourself. Aloud."

During my time in Hollywood, I witnessed so many examples of women living on purpose, creating their own experiences, one gold whistle at a time. I now understand that self-confidence isn't something that's ever going to be handed to you. You have to fight for it. And take it.

THE SECRET OF SELF-WORTH

What we allow is what will continue. In my younger days, without realizing it, I was teaching other people that they could undervalue me, because, after all, I did. Until I was willing to take a stand, I allowed producers, and some people in my personal life, to mess with me and not honor my boundaries.

Here's how I got past putting a lid on my self-worth. It's just like Anaïs Nin wrote: "We do not see things as they are. We see things as we are." If you think you're not worthy, if you're negative, suspicious, disloyal—you name it—that's how you're going to see the world coming back at you. Take a good look at who you are—and how you are—and if that doesn't accurately reflect who you want to be, you (and you alone) can change it. The ones who have the audacity to believe they can change are the ones who do. No magic, just habits.

CHAPTER TWO

Pee on Your Own Turf
(Focus)

There will always be someone richer, prettier, smarter, skinnier, with better hair. Comparing degrades and diminishes your own journey. As I like to say, "I'm so busy watering my own lawn that I don't have time to see how green your grass is." Instead, focus on what you have that can always be greater than what everyone else possesses and last you a lifetime: passion for your own path. I call it peeing on your own turf. Think about how it's such a natural thing for dogs to spray their territory and claim it, even if it's a micro-Maltese going up against a great Dane. They are not comparing. They are marking their territory.

Passionate people have no trouble claiming what's theirs, and they have the real power because they work harder than anyone else. At the end of a person's life, the Ancient Greeks measured its worth by asking simply if the deceased had passion. If you've got it, you are engaged, and you are engaging. Think about it in Maya Angelou's words: "Life's a bitch. You've got to go out and kick some ass!" There's no way that's going to happen without passion. The great news is it's innate. Yes, everyone has it, but not everyone brings it out. It's as simple as this: Find your strengths; your passion is tethered to them. Strengthen your strengths and you can't help but get ahead.

Here's a strength that always came naturally to me: focus. I believed that as long as I worked harder than everyone else, I could always deliver, even when it didn't seem obvious to anyone else. And so my mantra became *I'll show you. If you can't see what I can do, I'll prove it to you over time.* With this approach, I always somehow managed to come through.

You don't have to look far to find lots of business leaders who swear by focus as a major source of their success. You know those KIND bars, which seemed to pop up everywhere overnight? They didn't. In fact, it took two decades and lots of setbacks to build this empire. Daniel Lubetzky, the CEO of KIND bars, describes in his book, *Do the KIND Thing,* how he actually keeps reminders of his past failures—products that didn't take off—in his office as a way to remember times when he tried to grow too fast, forgot his central mission, lost focus, and nearly derailed his business. He also acknowledges his failure while it's happening, no matter how embarrassing or painful this may be. It's sort of like when I talk about setting a place at your table for pain and asking, "What have you come to teach me?" Everything shows up in our lives for our own best interest, whether we can see it at the time or not. I love Daniel's idea of having an ongoing dialogue with your failures. They remind us of the mistakes we don't want to make again. But somehow I can't imagine lining up the *Gone With the Wind* Barbie dolls I'd tried to sell through an infomercial and pacing back and forth in front of them, asking them why it didn't work out so well. Maybe it's because part of me would expect the Barbies to talk back and tell me, "Leeza, just because you grew up imagining your Barbies as reporters who ruled the world doesn't mean your passion for your imaginary Barbara Walters Barbie can help you sell this Scarlett O'Hara doll." And maybe they'd be right. My focus got a little fuzzy on that one.

I always figured real life began when someone raised the stakes. That meant always being accountable for who I was and what I was doing. Responsibility may not be something that seduces every young person, but I always rushed to make it happen, and I was pretty sure real life was just around the next corner. I couldn't get there fast enough. People always thought I was in such a hurry to get to my next goal, and I guess I was. After completing my high school requirements in three years, I did a fourth year just to be a senior. I graduated from college in three years, too. Not because I wanted a free year to backpack around Europe or surf in Baja. No, I wanted to work. To me, nothing could be better than landing a job and starting my "real life." Being in fast forward, though, doesn't miraculously conjure up confidence. I was about to find out what did. At least for me.

Don't worry if you don't have focus, because it's a quality

that can easily be cultivated. You don't have to have a pedigree or a genius IQ to achieve more in your own life; you just need to focus on what you want while being grateful for what you have. "What you seek is seeking you." This quote from thirteenth-century Persian poet Rumi keeps me focused on making it happen.

FAKE IT TILL YOU'RE FEARLESS

You always remember your first. Especially when it happens in Rio. I was on assignment, covering Carnival for *Two on the Town* with my cohost Robb Weller (a great guy) and my producer/best friend, Andrea. That's why I loved this job, even if I still hadn't figured out living in New York City, and I was definitely not in line to become one of the PIB (People in Black). My work took me all over the world and allowed me to be way more courageous than I ever would have been on my own time. If the camera was pointed at me and the red tally light was on, I was fearless (or at least able to fake it). I honestly think I must have envisioned myself possessing special powers or something because I did the most insane and fabulous things. Years later, I would shout, *"Yeeeesss!!!!"* when I read what Tina Fey wrote in her book *Bossypants:* "You can't be that kid standing at the top of the waterslide overthinking it. You have to go down the chute." Back then my job forced me to go down the chute, or in the case of my Rio assignment, off the cliff.

It was a gorgeous day in one of the sexiest cities on earth. I'm told the man who was instructing me to jump off a perfectly good cliff was sexy, too. I have no idea. I was trying to settle my nerves and envision landing on Pepino Beach, far below. This was *the* spot for hang-gliding daredevils in Rio to take flight and absorb views of the seductive city, and I was about to be one of them. The cameras were rolling. I got my cue from the director, and that meant I had to cue up my courage. Andrea was producing this segment, and there was no way I was going to let her down. *Run, run, run . . . right to the place where the earth drops off below you, and the wind catches your sail.* As I hit the sweet spot, the only instruction I remembered was "Whatever you do, don't stop running when you reach the end." So even after liftoff, my feet were still in action beneath me as I hung from the harness in the bright blue sky. I was too scared to enjoy much of the vista. When I landed safely, I was about to say a prayer of gratitude, when Andrea rushed up to me, all smiles but no nonsense.

"That was great! Okay, now you have to do it again so we can get our camera angle from the beach this time," she said.

Seriously?

Whatever. At this point, my courage was locked and loaded, and I was ready to go as many times as they needed.

When I finally returned to my hotel room to freshen up for dinner and prep for the next day's shoot, I was proud of myself and happy about the footage we'd gotten in the can. There was a knock at my door. When I let Andrea in, I couldn't help but notice her strange, serious expression that was so *not* Andrea.

"Leeza, the show was canceled," she said.

"What do you mean?" I asked. "Just like that?"

"Apparently," she said. "I just got a call from New York."

"I can't believe they don't even want to see all the great stuff we shot down here," I said, too shocked to fully understand I'd just lost a lot more than one assignment and a bunch of great video.

"I know," she said. "Some goodbye, right? At least they're letting us stay in Rio awhile."

"Oh, not me, I have to get back," I said, already updating my audition reel in my mind.

"Really?" Andrea said. "You're not going to take a free vacation in Rio?"

"Nope," I said. "I'm gonna find my next job. I mean this is sucky news, but I'll find something even better. I'd rather just get on with it."

"All right, you go, girl," Andrea said. "I'll drive you to the airport. I'm going to stay here and party."

That was the first time I ever got fired.

"Don't hurry back," the station manager said to me. "We've already packed up your office, and your stuff is in a box by the door."

Of course, I was stunned. And confused. And sad. All of the feelings that emerge after any kind of a breakup.

For about five minutes.

While Andrea stayed in Rio, living it up for the next two weeks, I flew back to New York and started searching for my next job. Of course, looking back at my very earnest twenty-two-year-old self, part of me wants to say, "Oh, come on. Have a few piña coladas. You're young. Free trips to Rio don't just fall from the sky." And part of me applauds my determination and focus.

Getting emotional was not an option. Not for me. If there was bad news, I wanted to face it, fix it, or move past it. I'm not sure how I got that kind of determination. It's not like I had a lot of life experience to give me this confidence. I guess it was just my way of handling hurt. "Things turn out best for those who make the best of how things turn out," according to the late John Wooden, legendary UCLA basketball coach. I think that's exactly right! I knew what I wanted: a life in television news. Nothing was going to get in my way. Not a show cancellation. Not a gorgeous beach with free drinks.

Life is full of setbacks and false starts. It just is. I wanted Happily Ever After with a white picket fence and monogrammed guest towels but that's not the way I made it happen. I've had *lots* of missteps on the way to finding both success and love. My dream of opening my nonprofit Leeza's Care Connection support centers in every city is ten years behind schedule and counting. I'd give anything to have coffee at my kitchen table with my mother again. I always thought I'd have one spouse forever, like my mom and dad did. Life comes with an automatic dream detour. There's no sense in wishing for it to be any other way. What we can control, though, is our attitude, and the self-respect we show ourselves by taking our dreams seriously. No matter how many times they change, they are our tracking device to our own happiness.

My mom always told me to stay in my lane and just do my best. She reminded me to put on my blinders, like a Thoroughbred racehorse, so I wouldn't be distracted by anyone else's drama or success. "Don't look at the other horses," she said. "Just run your race." And so I never worried about what anyone else was doing or how I compared. I put all of my attention on my path and I tried not to lose time or energy worrying about anything, or anyone, else. This is what I'm kind of naturally wired to do, but I can see lots of ways that I've become aware of the value of this approach, so I've set out to perfect it over the years.

In *Lean In,* Sheryl Sandberg talks about "ruthlessly prioritizing." It comes down to honoring your journey, working on what you can improve—your deliverables and relationships—while giving as little thought (and even less worry) to the things beyond your control (gossip, bad hair days, the competitiveness of others). When things don't go your way, or can't be improved, move on. Of course, be accountable and present in your life, but don't lose time or energy on aspects that don't serve you.

Don't worry about the C-R-A-P, which I've learned stands for Criticism, Resistance, Assholes, and Pressure. That'll all be there without you having to focus on it, so don't. If you focus on crap, you're only gonna get more of it. Instead, focus on what you can improve: you. Wherever you are in your life, you should be able to expect respect and get it, but it doesn't come without you creating the blueprint. Every time you ignore negativity you build an invisible protective barrier around you. If you can make the sources of nastiness irrelevant, they will usually atrophy and die. That's what happened with a news producer back in South Carolina who suggested I wear tighter shirts. He actually said, "You're cute as a speckled pup, and if you could just dress in a way that shows us you're a woman, you're probably gonna go far." I decided to ignore him and focus on what I wanted, which was out of there. When I didn't react or respond, he had no cause to continue fencing with me. He put down his sword, and I got on with it without making a scene. I think he's selling cars somewhere in Phoenix right now, probably trying that same line on his new hires.

And so, yes, when our show got the ax, I did go back to New York City, get my resume and reel together, and start talking to my agent about getting back to work. And, yes, a promising opportunity did come along. Within the month I found myself interviewing for a job at WBZ in Boston.

I CAN DO THAT

Looking back at my career ups and downs, and my somehow stalwart confidence, more than anything else I'd say to my former self, "You've got this, honey!"

During my stint of unemployment following *Two on the Town,* I holed up in my cute little brownstone on West Seventy-Eighth Street (the one I'd bought because I thought it was *so much* like Marlo Thomas's place on the TV show *That Girl*). While watching TV in my oh-so-chic exposed-brick living room one day, I got up and changed the channel (this was back when you actually did that) and a new show caught my eye. There was Mary Hart sitting behind the anchor desk on *Entertainment Tonight*. It had become an instantly popular source of celebrity news when it launched the previous year. A new show feeding America's already insatiable need for celebrity. Glitzy, fresh, and often fun. And no one wore black!

I can do that, I thought.

I have no idea what inspired this epiphany, which I turned into a sixteen-year career as an entertainment reporter. Sure, I'd read *Tiger Beat* and *Seventeen* as a teenager, but I didn't follow Hollywood or know any celebrities by sight. And yet, I was pretty sure I could figure it out.

I flew out to Los Angeles hoping to set up an interview at *ET,* appearing at the show's offices with my audition tape in hand, only to be asked to take a seat in the waiting room. And so I waited, and I waited, that whole first day, until everyone went home in the evening. Nothing. I went back the next day and waited until, finally, the receptionist took pity on me. She motioned me over and held out her hand.

"Why don't you go ahead and give me your tape?" she said.

"Wow, really?" I said. "Thank you."

With my experience now, of course, I know she was just shining me on. After all, what else could she do, arrest me for loitering? I'm not sure she ever showed my tape to anyone. I'm not even sure the woman I met was the actual receptionist, and wasn't just a temp. But the gesture at least made me feel a lot better. I was grinning like an idiot as I walked out of there that day.

Ultimately, my agent arranged for me to come in on an actual audition. It wasn't for *ET* but I was still very excited. I was shooting ad lib scenes with my now dear friend, Steve Edwards, who was (and is) a huge star in L.A. Steve hosted the west coast version of *Two on the Town* and had previously hosted *Good Morning America* and *ET,* among other top shows. I knew shooting with him was a big deal, but he made it effortless and allowed me to be me. He showed me a lot of empathy and was one of my first examples of the power of being kind and considerate. Now we laugh about our initial on-camera collaboration and about how I was just so darned eager to please. We taped our banter at a little strip mall called Gower Gulch, a short walk from Paramount, where I would ultimately take root.

But not that day. That day I was being used as leverage to get Melody Rogers to re-up. At least that's what Steve later told me, and it makes perfect sense. Apparently Melody was in contract negotiations for her role on *Two on the Town* with Steve. I don't know if parading me around had anything at all to do with it, but she did sign a new deal, and by the time I got the call that the opportunity was "no longer available," my love affair with Los Angeles was already in high gear. My gut told me this would be my new home. So now I refocused on *ET.*

Ultimately, *ET* did hire me, but it was not like I'd landed a multiyear commitment with a company that just *had* to have me on their team. When I met with the executives in New York, they made an offer, but it was vague and weak, and it came wrapped in a high-stakes challenge. I would have to leave New York and move to Los Angeles for only thirteen weeks of guaranteed work. That was it. And that's pretty standard. If they didn't like me, or if it wasn't working, I was out.

I knew I would just have to parlay that opportunity into a secure position by working hard enough to make myself indispensable. I knew I could do it, too. I could already see it. Just like when Walt Disney built Disneyland and he told the workers to build the castle first because it was the vision that would help build the rest, I already had my vision of life as a successful journalist in L.A. I built that first. Just like I had told my classmates back in college. But now that the moment was here, I was afraid I wouldn't get the opportunity for growth that I needed from the position, as offered from *ET,* so I told my agent if he got the contract, we should pass.

For real? Looking back, that kind of chutzpah seems ridiculous. I mean this was a hot, national show. I was a relative newcomer. Sure, part of my brain told me to just smile and say, "Thank you. Where do I sign?" But I was pure focus. On a mission. The stronger, more optimistic part of me knew what I wanted, and that this might be my only chance to go for it, and I needed to hold out for a better offer.

We went around and around for a bit, more meetings, phone calls, and the usual negotiation tactics. Finally, I received what I felt was a fairly solid offer with the promise of a shot to anchor. It was still a thirteen-week trial, but that was good enough for me.

I called my mother with the good news, but she wasn't so sure.

"You can't take this," she said. "You have other job offers that are better than this and are much more secure."

She was right, of course. I did have more secure, lucrative offers on the table, but I knew I was supposed to be in L.A. I was supposed to be at *ET*.

"I know it's just thirteen weeks, Mom," I said. "But that's three months. That's more than enough time. Why don't you just pack your things, meet me in New York, and we can drive cross-country together?"

Just because I knew I could do it doesn't mean I wasn't apprehensive. But I've always known there's a big upside to facing the downsides in life (in this case, fear). As with working hard, facing down your fears instead of letting them constrict your possibilities is the surest way to create a positive outcome, first of all by convincing yourself, *My fear is just my courage looking for a way in. I'm going to be able to deliver. I'm going to be proud of myself. I'm going to make it work.* I knew I had a choice about how I was going to look at my fear. I wanted those four letters to stand for "Face Everything And Rise." And so, that's what I set out to do. Steve Jobs famously said, "People think focus means saying yes to the thing you've got to focus on. But that's not what it means at all. It means saying no to the hundred other good ideas that there are." You already know that I learned the value of no in the woods behind Aunt Wayne's house, so walking past all the other great ideas out there to stand with the one that's right for me was something I had begun to get the knack of early on.

I really think it was my sheer focus that pulled me through the uncertainty of my early days at *ET* and got me to where I was supposed to be (well, that, and maybe the naïve bravado of youth, which has its benefits, too).

THE ART OF THE DONALD

Focus has definitely always come naturally to me. But plenty of stuff doesn't. Like singing. And dancing. And relaxing. I also knew that focus wasn't enough to get me where I wanted to go, and that one of the best ways to ensure success was to study the methods of those who'd already achieved it. Since "success leaves clues," I was like a detective examining every case for what I might learn. And so, yes, I was influenced by The Donald decades before I ever entered his boardroom as a contestant on *Celebrity Apprentice.* When he published his first book, *The Art of the Deal,* back in 1987, I eagerly read his advice about getting ahead in business. It was thoroughly Trump— entertaining and exasperating; long on wisdom, short on modesty. I devoured it. Those pages contained some gems and tips that I still use to this day. The first is a personal philosophy that goes something like this: plan for the future by focusing on the present. The second is a technique that may seem counterintuitive for a control enthusiast like me, but has served me better than maybe any other approach I've adopted in business. Trump says you can't be entrepreneurial—or imaginative, even—if you're too structured. Even now, as a presidential candidate, he rarely reads off a teleprompter or cue cards. He just lets it happen, remaining open to comment about a mic that's not working or to riff on a competitor. His campaign advisers got it right, I believe, with that motto they adopted: "Let Trump Be Trump." I think that's why so many people respond to his energy, what they perceive as authenticity. I can't really think of another public figure who is more unapologetically himself than Trump. Whether you like it or not, he owns it.

As he explained in his first book, using several examples from his own life, he approaches his business with a lot of fluidity and flexibility. I saw the wisdom in this, and I've tried to take the same approach in my business deals and in dealing with all kinds of relationships. I can always be flexible and am ready to pivot when I need to. Sometimes I'm sure it frustrates those who work with me. I know. People like to be sure of where they stand and what's coming up next. But I can't always give them specifics. What I know for sure is we're going *up* by being better and stronger. Beyond that, I usually prefer to keep the details open, in both my schedule and my expectations about how the next steps may happen in my business life.

In my staff meetings for Leeza's Care Connection, our team has sometimes complained of motion sickness because the view keeps changing! I may start out discussing a plan to offer a new support group for families struggling to accept life after a devastating diagnosis, and the next thing you know, I'm talking about a different program with new partners and new ways of looking at their needs. I always want to explore the "what ifs" and take the detours along the way. When you remove the risk of being judged for such an unbridled creative approach, others are inspired to think about the "what ifs," too.

One of my business heroes, Sir Richard Branson, the English entrepreneur who created Virgin Airlines, the Virgin megastores, and several other Virgin branded businesses, described using a fluid approach in his book, *Losing My Virginity*. His entire business structure is to be unstructured. When others try to tell him his approach won't work, his famous comeback is "Screw it. Let's do it." (The title of another one of his many books.) He has written his own rules for success, and we can, too.

Hemingway has been quoted as having said, "The world breaks everyone, and afterwards, many are strong at the broken places." I don't think that's completely true. I believe the world tests everyone, but if we are flexible, we'll bend and not break.

YOU CAN'T BOTTLE IT

Before I wanted to be Beyoncé, I wanted to be Dick Clark. I'm always attracted to people who wield their power with grace and strength.

When I was sent to interview Dick Clark not long into my time at *ET,* I hit the legend lottery. Did the assignment editor have any idea of what was about to happen? I was about to meet the man who was at the top of my inspirational dream team.

The first thing I noticed when I walked into his office was the vintage jukeboxes. The vibe seemed loose and fun. The people who worked there seemed happy and committed to excellence, which was Dick's way.

Perhaps no one has influenced me more, not just as a professional, but also as a person, than Dick Clark. Of course, when I was coming up as a broadcast journalism major who worked as a radio DJ and loved Wolfman Jack, Dick Clark was pretty much the apex of what I might possibly do with my life one day. I also had Diane Sawyer as a pacesetter, as well as Barbara Walters (hence my reporter Barbie named after her), and coveted their reputations for being strong competitors with an unmatched work ethic. But there was something about Dick Clark that transcended it all for me.

I was about to shake hands with my reason for being a broadcaster. Now, the standard in Hollywood would be to have an assistant offer me coffee or water while I waited to see the king, but within a few minutes Dick himself came out and greeted me. He was dressed in a casual sweater over a button-down shirt.

When you're meeting a hero for the first time, there's always the danger of being disappointed. But there was no chance of that happening in that moment because I could instantly tell that Dick was exactly who he appeared to be on camera. Okay, he was a bit shorter than I'd imagined, but he was still larger than life to me. I had spent time in the hair and makeup chair at the studio that morning just for the occasion. Our wardrobe stylist, Julie, had given me a teal knit top that zipped up the front. When I saw him, I was glad I hadn't worn the little conservative suit I was considering. There was nothing stuffy about Dick Clark. He made you feel like you were exactly the person he wanted to see at that very moment. He wasn't putting on an act. Nothing rushed or phony. It was just as if I'd been a guest on *American Bandstand* and he was putting me at ease. I think, more than anything, it was his voice. With that friendly, famous voice, he actually told me that he enjoyed my work. The next thing I knew, he was basically interviewing me, until I snapped out of it long enough to introduce the rest of our team. He was Dick Clark, through and through. An American icon who just happened to come off as a regular guy.

As a TV producer and entrepreneur, for me Dick was in that most rarefied air, alongside Barbara Walters and Oprah Winfrey, where inspiration flows freely. When I was building my career in the 1980s, Dick had shows on all three networks. Now Dick Clark Productions is the world's largest producer of live televised events.

The first time I got to host one of these live events with Dick was the Miss USA pageant in Wichita, Kansas, in 1990. Interestingly enough, in 1993 I was again hosting the pageant with Dick, when Miss Michigan, a beautiful African American woman named Kenya Moore, was crowned Miss USA. I wouldn't see Kenya again for twenty-one years, when we both ended up being contestants on *Celebrity Apprentice*. Truly, a small world! Over the years, Dick hired me to host or present at several of his big live productions, including the Academy of Country Music Awards. Cohosting with Dick was not only a thrill because of sharing a stage with him; I was also seeing firsthand the work ethic and ambition fueling this deceptively laid-back icon. What I witnessed was a man who was the master of focus and had a very special relationship with the audience, especially live in the studio. It was poetry in motion. He knew audiences, as simple as that. I watched him look people directly in the eye. He would smile and appear casual while at the same time being all business. I swear audiences would stand up and take their clothes off if he asked them to! He made them feel that safe. Dick was in charge; what could go wrong? He deepened this rapport by doing a behind-the-scenes play-by-play, letting the audience know what was coming up, or if the production was running long, so they became a part of the production team. Dick's focus never failed when giving what I call teachable feedback. If you were missing the target, Dick would let you know. I was always happy to take the note. Owning your power is never wrong, especially if it comes with a guide on how to hit the bull's-eye next time.

I always love doing live television. There's such a rush, knowing you only have one chance to get it right. When I did my first live broadcast with Dick, I found myself standing up a little taller because he was so on top of every little detail. I wanted to overdeliver for him and bring that exceptional care to the show, too.

After I got to know Dick a little better, I realized I had to make good use of my access to him. It wasn't enough to simply learn by observing. I wanted to really know how he did it, and so I started looking for those moments when the cameras weren't rolling and I could ask him questions without interfering with his job.

"Dick, what's your secret when it comes to timing and pacing?" I asked.

"So much of it is intuitive," he said. "You feel it."

I nodded my head, wondering if I'd ever hone my instincts like he had. From there I began asking him for business advice. As my high-profile position at *ET* brought more and more opportunities my way, I wanted to make sure I grew my business as strategically as Dick had. He advised me to branch out and create multiple income sources while never alienating my base. Using his example, I created and owned my own radio business modeled on what he had achieved. Before I knew it, in the early 1990s, I was cohosting *ET,* hosting my own show, *Leeza,* and running three nationally syndicated radio shows. I had one radio studio at Paramount and one at home, and I used to record my radio shows at all hours of the day—and night. I'd even do "pickup lines," or short script changes, during fifteen-minute breaks while filming *Leeza.* My soundproof booth at home earned the nickname "the screaming room," because when the kids were little and needed a place to melt down, I directed them to my little tricked-out announcer room, where they could yell as much as they needed to without being heard outside.

I felt like Dick had become a mentor, and I aimed to make him proud. And so it was an incredible honor and thrill when I got my star on the Hollywood Walk of Fame in 1998 and Dick came to speak on my behalf.

"You know, you can't teach it, and you can't bottle it, and you can't give it to someone," he said. "They've either got it, or they don't, and Leeza has it."

The honor of the star itself was fantastic, but then to have Dick speaking so highly about me still makes my spine tingle when I think about that moment today. Who gets that? To not only meet one of your heroes, but to have him come and support you in such a way? It was an incredibly special moment.

Dick's other favorite piece of advice was this: Always be respectful and have gratitude. Those are the basics that make sense to me and always have. I think that's why you get invited back in the beginning and, eventually, why you get to stay at the top. Dick was a prime example of living these qualities to the fullest in his own life, and I can't think of anyone in our orbit who was more beloved.

SAY YES

Good thing I've always done well on no sleep (and lots of coffee). I was already juggling a full schedule, plus being a single mom, but I was fully embracing the Dick Clark model, and so I looked for unconventional ways to continue building opportunities. It occurred to me that I was only using a fraction of the footage I taped when I interviewed celebrities, and so I went to *ET* and asked them if I could repackage the extra material into content for shows like *Good Morning Australia* and *Late Night Australia*.

As far as the folks at *ET* were concerned, this setup would mean greater exposure for the show without any extra expense or effort from them, and so they agreed. I snagged Billy Olson to help me with the copy, adding it to the mix of material I had to regularly generate, making me what he called the "first entertainment reporter to cross international waters." This move just showed there was a hunger for this kind of news around the world.

It was an easy layup for the studio. Not so much for me. It wasn't producing or editing the packages that got me. It was the time difference. Once I had my story, I had to get to my Hollywood sign backdrop at the studio, or to the CNN building rooftop, *in the middle of the night,* to do a live intro for the show in Australia.

I didn't care. For me I was right on track, taking advantage of all the opportunities that were being laid at my feet and hustling for new ones. With all due respect to Steve Jobs' focus formula of saying no to things that weren't right, as long as it made sense for me, no matter how big or how small, I always tried to say yes to any chance to grow my business. I knew that's where my focus needed to be and that no other approach could ever be more right. I developed a strong radio presence. I hosted pageants, fundraisers, the Hollywood Christmas Parade, the Rose Parade. I even landed my own Lifetime show, *Growing Up Together,* about being a mom. I was *busy* but I never lost sight of where I was going and I knew that all my efforts had landed me right smack dab in the middle of the life of my dreams. No way was I going to complain about being exhausted. I was having a ball.

LOVE YOUR HATERS

"Well, I don't think I'm going to do an infomercial, but I'd love to meet Tony Robbins," I said.

Little did I know when I spoke those words to my agent that Tony Robbins could, and would, persuade me to do what I'd vowed not to do, and that I'd end up knowing he was right. I was already a fan of Tony, having discovered him when I first moved to Los Angeles. I was watching TV one night when Martin Sheen caught my attention. He was talking about Tony Robbins and his personal growth program, "Personal Power," and how it had changed his life. Since I was always looking for a new way to change *my* life, I called up and ordered a copy of the audio program.

Tony's whole message really worked for me, and I felt it immediately add value to everything I was trying to accomplish. I always kept my library of cassette tapes (this was the 1990s, remember?) in my car, and I purposely arrived at shoots early so I could finish listening to the rest of a tape. I did everything he advised, kept my little workbook close, and went about my life. Often I would think about a lesson I'd learned from Tony, like: "If you do what you've always done, you'll get what you've always gotten." Or: "You get what you focus on." Whenever I felt challenged, I was grateful to have these kinds of tools in my box, which helped me to get on with the business at hand.

Nearly a decade later, things were clicking for me. I'd internalized Tony's lessons, and my career was going great. That's when one of my agents called to say the folks at the direct marketing giant Guthy-Renker wanted to talk to me.

"They want you to do an infomercial interviewing Tony Robbins," he said.

Now, at that time nobody in my business was doing infomercials. No Cindy Crawford and her Meaningful Beauty, no Britney and Bieber or Adam Levine speaking out for Proactiv. I wondered what doing an infomercial would signal to those in my profession. Maybe it would look like I had no career, or needed the money. But my career was in full gear. I was making real money. More than anything, I still wanted to be taken seriously as a journalist, and at the time this was a step no self-respecting journalist would make.

It was arranged that I would meet Tony at a café in Westwood, and the next thing I knew, I was in the thrall of his full persuasiveness and all seven feet of his personal power. He told me about working with Princess Diana, Nelson Mandela, Bill Clinton, even Mother Teresa. One thirty-minute conversation and one cup of coffee later, I was all in! I'd agreed to go to his personal island in Fiji to tape the interview for the infomercial. I would have gotten on the plane with him right then and there if he'd asked me.

I called my agents as soon as I got home.

"I want to do it," I said. "I'm in."

But it was far from a done deal. This was a major risk, a crossroads.

At the time, my only concern—and my agents' *major* concern, which they expressed to me in daily conversations while I was deciding—was: *How would this look? Could I do an infomercial and still be considered credible by those within my industry and the public?* Everyone I turned to for an opinion warned me that I probably couldn't, and that I might never get another reporting job, much less a mainstream news job. *Hmm, my news director in Spartanburg had said the same thing.*

Well, I didn't see it that way. I believed it would actually enhance my credibility. Not that I was simply letting wishful thinking rule the day. Not at all. I knew it was risky, but I loved the whole direct-to-consumer model, and I believed in Tony and his message, knowing how valuable it had been to me. This was my chance to not only learn from Tony, but also to contribute and affect other people. Taking the chance felt dangerous, like a dare, which was extremely appealing to me. Oh, and the deal would pay me a lot of money. If our collaboration worked and the infomercial was successful, it would mean even more money. That wasn't part of my decision-making process; my integrity and career longevity were more important to me than any sum of money, but sure, that was on the table, too. Money is a powerful incentive, and there's no shame in admitting that you're striving to run a profitable business, as long as you're running it with your values intact.

I thought about how the people I admired most always wrote their own rules for success. I remembered Dick telling me, "You've gotta feel it." And I did. Of course, at the time I didn't know this decision would cause much bigger problems, including being sued by Paramount. It never crossed my mind that anything could truly derail my career. I'd worked too hard, and I believed in myself too much.

I figured the worst (or best) thing that could happen was I'd end up like one of my other business inspirations, Suzanne Somers, and her Thighmaster, a stroke of marketing genius. She set the pace for me with this one. Suzanne didn't care that she was initially laughed at for selling this product. She remained confident that she knew what was right for her and her audience. She made a fortune. Plus, that decision opened up a whole new career for her, selling all kinds of things for the next thirty years. No one is laughing at her now.

With all this in mind, I knew the infomercial was the right decision for me, no matter what anyone said. Although I was always polite to my team when I disagreed with them or wanted to go in a different direction, I was firm about what I wanted and how I expected it to happen. Nice means pleasant. It doesn't mean meek. And, yes, I had that same intense focus and fierce optimism that had carried me through so many uncertain moments in my life, so I moved forward. Game on.

Everything about shooting the infomercial with Tony was great. We had a hit. The program was well received and it didn't take long for Guthy-Renker to approach me directly about developing products of my own. Here was an instance when staying focused on my own goals and instincts, and ignoring others' negativity, was absolutely the way to go. People get off track when they "major in minor things," as entrepreneur, author, and motivational speaker Jim Rohn said. There was no way I was going to give detractors major focus. That decision led the way to the podium at the Direct to Consumer convention in Las Vegas.

LET THE REAL YOU SHINE THROUGH

"If I stand for something," I said before the crowd when I accepted the 2015 Icon Award from my peers in the direct response industry, "I'd like it to be gratitude and optimism."

I have Greg Renker and Bill Guthy to thank for that. My first TV project with Tony was really the launching pad for getting into business with Guthy-Renker, the company that originally saw Tony Robbins's potential and essentially gave the world the infomercial as we now know it. My relationship with them is now the longest-running partnership in the direct-to-consumer industry, generating more than a billion dollars in sales.

Bill and Greg are amazing pioneers and visionaries who have modeled risk-taking qualities for me along with focus and flexibility. Guthy-Renker knew they had a hit with "Personal Power" and they thought there was more for us to do together.

"Do you think you'd ever want your own products?" they asked. "If you do, we'd like to have that discussion."

"Thank you, but I don't really think so," I said.

Selling life improvement was one thing. Selling jewelry or cleansers was another. But wait a minute: *I was being offered an opportunity by one of the most successful business partnerships out there. Was I really going to say no?* It's like what Sheryl Sandberg says: "When someone offers you a seat on a rocket ship, don't ask what seat." Maybe, just maybe, it was simply a matter of keeping the same tight focus I'd always applied to other areas of my professional life, and finding the right product for me. The more I thought about it, the more I realized that whatever I sold would have to be transformational, like Tony's program. I didn't see at the time how beauty products could match that criterion. I wanted to build a deeper relationship with buyers by speaking intimately to them, and I wasn't sure I could do that as a BFF who was sharing her beauty secrets.

Enter Pauline Youngblood, an aesthetician who had developed a product for people with birthmarks or other imperfections that were difficult to cover. I had actually heard about this product on production sets where it was used when actresses had to have their tattoos covered for a love scene. Not only could it successfully camouflage a tattoo—or anything else; it was also good for your skin and could even be worn by people in various stages of laser procedures to remove birthmarks, or other treatments that left the skin delicate or fragile. Addressing a genuine need in the marketplace, delivering on a promise . . . that all sounded like a solid business model.

But if I was going to stake my reputation on something, I had to be sure. I didn't need to hear any more about just how great the product was. I wanted to see it with my own eyes and have real customers show me how they used it and why. So I invited in some women with birthmarks, pigment variations, rosacea, and everything else you could think of, and I had them put on the makeup, *themselves, in the natural light of my office.*

The results were incredible.

Bingo! That's the product, I thought. *First of all, it works. And for those people who feel they can't be confident because of an imperfection that's making them self-conscious, this new beginning could be truly transformative. That's all makeup is for any of us: a chance to feel better about ourselves. When we feel better about who we are, we become more powerful in our own lives. This product could totally deliver on its promise, a message I've always believed in, to "Let The Real You Shine Through."*

That product ultimately became Sheer Cover Mineral Makeup, which I sold through infomercials and on the Home Shopping Network (HSN). Not only was it successful, it also brought me to a new audience that I hadn't connected with through my entertainment reporting. Many people can't relate to celebrities, but vulnerabilities about the way we look are something almost everyone can understand. And the truth was, although it was a product, it meant more to me than a lot of the reporting I'd done on assignment. I loved having a portal, a reason to start conversations with women about what I *really* care about: my message that who you are today is not who you have to be tomorrow. That was the promise of this product. The possibility of transformation wasn't limited to the exterior. I made this truth a part of my message. Women responded by the thousands. It was an incredible feeling.

I took my Sheer Cover business very seriously. Even though I still had all of my regular commitments from my broadcasting career, I knew I had to put careful focus on this new segment of my career as well if I wanted it to succeed. So I set aside time to go through emails we'd received from customers and to cold-call as many of them as I could. Of course, many women thought they were being punked when they heard that I was on the phone, wanting to know about their Sheer Cover experiences. "Come on, is this really Leeza Gibbons?" I heard, again and again. "Why do you want to talk to me?" As soon as I told them how important it was for me to get their feedback, we had surprisingly intimate conversations about fears and disappointments, and the power of possibilities. I'm a storyteller, and their stories nourished me, just like when I do interviews on TV. I felt a great sense of satisfaction, knowing these women could now show up in their lives with more confidence and power.

REFOCUSING IS ANOTHER FORM OF FOCUS

Even when a venture is successful, it's crucial to be just as cautious and exacting in your decision making at every stage of the game. When I wasn't, I paid the price.

As the years went by and Sheer Cover continued to be successful, HSN encouraged us to expand the brand and do more with it for them. HSN said they needed more variety in the line. Beauty, they said, is like the fashion business: customers want something new every quarter. They're right about that. I mean look at successful makeup lines. They've usually got a warehouse full of tantalizing new colors. The development team at Guthy-Renker presented the products they thought I should sell along with our problem/solution concealer and mineral powder foundation: lip gloss and eye shadow.

Now, this had nothing to do with my original mandate of promoting a product that genuinely helped people and brought transformation and renewal into their lives. I expressed my doubts, but HSN kept pressing, and we had to give them something or else risk losing our spots on air. Because they were the experts, I deferred to the marketing team. *I've never developed a brand on a shopping channel before,* I thought. *They have. If they're telling me that this is what we need to be offering, then let's go with that.*

When the lip gloss and shadow were not the major success the core products had been, I blamed myself (just like in the Amy Schumer "I'm Sorry" skit). *I'm missing it. If I just try harder to sell these products that they obviously think are the right products, then the numbers will be better, and everybody will be happy,* I thought. *And then we'll get to move on.*

Unfortunately, sometimes there's a limit to how much you can do with work ethic and willpower alone, and none of the color products in the line extension ever really took off. In retrospect, I should have trusted myself more and pushed back harder. I could have respectfully and politely shut the door on this direction, and potentially saved all of us a lot of anxiety and extra effort. It was still all about trying to sell products, but before I had sold my relationship to—and belief in—the products. Lesson learned (again): stay focused on your game, trust yourself, and be true to your gut, even when other people doubt you.

I've realized that I owe it to myself, and everyone involved, to give my honest position on a product, show, or service, regardless of whether I'm an expert on the subject or not. I've begun to listen more, and to get the information I need, by being patient as answers are revealed. I learned a lot about this from Greg Renker.

I love to take business meetings with Greg. Just to be in casual conversation with him is to witness someone highly skilled at controlling the energy. Many times he does it by being silent. Let's say I'm in the room with my husband, our agent, a producer, a director, and someone on the creative team for a new product we're discussing. Greg is polite, charming, and engaging but manages to run a meeting that's all business by utilizing what I call the Clint Eastwood approach. He sets an agenda and has everyone "empty out" about their ideas, feelings, and opinions. He listens intently, with very little emotion and even fewer words.

When he does talk, he's usually gathering more information by probing: "What's your beauty routine? Is that something that makes sense to you? Have you even seen anyone who does it that way?" There are very few "I" statements. When you leave the room, you realize Greg has made everyone feel great and valued, but he has not tipped his hand at all. Listen more than you talk. Check. Give everyone something to feel smart about and allow them to own their positions. Got it. Treat everyone with dignity and give time and attention like you have a surplus of both. Duly noted. Now, in business meetings (and later on *Celebrity Apprentice*), I've learned to wait it out and hear other opinions before offering mine. People are less likely to mistake silence for not having a position, or for being ignorant, if you make your words count. When I'm in meetings with those like my mentor Greg Renker, I recognize this skill in action, and I rarely think that because someone is kind, they will be weak.

Oh, and by the way, I'm still working with Guthy-Renker. Our relationship continues to be dynamic, challenging, and financially rewarding. I'm still speaking directly with audiences and customers about how to live their best lives. All bases covered on that one.

WHEN YOU WANT TO DO YOUR BEST, FOCUS

Two thousand and two was a very rough year for me. My mother's diagnosis of Alzheimer's disease left me grieving and sad. I had finally realized that I couldn't fix it and that I would eventually lose my mom the same way she had lost hers. I felt so powerless, and I was very vulnerable. At the same time, I felt destiny-driven to honor my mother, and to make my life stand for something by sharing our story and helping others who were suffering as my family was. I felt empowered to step into what I knew was an important place of purpose for me, but I also had a lot of questions about how to do that, and I was just very raw. It was within this hurricane of emotion that I started my nonprofit foundation.

During this time, I was a guest on *The Larry King Show*.

I had shared so many of my personal beliefs and so much of my life—including the story of my mom's illness—on my own talk show, and yet I worried that I wasn't in a good place to talk coherently about how the foundation had risen out of my loss. This new path, though, was emerging as more important to me than anything else just then, and so I decided to try.

As soon as I sat down across from Larry, I was so glad that I had. Something about being there with him, in his suspenders with his elbows on the table, opening up the dialogue for me, allowed me to exhale. *Okay, Larry's in the driver's seat,* I thought. *He's so good, and I trust him, and this is so where I'm supposed to be.* For once I was able to avoid doing the thing I always do, which is to get stuck in my head, overanalyzing and overproducing everything. Ruminating about outcomes, choices, consequences, and all the rest is not focus. It's a trap. How many times had I played out the way segments should go, what I should wear, when it should all happen? Planning and being strategic is one thing (and a very smart thing) but when you're in a constant loop of analytics about everything, it's time to walk away from the control switch, honey. Now I had arrived at a place where the emotional side of my brain finally won over the control enthusiast. I liked it in the way that dangerous things are compelling. I felt very privileged to be there, telling my story in a way that was authentic and pure. It wasn't about me. That's when I began to elevate Mom's wise words, "Show up, do your best, let go of the rest," to mantra status. It was an honor, a few years later, when Larry asked me if I would fill in for him for a time while he was away. I knew these were big suspenders to fill, but as I've always loved a challenge, I couldn't wait to try.

I was so excited about the opportunity that I'm sure I badgered the producers way too much about how I could best get myself ready, and who our guests were going to be. I really wanted to be on top of my game. As I've always done, I overprepared so I could have the luxury of not having to worry about being caught underprepared when the cameras rolled. Of course, as I was soon reminded, none of my preparation was relevant in the moment, because when you're on live TV, it's unpredictable, and you almost always end up going in a different direction anyhow.

After my time as guest host ended, I wrote the show's producers a note, thanking them for letting me be there, and for working with me and supporting me.

"You know, we've been doing the show a long time, and we've never had anyone send us a thank-you note," one of the producers told me. "Larry gets them, but not us."

I was so surprised by that fact, not only because it had felt so natural for me to express my genuine gratitude to them for the opportunity they'd given me, but also because fundamental good manners are something I've always believed in. Nice people do nice things to show appreciation. After all, one of the first books my mother gave me was *White Gloves and Party Manners,* which I read cover to cover and still keep on my bookshelf at home. I'm not a big memorabilia collector, but Larry sent me a pair of suspenders in appreciation for guest hosting his show, and they are among my favorite keepsakes. Not only was it cool to receive them, but the gesture also reinforced my belief in expressions of gratitude. Larry later provided the foreword to my book *Take Your Oxygen First: Protecting Your Health and Happiness While Caring for a Loved One with Memory Loss*. He wrote, "She has been one of the few people to whom I have turned to guest host my show, because I know Leeza puts her heart and soul into everything she does." Takes one to know one, Larry. Thank you for all you've taught me.

When I think back to what I've learned from Larry, it's almost the exact opposite of what I learned from Dick Clark, who was always planning and preparing and bringing his perfectionism to bear on everything he did. Larry taught me that there can also be a great value in homing your focus in on the moment, which allows for spontaneity and intuition to take over. I came to see that when I've overprepared, I've sometimes become too rigid and tripped myself up.

Larry knows when to veer off the standard path, which of course is where the real gold is mined. I'm not sure whether it's intuition, or being able to read the body language of others, but after so many decades of interviewing authors, directors, newsmakers, and scandal survivors, he's really learned the things that telegraph people's thoughts so he can jump on a clue and move the conversation in an authentic, dynamic direction. I don't think Larry ever worries about looking naïve or ill-informed or silly, and that's got to be very liberating. I've not yet reached this point myself, and I'm not sure I'll live long enough to completely get there, but I'm working on it. I guess you could say it's an emerging skill, this lack of self-consciousness. I sure could have used it on *Dancing with the Stars*.

FOCUS WITH FLEXIBILITY

Real friends will help you put on a holiday musical revue—sometimes in drag—with hot pants and a bustier, no less. At least if you're friends with me! (More on that later.) And real friends will always shoot straight with you.

Many of my best friends in the world are people I once worked with—former producers, assistants, and writers—who labored in the trenches with me day after day, while we built our lives and careers. We are devoted to each other, which has been a wonderful gift. They are also unfailingly honest with me, which is incredibly valuable, even if it sometimes stings.

I have heard from my former-employees-turned-friends that they've sometimes wished I'd been narrower in my focus over the years. From their perspective, because I was so ambitious, and so excited to stretch myself and grow, I was always looking for the next venture. When I was hosting the TV newsmagazine *EXTRA,* I was passionate about looking for ways to use my talent and business opportunities to help others deal with the new normal that comes when someone you love and care for receives a serious diagnosis. Learning that your wife has cancer, your husband has Parkinson's, or your mother has

Alzheimer's can leave you with a kind of fear-driven inertia and aching that changes everything. This was a cruel reality I knew firsthand, since my mother was bravely battling the theft of her memories by Alzheimer's disease, after seeing it claim her own mom, my granny.

Around this time, I saw an opening to help those like my family by developing an Internet life-coaching business and I pounced. I knew it was the right opportunity at the right time. I was dead-set on connecting families with the mental health providers and other professionals they needed to move forward with faith and focus. Yeah, but see, that's the thing. I was so hot to make this happen that I didn't want to hear anything other than yes. My attention was stubbornly on getting services into the lives of those who were hurting, and not enough on the roadblocks along the way, and the business never really took off. My team could see the derailment looming, but I kept the faith we could persevere. I got distracted with layouts for the website and colors and language for the brochures and didn't want to face the fact that the distribution system couldn't sustain the business. Well, you can't will things into existence, no matter how much you try. As in our relationships, our business ventures need our 360-degree dedicated focus to thrive. I always want to look at the "good" parts, or the parts that are working, but that's not enough on its own.

And so, while I can point to moments when I've been proud of my focus, it's really the quality of staying *consistently* focused that I strive to develop even more in my own life and business landscape now. I'm telling you this, because someone cared enough to tell me. The candor of my employees has given me the chance to see myself through their eyes, and to strive to do better. This is an incredible growth opportunity to step back, refocus, and retrain for the next big thing, which may mean aborting some or all of your original idea. Being distracted by the shiny paint on an engine that doesn't run is a shortcut to failure. Lots of entrepreneurs get stuck here because we are addicted to the excitement of creating something new and dynamic. Consistent or corrective focus is the antidote. Here's what I know for certain: your bounce-back quality is what determines success. We rebound by doing, not by thinking, so the thing I began to do differently was to ask questions. "How did I mess up? What could I have done better?" I hope you'll find ways to open the door for corrective focus in your life, not only by investing in friends and coworkers who respect you enough to tell you the truth, but also by developing your ability to hear criticism, or an alternative opinion, and embrace it. Going into defensive mode and getting your feelings hurt will only destroy your best shot to make things better. Winners don't micromanage. They focus on what they're good at and do more of that, delegating to others the tasks or responsibilities that are focus-diffusors for them.

Bottom line: focus is crucial but can also become a trap if you cling to one idea or goal too ferociously or try to focus on too many things at once. Acknowledging when it's time to take a different approach or go in a new direction gives you focus with flexibility, which is the best, most winning combination of all. For me it's meant I've never been without work, well, not since I got that call in Rio telling me it was time to hit the beach (or the employment line).

THE SECRET OF FOCUS

As you are hoping, wishing, praying, dreaming, strategizing, learning, and preparing for success, you have to find a way to focus on being okay with where you are now, even while you're striving. I was missing this aspect of my focus in my younger days. I was so worried about looking ahead, creating a life of substance, I didn't stop to realize I actually had one already, and if I wanted more, I needed to start by being grateful for what I had. I now have "Gratitude is the foundation for abundance" written in several places, from my car to my phone, as a reminder.

If you are constantly seeking better and greater opportunities without being content with your starting point, then you've missed the most important aspect of fulfillment. It's like a neutralization of the starting line; the farther you keep moving it up, the farther away your ultimate happiness will be. In fact, you may *never* reach your ultimate happiness.

Even though most people are economically better off now than they were a few decades ago, research shows that they are less happy. And so there you have it. I love money as much as the next person, but if that's how you measure success, it will feel like opening an empty box over and over. You're not gonna find contentment inside. I remind you to "pee on your own turf." Put your first focus every day on loving who you are and valuing where you are now—even as you're taking steps to make it better. I love the *Velveteen Rabbit* quote: "You become. It takes a long time. That's why it doesn't happen often to people who break easily, or have sharp edges, or who have to be carefully kept." Be open to shifting your focus to "becoming" who you need to be.

CHAPTER THREE

Built to Last (Resilience)

What do Madonna and Dick Clark have in common? During my years reporting on the entertainment business, I was always on the lookout for those who managed lasting, meaningful careers, and the lessons of how they did it. As far as I could tell, there were two main camps: those like Dick Clark and Barbara Walters, who established a persona and never failed to deliver what they were known—and loved—for over the decades. And those like Suzanne Somers and Miley Cyrus, who became known as much for their constant reinvention as for any one particular chapter in their careers. I could see the benefits of both ways of being, and that both approaches actually had something in common: these masters of resilience always found ways to bring what they had to offer into the present landscape, rather than dwelling on the past, whatever its glories. They knew how to capitalize on the right now, realizing that the best use of this moment will prepare you for the ones ahead better than anything else.

Staying excited about today—and tomorrow—is really important, not only as a way to remain relevant and continue to grow and achieve, but also because being fully engaged with the present moment is where real happiness lies. This lesson was brought home for me during my time at *ET* when I was sent to interview so many stars and public figures at all different stages of their careers. I think about Warren Beatty, Tom Cruise, and Bill Clinton as among those who were always focused on the present. I'd submit that this was a prime reason all three of these men were able to weather so many ups and downs in their careers and bounce back from a variety of scandals and tabloid tsunamis. Rather than hiding out, or trying to silence their critics, they've held their heads high while creating fresh focal points in their personal and professional lives. That is the definition of resilience, and I think each time you reemerge or bounce back, it brings you closer to who you really are.

What's thorny about buoyancy like that is that it's often easier to cultivate and maintain in the areas where we're already strong, and trickier for us when we're dealing with matters that are more challenging. I know this was the case for me.

At work, I had this down. Professional obstacles and setbacks often came to feel almost like blessings because they inspired me to dig deeper and prove myself by chasing success even more. But, as you're about to see, when it came to my personal life, these natural traits, which I obviously still had when I drove off the Paramount lot after work seemed to deactivate. They weren't enough to keep me from suffering heartache and disappointment again and again.

Kids change everything, and they always come first. By the time I was juggling hosting duties on my own shows, on TV as well as radio, and my own production company, I also had three children, who were my top priority, emotionally, but it required a mama bear's ferocity to keep them at the top of my list every day. As busy as I was, I rarely missed any event at my kids' schools, including being a homeroom mother, chaperoning field trips, and bringing treats. I'm not looking for credit or glory here. Most working moms will tell you the same. But even though I was involved at school, I sometimes felt like an outsider among the stay-at-home moms. Check out this example of how a conversation on the playground went down, when I asked what I should bring to an upcoming bake sale.

"Oh, you don't have to do anything, Leeza," another mother said. "We know you're busy with work, and you know, we don't allow pink bakery boxes. Only homemade."

"Oh, I'll bake something myself," I said with maybe too much defiance. "I make a great peanut butter cookie!"

I wasn't about to guilt myself over this. It had nothing to do with my parenting. I proceeded to stop by the bakery, where I picked up two dozen cookies *in the pink box*, transferred them to ziplock bags, and moved forward. I wasn't going to let them diminish what I had to offer just because my home life didn't look just like theirs. And I wasn't going to try to diminish them, or their offerings, either, just because it might have made me feel better in the moment.

This is sensitive stuff, I know. When I hosted a *Leeza* show about moms in the workplace, our crowd reached near riot levels. There we were, a group of mothers pointing our fingers, whipping our hair around, and acting like the women on the other side of the issue were criminals who had no shot at rehabilitation. There was so much tension and division of thought, it felt like the soundstage would explode. And so I'm all about being open-minded and empathetic toward all ways of being, in this controversy and others. We've fought so hard for our work-life options and our right to decide what's best for us, that to battle each other along with the world at large seems insane. Let's support each other, for heaven's sake. When we can do that, we'll make it better for everyone, and maybe we'll even stop being targets. I agree with Madeleine Albright: "There is a special place in hell for women who don't help other women." Girls compete with each other. Women empower each other.

In my case, the situation at home was complicated by the fact that when I was married to the men with whom I had my children, I was the primary breadwinner. Years later, I could totally relate to Anne-Marie Slaughter's article in *The Atlantic*: "Why Women Still Can't Have It All." Realistically, it shouldn't matter where the money comes from, and both members of the marriage (or partnership) team should be willing and able to be the lead parent, or be allowed to follow the things they decide best support the family and provide the most opportunity (which isn't always about the money). It's just difficult to reverse years of built-in hardwiring that says men are the providers, and that if they can't bring in the money, they lose points in the man-club. Even well-intentioned guys, who just want everyone to get along, can get stuck here. My rearview mirror now shows me that both the men I chose to have children with were likely struggling with my success and probably acted out because of that, often sabotaging me with irresponsible, hurtful, or destructive behavior. I don't think this was necessarily deliberate, or even always conscious, and I'm sure there were plenty of times when I didn't make it any easier, but I didn't respect myself when I played it small and turned down opportunities that supported us all.

I loved what I did so much, and it allowed me a lot of flexibility as a mom, but I often felt as if I should feel ashamed or guilty for succeeding. I never felt that way when I was single. You know the story: We applaud men who don't let anything steal their dreams, and yet women often get labeled as selfish or uncompromising for the exact same behavior. I don't think I fit either of those two labels, but I felt strongly that being a role model for my daughter (and sons) meant demonstrating for them that work and life are fluid, and that career success can be an important component of overall happiness. It sure was for me. Slaughter had it right. As long as we are saying "working mothers" (which is a redundant term if you ask me), and not "working fathers," we are still missing the point. As I later came to discover, if you're lucky enough to find your career voice and your mission, the right life partner can only make those victories sweeter.

This was my blind spot for many years. Even when my marriages faltered, I just kept trying, while redirecting the mounting tension, thinking the honor, the glory, and the ultimate prize (balance) came to those who stayed the course. While I look back with sympathy for the young woman I was, and the pain I encountered, I also have to respect the way I kept my head down and just how hard I tried. I stayed on course even when I felt like I was being run off the road. Don't get me wrong. I take full responsibility for the part I played in the decline and demise of my marriages. I should have had better boundaries and made better choices. But the question remains, should women—or anyone—feel bad about themselves, and acquiesce to make someone else feel better? Slaughter wisely says: "Perhaps the problem is not with women but with work." Touché.

Because I loved my work so much, and found so much sheer joy in the day-to-day duties that kept me going, it was easy to hide out there when things weren't going so well at home. It was like living inside a blender stuck on high. And as a working mom (and at times a single, working mom), I felt added pressures that often made it difficult to stop long enough to even see what was happening in my personal life, let alone improve it. Constant motion was the great pacifier. Like the white noise in my life, I got used to it. It created a kind of veil, putting things in soft focus that should have been sharp. I know I'm far from alone in this struggle, which is why I'm opening up about aspects of my own resilience I've never discussed publicly before.

The complicated intersection of professional and personal duties in the lives of working moms is presented so well in the recent Nancy Meyers movie, *The Intern*. While watching this one, I was totally talking back to the screen, cheering on this young entrepreneur, wife, and mom, played by Anne Hathaway, who almost gives it all up because she can't seem to sync it all up for everyone. Her character is subject to all kinds of judgment, in the boardroom as well as on the playground, with both camps assuming she's bound to fail. This felt like my story, a story that belongs to many of us women who work. As was pointed out in a *Washington Post* blog and in other articles, the movie is like the bookend to Meyers's 1987 film, *Baby Boom*, starring Diane Keaton as a female executive facing the same challenges thirty years ago, only worse. I saw that movie two years before I had my first child, never imagining it would ever have anything to do with my life.

When taken together, I believe these films show how working moms are set up for criticism in our society because we've allowed it to be that way. Sure, advances have been made, but not enough to allow women to enjoy the respect and authority they deserve. We have to change our expectations about balance. I say balance is bogus. It just is. If you're chasing it, you will always feel like an epic failure in your own life. There's no genuine balance possible between family and work, so I say don't try to balance your time, invest it. Invest in the right things (especially in yourself) and the dividends are huge. One day women will be able to claim our need for achievement, and not apologize for wanting success and a happy marriage and family, or a fulfilling personal life of our choice. We will be able to expect our mates, employers, and coworkers to honor our choices, knowing that validation cranks up our desire and ability to deliver on all fronts. (Until then, maybe just get better at playing the game.)

This isn't just a Hollywood problem, either. It could just as well happen to the young woman who goes to night school and studies to reach her dream of being a salon owner, only to be judged by her friends for not spending enough time with her kids, or blamed by her husband or boyfriend for neglecting her duties and not having dinner on the table. Or all those people who pursue goals that take them away from their day-to-day responsibilities, causing resentment from their loved ones. This is when we need to see that investing in education, opportunity, or growing yourself may not create balance, but it can create dividends by ultimately making you a stronger parent and a better partner. That's a great payoff. No matter what anyone else has to say, it's important to stay true to yourself and your dreams, and to remember that even when you get knocked down repeatedly, dreams are serious stuff (so don't leave your dreams along life's highway like roadkill). Dreams make us better. They'll help you find greater resilience and they may help you learn to be more flexible, collaborative, and patient.

Statistically, women tend to find that happiness eludes them more often than it does men. Sheryl Sandberg, Mark Zuckerberg, and many others are shifting the conversation by promoting partnerships that are more equitable. But for now, society expects women to succeed domestically and professionally, and if we don't, we are judged and likely made to feel guilty. Women are especially tough on each other. Tina Fey was right when she said, "Girl-on-girl sabotage is the worst kind of female behavior."

When I gave birth to my first child, my daughter Leksy, I had quite a bit of maternity leave available to me. Before delivery, I thought that was fantastic and was certain I would need even more time and would lament the day I had to go back to work. Just the opposite happened. I had never been a mom before. As a first-timer, I didn't know what I was doing. The target for success kept moving, and I didn't feel comfortable yet with knowing that's the point (not just in parenting, but in life). I had just figured out how to get her to latch on for breastfeeding, when sleeping became the problem. The point is, no one was surprised when I called up the studio after just two weeks and said: "Is it okay if I come back to work now?"

Working was what I knew. It was where I was sure I could be successful. Being a great mother came over time, but initially I felt I was failing. Once I got back to my comfort zone (I was lucky enough to be able to bring my baby with me), I could relax into this new motherhood role and be better at it. Work was actually a huge part of what gave me the confidence to segue into motherhood. Of course, I recognize it's not the same for all women. And that's the whole point. We should all be free to find what works best for us. Without shame. And without judgment. But look at what we're still doing to each other, with the labeling and judging. I believe that this kind of behavior is just plain antifeminist.

RESILIENCE LESSON NUMBER ONE

"Listen, kid, this thing with your fiancé is not gonna work out," producer George Schlatter said to me over coffee one day at Raleigh Studios in Hollywood. "I know you love him and all that, but he's a starfucker, and it's gonna end in heartbreak. I've had to have the same kind of conversations with Goldie."

George had hired me for a summer replacement series, *Funny People*, along with comedian Rita Rudner and two male comics. I knew I wasn't necessarily funny, but George had created a hit with *Rowan & Martin's Laugh-In* and *Real People*, the latter, which aired on NBC from 1979 to 1984, was the forerunner of today's reality shows. *Funny People* came along during a writers' strike and that seemed like the perfect time for a budget-friendly reality show that didn't depend on writers. George thought I could be this new show's straight woman, so that was good enough for me. I could do it.

Well, no, unfortunately, I couldn't. Or we couldn't. The show got very lukewarm reviews. *People* Magazine gave us a C+ and urged the writers to go back to work so we wouldn't get any more shows like these!

I don't know whether it was a bad blend of chemistry, or the fact that I shot the premiere episode sporting a purple satin culotte getup and a gigantic fever blister on my top lip, which was all I could think about. Maybe it was some inherent flaw in the format, but the show was off the air following only a handful of episodes.

Thankfully, I was able to put it all in the right frame and not be too crushed by the disappointment. I'd tried something different, and it hadn't worked out, but people respected George, and our effort, and I'd learned a lot. But my upcoming wedding was another matter altogether.

Wonderful George was trying to help me avoid a disaster, but I didn't feel alerted to anything. I just felt a sense of overwhelming sadness. My throat tightened up as my eyes began to fill with tears. Then, as I always did when confronted with a harsh reality I didn't want to see, I put all of this crazy talk into a shiny pink bubble that I floated off into the sky, and I got on with what I'd intended to do in the first place. Denial, anyone?

It wasn't just my professional life that I ran according to a tight schedule. I also had a very specific timeline for my personal life (ah, that sweet bird of youth who thinks the universe can be set like a stopwatch). When I turned thirty, my biological clock kicked into overdrive. I'd always wanted a family, but suddenly I wanted one *right now*. I often warn female friends around this age to beware of being "emotionally drunk" for these reasons. Me? I thought I was stone-cold sober. In control. Just how I like it. My friends, of course, knew better.

Around this time, I flew to New Zealand to take part in a national on-air telethon. Right there on camera, for the whole world to see (or at least the local population of Kiwis, Aussies, and Brits likely to watch this telethon), Cupid struck me with his arrow.

The man was an English actor and one of the stars of the British hit show *Coronation Street.* He was cute and charming, and he demanded that people notice him. You know those guys who take up all the oxygen in the room? Yes, he was *that* guy, and then some. I was immediately in full swoon. Although my friends and family warned me I was rushing things with a man I barely knew, who happened to have a playboy reputation, I was getting married, and I wouldn't be dissuaded.

A story ran in a British newspaper, my picture featured with dozens of other women, all of us circling around Britain's Bad Boy du Jour. This article and others basically said: "Don't do it, Leeza!" This, finally, was a little alarming.

"Oh, you know, they just do that to sell papers," he told me.

I assured myself he was right and felt guilty for even questioning the man who would become my husband. See what I mean: emotionally drunk. I was getting married, and I was going to live happily ever after, and no one could tell me otherwise. Not that plenty of people didn't try, and not just George, either. Although my parents tried to be supportive at the time, I knew they had misgivings that I'd rushed into marriage without really getting to know my groom. And, as I later found out, my former-producer-turned-best-friend-Andrea told me she received a phone call from Robin Leach the night before my wedding. She was a producer for his show, *Lifestyles of the Rich and Famous,* and he actually wanted her to convince me to call off the wedding because of my soon-to-be-husband's reputation. Of course, she was my best friend and just hoping for the best, so she didn't do anything of the kind. She dutifully wore the horrific cream brocade bridesmaid dress featuring a high-low hemline and smiled.

I was oblivious to all of this at the time, but I did notice a *minor* red flag on my wedding day, when we couldn't get my new husband off the stage at our reception to take me on our honeymoon. Eventually we did leave, and on our honeymoon, I got pregnant. Now there *really* was no telling me everything wasn't going to be perfect. What I was too young, too naïve, or just too headstrong to understand at the time was that, unfortunately, focus doesn't always guarantee the same success and positive results in our personal lives that it often does in our professional lives. It would definitely take me much longer to gain the kind of clarity and confidence in my romantic relationships that came so naturally to me in my business dealings.

Not long after our wedding, someone at the *National Enquirer* was kind enough to tell me that my husband had been seen doing all kinds of tabloid-worthy things. (I know that may not *sound* nice, but she was doing me a big favor by giving me a heads-up before I saw it in print.) Still, I shut her down and I wouldn't hear anything about it.

This was one of several moments in my life when, I can see now, my intense, unwavering work focus became something of a double-edged sword. I was ducking. My personal life was out of control, so I threw myself into my career, where it felt safer. It was a solace for me, and it let me hide out and avoid admitting what was really happening at home. A friend of mine took the initiative to wake me up by actually hiring a private investigator, and he dropped off photos on my doorstep. *Stab. A picture is worth a thousand words, and a thousand shards of heartbreak.*

I was still figuring out what I was going to do about my marriage when *ET* sent me to Mexico for an interview with Kevin Costner. While I was away, apparently there was a veritable orgy at the home I'd bought for us in Beverly Hills. At least that's what the *Enquirer* told me. They painted quite a scene: men wearing my lingerie, and all sorts of stuff you don't read about in Martha Stewart's books on entertaining. They wanted me to comment. How do they find out stuff like this? Maybe it was the two dozen Harleys and other motorcycles parked on our street in the flats of Beverly Hills that tipped them off. Or the music the neighbors told me was blaring from the area by the pool, where people were apparently swimming in the nude, or in my bras and panties. Somehow the tabloid always seemed to know everything unsavory there was to know.

It got worse. That wasn't all they were going to print. When I heard their plans for the story (this time from an anonymous source—thank you for the kindness of strangers) my first thought was of my parents, who might innocently stumble upon the tabloid at their local grocery store and learn the worst, including information that absolutely wasn't true.

Feeling awful and ashamed, I called my parents to give them fair warning. Chalk this up as one of the hardest and most awkward conversations I've ever had, and my career has been pretty much all about handling uncomfortable topics with grace.

My father answered the phone. "Dad, I have to tell you

something," I said. "There's going to be an article in the *National Enquirer,* with a headline to go with it, saying I'm scared that I caught AIDS, and that my unborn child and I are at risk."

"Oh, honey," he said.

"It's not true," I quickly said. "So I don't want you to worry."

Of course he and my mom *were* worried, not that I had AIDS, but that I had come to the end of what I was convinced would be a fairy tale, and now I would have to face the hurtful reality of my choices. That whole year was so difficult, but telling my parents was the worst part. It was just awful. I knew they'd been right all along. Now that I have kids of marrying age, I can't imagine how painful it must be to see your child walk so stubbornly into a mistake. Let's hope I never have to find out how it feels, or that if I do, I manage to remain as calm and loving as my parents did during this time.

I couldn't hold on to my fantasy of our marriage anymore after that. All of my focus was on bringing our daughter safely into the world, and once she was here and healthy, I told him I was done with our marriage. But we had this beautiful little girl, and so I let him know that I would always encourage him to stay involved in her life. It was incredibly disappointing when he not only left our marriage, he also left the country to return to his native England, without any real plan to remain responsible for his daughter.

This was one of my best lessons in resilience and forgiveness. It wasn't about me now. It was about our daughter and her happiness. I'd always been a daddy's girl, and I felt sick that Leksy might not have the joys of a daddy who was present and adored her, doting on her every move. I knew having a dad who appeared to "abandon" her would leave a hole in her heart that would be hard to mend. I can see my daughter still grappling with this part of her story. It's not just me who got a lesson in resilience from this chapter in my life, but also my daughter, and I can only hope that I can help her to learn it as well as I did.

KEEP THE CHEESE; LET ME OUT OF THE TRAP

My good friend John Mcgill has always encouraged me and believed in me professionally, since long before either of us knew what we were doing. Okay, it's not fair for me to paint him with the brush of my own inexperience, but we really were only slightly better than *Dumb and Dumber* when we started working together.

When John called me to come to Dallas to host the local segment of the national telethon for March of Dimes, I jumped. I had just left Dallas for New York and was so grateful for some Texas love. John was writing and producing the segments, and it became clear we shared the same wicked, take-no-prisoners sense of humor. John has always told people I don't giggle; I go straight to a laugh explosion. He's right, and we've had lots of things to laugh about over the years!

John always looked for ways to work me into projects he

was doing in the Big D. Like ArtFest, an annual multiday event celebrating all things art. I became cochair, along with George W. Bush, but first, John had to convince the board to name me. They told him, "We love Leeza and all but what does she have to do with ArtFest? She's not a performer or an artist." *Well, we can fix that,* we both thought. He satisfied their skepticism by arranging for me to become a performer. I jacked up my hair like one of the B-52's, threw on a mini, and took to the stage to sing backup with an Elvis impersonator. Game on.

At the time, George W. was the co-owner of the Rangers. His father was president, and the secret service put him in the back of a big black van to drive to KVIL, the most popular radio station in Dallas, to promote ArtFest. My buddy John was with him prepping him for the interview on the drive over when it became apparent Mr. Bush didn't know who I was.

"Leeza Gibbons is your cochair," John said.

"Who?" Bush replied.

He was then told I did *ET,* which apparently didn't ring a bell either. This had John a bit worried, so Bush was quickly shown my picture before being taken up to the studio. During the interview, the host Ron Chapman said, "So tell me, what do you think of your cohost Leeza Gibbons?"

Without missing a beat, Bush said something like, "She's going to be great . . . looks like a Texas woman."

He then shifted the topic and winked as he glanced over at John, who later told me, "It was kind of brilliant."

I had lots of exposure to people in the public eye at the time who also knew how to wing it, create moments, and save themselves in a tight spot. Tastemakers, influencers, celebrities, authors, and more. I was often pretty full of myself, thinking I had some kind of inside track to the day's most fascinating information, obtained through my interviews. One day over lunch at the Adolphus Hotel in Dallas, I was regaling John with the latest psychological insights I'd obtained through a writer I'd interviewed about why men like oral sex. It was a drop-the-mic moment. Not only is the answer obvious, but I asked the question without a hint of a giggle, no smirk, nothing. Just deadpan, as if I were simply seeking straightforward knowledge that I *must* pass on, along with advice for women who had an issue performing, which included naming the penis. Like "Little Andrew," for example, if that was the man's name, I earnestly explained. Good heavens, I was ridiculous!

John and I have shared a lot of fun stories like that over the years, but he was also there for the not-so-fun ones, like when I was ending my marriage to my daughter's father. I told John I would do whatever I must to get out of the relationship (with my dignity intact) as quickly as I had gotten into it. "I can always make more money," I said. "I can't replace the time I'd lose trying to untangle it. He can have the cheese, just let me out of the trap."

Of course, raising my daughter on my own wasn't easy, and John witnessed my attempts to do it right. He laughs about being out to dinner with us one night at an Italian place when Leksy was about eighteen months old or so, and she was throwing her plastic dinner bowl. After it happened several times,

John was going nuts, so he put the bowl firmly on the table and said, "No!"

Oh, clutch the pearls, I was horrified!

I jumped right in there and said: "We don't really tell Leksy, 'No.' We just try to redirect her."

John rolled his eyes while thinking: *Who says that? She's been in L.A. too long.*

In truth, he was right of course, but as with everything, I took my role as a mom very seriously, and I truly thought this was the best plan for developing a better baby.

"You always worked hard and were all about a strategy," he later told me. "That's how I knew you would win *Celebrity Apprentice.*"

Note to self: flexibility and some self-awareness can go a long way, too!

When I say I have learned over time how to be fluid and flexible, I always think back on this period of my life as the moment when I was learning it the most aggressively. And it was essential for me to offer myself forgiveness for being inexperienced, impractical, and a bit righteous as I grew into the best woman and mom I could be.

STRADDLING PIANO BENCHES IS NOT AN OPTION

Back in the days of *Entertainment This Week,* I may have been only a few years into my Hollywood career, but I already had the boundaries of an industry veteran. During a press junket in New Zealand, a photographer tried to coax me into straddling a piano bench so he could get his dream shot. "It'll be great," he said. "Just put one leg on either side of the bench."

"I don't do cheesecake," I said, shutting him down without a moment's hesitation. Of course, it may well have been a great shot, but it felt uncomfortable to me.

Why couldn't I find that same strong, vocal girl in my personal life? The one who had a specific boundary and had no hesitation about claiming it. Why were my insecurities running my love life, and why couldn't I know then what I know now? Well, that would be handy as we get older, right? It took me years to realize that denying parts of who we are in relationships of any kind makes us unrecognizable to ourselves, until we risk burying our authentic identity altogether. And for what? So we can pull off some façade, believing another person's image of us is who we should be, and that we should deliver that version of ourselves to the relationship?

The truth is I could fake it most of the time, and I did. Oh, I may not have even been aware of it back then—or I didn't dare admit it—but I was trying to convince myself that in order to be "enough" (whatever the heck that meant) I had to morph into the fantasy others had of me.

Have you ever heard yourself respond to the question "How are things going at home?" and been shocked by the answer you're giving? Do you go into automatic positivity mode and describe how you *wish* it was, rather than the life you're actually living? Or am I just projecting here? I don't think I am. It seems to me there are lots of us who have been stuck deciphering the difference between being *optimistic,* expecting the best of ourselves and everyone else, and actually *lying* to ourselves about how we are showing up in our lives.

My ability to begin to give up the fantasy came only when I realized that I just couldn't do it anymore. I couldn't survive emotionally in my faux reality anymore because it hurt too much and I was ashamed of myself. That's right, good old-fashioned denial was protecting me, like it does so many, until it wasn't anymore. The disappointment of facing how far I'd fallen from my own ideal bolstered me into finally facing the truth. As painful as it was, that's when the real growth began.

HOW DO YOU SAY RESILIENCE IN RUSSIAN?

What do you get when mommy guilt meets professional failure with a little foolishness mixed in? My trip to Russia. I was invited to what was then the Soviet Union on a cultural exchange program, and I decided to take the baby with me. Even though she was not yet walking and it was the dead of winter, it never occurred to me not to bring her. She was my child, and I wasn't going to leave her at home. I wanted her to go everywhere and experience everything, and boy, did she ever.

Remember, this was twenty-five years ago. We'd been

warned not to drink the water in Russia or we'd end up with dysentery and vomiting, so we'd packed enough bottles of water for our entire stay. Because Leksy wasn't eating solid food yet, and I had to drink lots of water in order to keep producing breast milk, this meant packing *a lot* of water. We prepared ourselves, like good Girl Scouts, and then, when our flight connected through London, the airline lost our luggage.

When we landed in Moscow, it was colder than cold. I bundled Leksy up in one of those thick snowsuits that made kids look like the Michelin Man, strapped her into her little car seat, and figured she'd be fine. Apparently the Soviets didn't agree.

As we were getting into the car at the airport, I noticed a few people looking at us and whispering, but I figured I was just being paranoid. And then, as we unloaded ourselves outside our hotel, a woman stalked up to me, glaring.

"Pochemu u vas etot rebenok vne doma?" she snapped, asking me: "Why do you have this child out?" "Kholodno." Or "It's cold."

"Thank you," I said, not knowing Russian, or how else to respond.

So, now, we're in our hotel room with no luggage, and that means no water. And because I'm nursing, if I don't drink water, and I get dehydrated, my milk will dry up. I panicked. *Oh my God, I'm starving my baby,* I thought.

No one over there had ever heard of *ET,* and even if they had, there wouldn't have been any welcome baskets of fruit and cheese. (This was during the Cold War, remember. Not to mention, up until the collapse of the Soviet Union in late 1991, food in the country was rationed.) When someone arrived at the door delivering a bowl of borscht that looked like something the cat threw up, we knew we were in trouble.

Luckily for me, I was traveling with my assistant, Kelly Duncan, who stayed calm and helpful, no matter what. (She's a cop now; I guess she really can take the heat.) We had a brainstorm. We had a bottle warmer in my carry-on luggage. Kelly, in a stroke of genius, had thrown a can of SpaghettiOs in her bag, which we heated up in the bottle warmer and ate for dinner. It was the best meal I've ever had.

After dinner we took turns walking up and down the hotel hallway while bouncing Leksy in our arms to keep her from crying, but that didn't solve the water problem. *I'm the worst mom ever*, I thought. I started to cry. "What if . . . ?" I said, through my tears.

"Shhh, don't cry," Kelly interrupted me. "That's precious hydration. You can't leak out the hydration."

"Oh my God, you're right," I said.

"And if you're stressed, your milk production will stop," she said. "Isn't that what the doctor told you?"

"That's right," I said. "He said stress can severely affect lactation."

And then I remembered that after I gave birth, the lactation consultant had told me that if I ever had trouble breastfeeding, I should just go to bed with my baby, shut out the outside world, and let her nurse on demand. So I decided that's what I needed to do.

"Cancel everything," I said. "I'm just going to lock myself up with Leksy. I've got to get my milk production up."

Kelly canceled my appearances for the day in the cultural program I was on, which had been the whole reason for this ill-fated trip. I didn't care about any of that. All I cared about was getting my baby girl home without starving her.

I did manage to keep producing milk, but our problems didn't end there. Because most of our luggage had been lost, we didn't have any diapers. We were in a communist country, where there was a massive food shortage, and I couldn't just go out and buy formula and Huggies. We had to find an alternative. During the day I spent in bed, we used the hotel curtains as a diaper wrap for Leksy, so we could save the few real diapers we had for the next day when we were traveling again. I truly felt like the worst mother of all time. It was like that Carol Burnett skit where she portrays Scarlett O'Hara and she whips off the curtains, rod and all, to make a dress. *I mean, seriously, did I just wrap my child in the hotel drapes?! What was I doing, coming here with my baby, just assuming we'd be fine?* I thought.

Now, with my youth in the rearview mirror, I can pull out the pictures of Leksy in her little car seat, all bundled up against the cold in Red Square, and smile at the scene, thinking I was so brave, and so resilient for adapting to being a single, working mom as well as I did. And yet so naïve. I was just grateful I had Kelly there with me. She was a rock. And we got home safely, if dehydrated.

RESILIENCE TRUMPS RATINGS

Unfortunately, you can't wish something into working. That's what I learned when *ET* host John Tesh and I had the chance to branch out and cohost our own show after I'd been at *ET* for almost a decade. I really liked John, and he and I felt *very* comfortable working together by this point. Perhaps a bit *too* comfortable. To sell our new show, we made a demo reel where John—or "Teshie," as I called him—went to the piano and started playing "I'm Too Sexy for My Shirt." I climbed up on the piano and sang along, like bad karaoke (really bad karaoke—remember, I can't sing). The producers took that tape out to stations and said, "These are your hosts. This is your show: *John & Leeza from Hollywood*." The tagline was "Talk about Fun." We had no content. But we had chemistry and chutzpah. And that was enough to sell the show.

Years later, we were in production for *Celebrity Apprentice* when Steven took me and my son Nate to dinner at this little Italian restaurant in Manhattan, right across from Trump Tower. As we were being escorted to our table, I noticed John Tesh and his wife, Connie Selleca. My teenage son is six feet three inches tall. Tesh is even taller. And as they towered above the other diners and shook hands, I flashed back to how far we'd come, including my experience watching John fall in love with Connie and being at their wedding, knowing this was a union not to be denied. I loved Connie, and I loved her for him. When we launched *John & Leeza from Hollywood*, they had just tied the knot. Seeing them that night prompted me to tell Nate about the time John and I did a talk show together, which we sold based on a Rod Stewart song. Like Nate needed more reasons to be horrified by his mother's behavior! But, for me, that impromptu reunion was really about how we never know what's coming for us, but it always truly does work out for the best. In marriage, and in our careers, we seem to end up exactly where we're supposed to be, even if it feels like quite the opposite during the transition times.

My show with John was supposed to be the west coast answer to *Live with Regis & Kathie Lee* and I had been very excited going into our launch. But it became clear quickly after its premiere that the show wasn't working, which was a huge disappointment. Up until then, my biggest career setback had been the cancellation of *Two on the Town,* and that had turned out to be a good thing because it was the layup for my job at *ET.* But now the stakes were much higher, and much more public.

John and I tried everything to make it work, but we weren't even sure what was wrong. After less than a year, a top producer came to my dressing room to talk to me. This didn't bode well. I braced myself for the news we were getting the ax. And then he surprised me by offering me my own solo gig. This all came down so fast: "Make a decision. Here's your contract. We need an answer in days." What? My head was spinning, and yet, there was a business arrangement to be made and pressure to sign the deal. When it came to this contract for this solo venture, I guess the idea was that I should feel grateful to have a show at all and should take what they were offering me. I was grateful. But I also knew that this would be a lot of pressure, and that if they believed in me enough to let me carry the show, I was going to work even harder than I already had to try to make it fly. I understood my value and asked for what I felt I deserved. That was the beginning of seven years on the *Leeza* show. These were some of the most fulfilling years of my life.

Obviously, this was a huge opportunity, but it was also a daunting prospect. At that time, there was no shortage of shows like they wanted me to do. In fact, there were seventeen single-hosted, single-topic talk shows, ranging from *Oprah* on one end to *Jenny Jones* on the other. Would I be able to make a name for myself in such a saturated market? Where would my show fit in that spectrum of very different approaches? What about Teshie? I had to make sure he was okay with the change.

"What happens to John if I do this show alone?" I'd asked the honcho in my dressing room as I first tried to let this news sink in. They assured me they'd take care of everything. That this was what he wanted, and it would work out better for him.

"Best to keep quiet about it for now," they told me.

John was blindsided by the news, which apparently he received while he was at Red Rocks Amphitheatre in Colorado doing a concert. I can't even imagine being in between sets and finding the studio execs had flown there to slam you with this news, and then you have to go back out there and be brilliant. But he was (and is) brilliant. That was his real passion—

music—and at least now he could devote more time to what he loved. It's true, he was actually happier in the long run, even if he had to experience a temporary setback to get there. When we find our passion, and let it lead us, we will never be lost (or at least not for long).

We had only about two weeks to get it together before we launched *Leeza,* and this was during the Christmas holidays, too. But failing wasn't even a passing thought. The thing about cultivating resilience is that it really allows you to put aside anxiety about impending changes and get on with what needs to be done, always expecting a good outcome.

I started studying my new format, and we began planning for our first episodes, bringing in test audiences so I could rehearse in front of them. Of course, by this point I should have known there's only so much you can do to prepare. The day we launched the show—January 17, 1994—happened to be the day the Northridge earthquake struck Southern California. An ominous beginning. And a major hurdle of the most unexpected kind. In the early morning hours, I'd been scheduled to do satellite radio interviews from my little home studio to pump up excitement for the show. Obviously, that didn't happen. We didn't even air in Los Angeles that day. Instead of talking about our lineup during the interviews that did happen, I reported on the earthquake. From there my producers and I did our best to get on with the show.

I didn't know anything about driving a talk show or handling a live audience. As I'd always done before, I figured all I could do was be myself. Or at least be the TV version of me.

Roger Ailes, now the chairman and CEO of Fox News and the Fox Television Stations Group, was then consulting to Paramount, and I guess he was put in charge of making sure I was relatable. He began debriefing me after shows.

"When you said you had Thai fusion the other day for lunch, people can't relate to that," he said, with a hint of laughter in his voice. "Say you had pasta. Noodles. Okay? And don't make any more comments about how you think your thighs are fat because America doesn't think your thighs are fat. Oh, and, Leeza, one more thing. Remember, you're not a black girl."

His tone was joking, but I knew he was serious. Nothing makes an audience squirm more than watching someone pretend to be someone they're not. (Unless they're watching an actress, of course.) He was absolutely right. My primary job was to be myself and trust that it would be enough. Forget my dream of being Beyoncé—or maybe even RuPaul. Even if I'd been able to make a lame attempt, and fake it for a little while, it wasn't sustainable. I took the note and took it to heart.

Those seven years on my show were like winning the lottery. What a tremendous gift in my life. *Leeza* came at the absolute right moment, too. Just as I might have started to get sucked into a Hollywood version of delivering coffee talk about hating my thighs and loving Thai fusion, Roger reminded me that to do that was not leading with my strength. He was reminding me that I was still the same good girl from South Carolina with the mall hair and the pink lips and fingernails. By going back to my roots and daring myself to be *myself* on my show, I not only connected very deeply with a lot of viewers, I also got the positive reinforcement that there was no better way to be. I really was enough.

Not that it was a seamless process. I've always had that pleaser streak. I think I may have been a founding member of the SPPP (Society of Perpetual People Pleasers), but that doesn't work anymore when you're the boss and the responsibility for a show's success or failure ultimately falls on you. Slowly, as I became more comfortable being myself, both as an on-camera host and a producer, I gave the green light only to the topics that made sense for me and that I knew I could effectively pull off. A good idea was a good idea only if it worked for me. Through this process, I became more resilient and less concerned with appearing to be in control, or always being perfect, and more open to just trying hard and being real. But it's definitely a work in progress—even still.

The *Leeza* show was a big job, and I loved it. I'd put in a full day at the studio with meetings and tapings, recording radio, and then I'd go home, have dinner with my kids, play with them, homework, bath time, and then put them to bed. After that I headed to my real sanity sanctuary and learning lab— a bubble bath—while I went over my notes for the next day and screened previews and teaser reels from the TV that hung in the cabinet at the foot of my tub. Afterward, I would often dictate notes and reminders to my staff and my assistant, often until 1 A.M. and sometimes later. I tried to sneak in as much sleep as I could—usually four or five hours—before getting up in time to pour plenty of coffee into my system, get the kids ready for their day, and then pile them into the back of my car.

(During these years, we had a family minivan, but I drove a white Porsche convertible with two car seats in the back for as long as they would fit. It was my indulgence and a symbol for me that I was making it, and of how much I loved Los Angeles and my life there.)

Whenever I whipped through the fabled Paramount gates and onto the lot, I just knew I was the luckiest girl alive. Once at the studio, I'd drop Troy off at the preschool on the lot and keep Nathan with me in the nursery on the stage. Leksy was in big-girl elementary school already. My day was scheduled around my kids' feeding schedule, when they were breastfeeding. And then, when they were older, it ran around their naptimes. No matter what else was going on, I always did my best to create a routine schedule for my children. Naptime was my favorite, and it was on my nonnegotiable list whenever we renewed my contract. I've always believed that children should be sung to, read to, and reassured by their parents on a regular basis. I wish every working woman had the flexibility that I had to provide all that for my kids. And I wish they all had hair and makeup pros, like Katherine, Keith, and (then) Dean, who kept me looking rested and fresh, even when I was far from it. They are geniuses of illusion, and kept me feeling safe and supported. (Sometimes the secret to faking resilience is a good concealer.)

In 1994 surrogacy was a fairly new concept, and it was one of the first topics we addressed on the *Leeza* show. The audience fell in love with my guests, husband and wife Kristi and Steve Welker. Who wouldn't? A fit, all-American-looking couple, they resembled the bride and groom on the top of a wedding cake, and they were deeply in love. They were also excited. Fertility problems had led them to start their family through a surrogate, and their twin babies would soon be born. Steve was skeptical about appearing on the show, concerned about what he called the "negative reputations" of some talk shows, but Kristi was all in, eager to educate audiences about surrogacy. The taping was so successful that Steve left the studio saying he "couldn't wait for the show to air." But he would never see the episode on which they appeared. Three days before it aired, an impaired driver hit Kristi and Steve, causing a near-fatal accident that gave them both traumatic brain injuries. Steve was blinded and would never see the babies who were born two weeks later. Kristi broke both of her clavicles and couldn't hold her boys, Dylan and Colton. We were crestfallen when we got the news, sending our best wishes and love to the hospital, but there was nothing we could do as this new family went about the next-to-impossible work of healing and moving forward. Steve said at the time, "I had but two choices: I could either crawl into my bedroom and never leave (and believe me, there were days when that's exactly what I wanted to do), or I could pick up the pieces of my life and move on."

They did more than that. They became "radically resilient," keeping their lives and their love together. Viewers were desperate for an update, so I went to Arizona to do a follow-up story. I was so humbled that they let me into their home to meet the babies. I was apprehensive about seeing Steve, since I knew just about every bone in his face had been broken. Astonishingly, he looked almost the same, and although he must have still been learning to negotiate life as a sightless person, he could have fooled me. I sat on the floor in their living room playing with their dog, in awe, hearing how Steve heated the bottles and fed the boys, and seeing how Kristi was the solid rock foundation of it all.

I was not surprised when Kristi went to graduate school and earned a master's degree in counseling, and then a doctorate in psychology. She is now a licensed professional counselor. Steve is an author and motivational speaker. Their boys are in college. They are still in love. They are experts on radical resiliency, and so they wrote a book on it. They teach others about needing a strong support system and *optimism*. They would be the first to let you know that they're on a mission. Kristi told me they "choose to enjoy what they have, rather than grieve what they've lost." Steve sent me an email recently, so I could see what he called the most beautiful picture of his wife and boys. He sees it all (and then some) with his heart. The only limits we have are the ones we impose on ourselves. Thank you, Steve and Kristi.

PREPARING TO PIVOT

Sometimes you don't have to bring your own drama to be the day's drama queen. In May 1998 I checked into the Sheraton New York hotel, I didn't get just a nice room, I was directed to the plush digs usually reserved for Dick Clark. It was a penthouse with four stories of lavishness, quite an unexpected perk. Even though I wasn't working with Dick, I was staying in the suite reserved for my ultimate role model, getting ready to do a live show. It's a good thing it was a big space because, as it turns out, I would uncharacteristically have plenty of turmoil to fill it.

I was hosting the Daytime Emmy Awards at Radio City Music Hall, which was a prime-time show. With me were my baby, Nate, who was ten months old, as well as my sister, Cammy, and my wardrobe stylist (and our friend) Julie. The next day, I had a scheduled rehearsal in the early afternoon, and then the show that night.

I had begun to get concerned before I left Los Angeles, when the gowns the brilliant designer Bradley Bayou had made for me were not finished in time for fittings. I got on the plane for New York already mentally prepping for a pivot. I knew Bradley was great, and I tried to calm my nerves about not having the dresses until a few hours before the show, but as *Women's Wear Daily* later reported, I was soon "in a tailspin."

At rehearsal we could see that neither gown would work. One needed too many alterations, and the other didn't have the right silhouette for camera. I'm sure they both would have been perfect eventually, but there was no time to get them tailored. Now I was worried about finding something to wear in the next few hours and also concerned that if I couldn't wear the Bradley Bayou custom designs, he might be upset. Bradley had flown in from L.A. for the event with his agent, and I didn't want him to be disappointed not to see the gowns he had worked on so hard.

"Well, we had months to get them ready, and now they're not," Julie said. "Bradley will understand. We should just be worried about what we're gonna do now."

This was a major pressure point for sweet Julie. She loved Bradley as much as I did, but there was no time to focus on what we wished we could do. We had to get in "go" mode. There was a cabdriver strike in New York at the time, so Julie burst out onto Fifth Avenue and headed in full gallop to Bergdorf Goodman, where Pamela Dennis was having a trunk show. Without even really hearing how bad the impending fiasco was, she let Julie leave with about a dozen gowns.

"I told the Harry Winston people to send different jewelry," Julie said, panting, when she arrived back with the loot.

I was already in hair and makeup at the time.

Oh my gosh, I'd forgotten about the diamonds.

They were coming at five so I could be on the red carpet, wearing the jewels, by five thirty.

"I let them know you're not gonna make *that*," Julie said.

We both just kept moving, each pretending not to be fazed by the fact that I had a show in three hours and no gowns.

I couldn't even figure out where anything was in the gargantuan suite. My sister, Cammy, had decided the suite had bad feng shui energy, so she'd rearranged all the furniture— like bad flow was really my problem at the moment! I was tripping all over myself, trying to find my stuff while still going over the script.

Never mind that I didn't have shoes that I'd ever tried on or walked in before, and I had to make a long entrance down stairs at the top of the show. We were out of time, so our posse hightailed it, single-file, out the door. *Women's Wear* later wrote that the "normally composed, eternally upbeat talk show host was plopped down on the floor of the hotel while four assistants tried to shoehorn her feet into a pair of pumps." It's true. The scene was Kardashian-worthy, there was so much attention on me.

Socialite Claudia Cohen walked by and shot me a quizzical look as my team was zipping, tucking, and fastening me into a skintight gray sparkling dress and a group of tourists was taking pictures and asking for autographs.

This can't be happening, I thought, and then, I went into a Zen zone. *Just breathe and imagine how great it's going to be.*

The next thing I knew, a panicked stage manager grabbed me, and I was on some sort of an elevator ramp lifting me in a horse-drawn carriage, from which I would elegantly descend and start the show. Julie had pulled off a miracle. The next day both of the dresses I wore were featured in several magazines and best dressed lists.

Julie, who now styles for Mario Lopez and the *EXTRA* hosts, could finally exhale, but she was actually headed into a situation that was much more dramatic than any backstage TV show panic. She was nosediving toward a crash landing with her very life.

Julie is a forever friend. A single mom, she works like a maniac, adores her son, and tries to fight for her happiness every day. And as I mentioned, she is also friends with my sister, Cammy, who appropriately dubbed her Twisted Sister to go with our Silly Sister (Cammy) and Soul Sister (me) monikers.

Around that time, I'd noticed that Julie wasn't herself at work. She was a bit erratic and had started keeping to herself. So I did what I do with people I love: I jumped in. It soon became clear she'd become an addict and was going to a dark place. She later told me it was so bad, she was doing enough cocaine to try to stop her heart. Embarrassed and afraid of losing her job, she begged Cammy not to tell me how bad it was.

"She already knows," Cammy told her. "And she wants to help."

I had found a rehab facility in Arizona that could take her. I had everything all set. Julie knew this was bigger than her and surrendered. The night before we left I told her to come stay at my house, where I had a hot bath and masseuse waiting for her.

The next day, on the drive to catch her flight, she cowered in the backseat like a little girl, trembling.

"This is going to save your life," I said. "But if you aren't okay with it when you get there, call me and I promise I'll come get you."

"Here, this will help look after you," Cam said, putting a "good luck" necklace on her. "Don't take it off."

In those days, they let you walk passengers all the way to the gate. When the airplane door finally closed with Twisted Sister safely inside, Cam and I just hugged each other without words.

It was a coincidence, but we later learned the emblem on

the necklace from Cammy was the symbol for fertility, and the rehab center discovered Julie was newly pregnant. Now that her son, Liam, is sixteen and healthy, and Julie is, too, we can smile about this moment and how only Cammy could impart her magic on someone without her even knowing it.

That was the first day of Julie getting back to Julie. We've been through a lot together. The death of my mother and her father. A steady stream of the wrong men, and moments when we just couldn't see any light at the end of the tunnel. I know she has sometimes thought she hurt the show, or me, but I would forgive her a million times over if she had. All of us can potentially get to a dark place. She let me into her life, and that's a place of great privilege. I think she is slowly beginning to forgive herself for all the things that weren't her fault. It was the addiction. I mentioned that I only have a handful of friends. Julie is one of them. She tries hard and cares more. And that's more than enough for me. She's says that I've been her angel. Well, if that's true then she's been my wings.

ROSE IS AN UNDERRATED COLOR

I might have been fooling myself, but virtually no one else was buying it. Although I had been cautious before marrying again, taking vows with my new husband only when Leksy was two and a half, and I felt strong and secure. Now, a dozen years into the marriage I'd thought was bulletproof, we had more than our share of rough patches and happiness was becoming harder to find. I was doing my best to make it seem like it was working, but for the most part, it wasn't—I coped the way I usually did, by continuing to deny that the cracks in my marriage to Steve, the father of my two sons, had deepened to the point where we needed to separate. I just put on a brave face and kept going forward. The denial didn't work on my kids, at least not on Leksy, my wise-for-her-age then-twelve-year-old, who wasn't optimistic about our potential to stay together. Steve and I had tried date nights and family outings where we attempted to salvage our connection. Leksy wasn't buying it: "Mom, what are you doing?" she said. "You're acting like a schoolgirl, and it's never going to work."

Looking back, I probably should have cleaned the lens through which I viewed my life sooner and saved myself some serious heartache. But that makes me think of one of my favorite lines from Oprah: "When you know better, you do better." *Nobody has it easy,* I thought, determined to hold on to my imperfect marriage and family life, and so that's what I did, for as long as I could. I will say this, though. I've always believed that rose is an underrated color. My rose-colored glasses may have hidden the truth at times, but that rosy view also allowed me to keep going, build a career that's made me incredibly proud, and helped me to create a home—and, ultimately, security—for my children. Even with the tears, and the heartache, I have no regrets about trying to stick it out. That time let me grow past the insecurities that had plagued me at the time, so I could become a stronger version of myself who was ready to open the door to whatever came next. Better still, I got two amazing sons.

But it wasn't always pretty. And sometimes there was no hiding the pain. You know, there are limits to what even the best hair and makeup pros can do, as I found out when it came time to shoot another infomercial with Guthy-Renker for my Mineral Makeup line. Following our initial success, this was the second infomercial for Sheer Cover, following our initial success, and it was a huge business venture for me, many years in the making. Greg Renker and Bill Guthy did everything first-class, and they had millions of dollars on the line. I surely didn't want to let them down. I needed my full concentration and every ounce of my energy, focus, and smarts.

Ups and downs in our relationship were now the norm, but during them all, Steve and I had never ruled out the possibility of getting back together (or at least I never had). Even though we were living apart at this time, I still wanted to be in love with him. I couldn't bear the thought of another failed marriage, and in my heart I thought it would be best to reconcile for our children. My blind spot had come back to haunt me once again.

Steve had been spending a lot of time at a property he'd bought in Hawaii, and so we'd decided that would be a good place to create a fresh start. The plan was I would fly to Hawaii after I was done shooting my Sheer Cover infomercial that day. We'd reconnect and come up with a new blueprint for our life, moving forward and reestablishing how we could be in a relationship with each other from this point on.

This was a tough one because during our time apart, Steve had started seeing another woman. We were separated, and I knew this was a possibility, but not if he wanted to put the marriage back together. I believed him when he said he would end it.

I was cautiously optimistic, but optimistic nonetheless. My friends, who'd consoled me countless times during the separation, weren't so sure. I think they sensed I was setting myself up for a fall but assumed I would go into my fantasy fairy tale pattern and fail to see the truth unless they hit me over the head with it. Julie, my friend and confidante, was about to do just that. Because I felt so guilty about not being able to make it work for our family, and because I thought it was the right thing to do, I was going to get on a plane that night to go meet Steve and give it my best.

Julie hadn't been able to quiet the voices in her head telling her something was wrong. She'd decided to do some sleuthing on her own. While she was getting me dressed in my show clothes on the Sheer Cover set, she sat me down.

"Leeza, I have to tell you something," she said. "Do what your gut tells you is right, but I found out Steve's girlfriend is with him. She flew to Hawaii the same day he did, on the same flight. This is what you're going to run into if you go. She's there, and you're going to see her. Or he's going to send her back to L.A. on the next plane, but she's there now. I just thought you needed to know what you were up against."

I still have no idea how she got that information, but it didn't matter. She'd unearthed the truth and there was no hiding it now.

Well, the truth crushed me. I felt so hurt, and so silly for believing we could still make it work. I felt undesirable, unlovable, and foolish. I was crying—sobbing, really—and I couldn't stop. Of course, there's never a good time to get news that rips your heart out, but this was very bad timing, since I basically had to be on set right then. Our live audience was in place. Alyssa Milano was waiting for me to interview her, as were the women who were going to do their personal testimonials for us. Everyone was in various stages of ready, except for me. It was awful.

Thank God for my team, who were like my family. They swept in to put me back together, so no one in the audience, or at home, would ever suspect I'd had this terrible moment I was just barely living through right now. My eyes were completely swollen up, so Keith (my dear friend and makeup guru) put iced Coke cans on my face to reduce the puffiness. I held them in place as Dean (my loyal hairstyling wizard and sweet friend) jacked up my hair a little higher as a distraction. As we sat, waiting for the cold metal to work its magic, a nervous producer, wondering why I wasn't ready, had come knocking at my dressing room door to hurry me along.

"Oh, you know what?" Julie said, all sweet reassurance. "The hem on her dress got snagged on her way out, and we had to rehem it. Sorry about that. We'll have her out to you in a minute."

Finally, they'd put me together as well as they were ever going to, and there was no more stalling. I asked everyone to give me a minute. Sometimes I have to stop and anchor myself before a big broadcast or meeting, and this was definitely one of those moments. Whether you're about to do a high-pressure TV taping, or you're about to have a difficult discussion with your kids, I think the real secret is to learn your personal operating system well enough so that you know what you need to be able to show up in that moment. There's always something. It's really personal and it might change over time. Mine has remained consistent and I always make space for it. Because my world moves so fast, I often need just a couple of minutes to give myself a little talking-to, in order to be as effective as I want to be in any given moment.

I took several deep breaths while telling myself to be grateful I was able to feel so deeply, and to focus on the love and support I received from my team. And then I pulled out the Louboutins Julie had purchased for me as part of my wardrobe for the shoot. These were much more to me than great-looking stilettos that were much more expensive than any shoes I've ever had. They'd become something of a survival strategy for me on this particular shoot. I put them on, and at the risk of sounding like a Disney princess at her moment of truth, I could feel their power.

All right, I am going to stand tall and proud in these heels, damn it, I thought. *I'm going to look sexy and confident, and I'm going to dig down deep and pull it together.*

Here's how that happened for me. When I worked with

Tony Robbins, I learned about NLP, or neuro-linguistic programming. Basically, NLP is all about the dynamics between the mind (neuro-) and language (linguistics), and how their interplay affects our body and behavior. It's about analyzing how we think, communicate, and act, in order to model and improve on our performance. Lots of athletes use it. I turned to this method now, and thankfully, it began working.

Tony also taught me to anchor myself by doing something, the same something, over and over until it became a pattern to signal my brain and my body that it's showtime. Years earlier I'd begun using a little jump and clap as that something to rev up my performance before I walked onstage. It's still the final thing I do before I go on to do most anything. For me it says: *Now you're here. Do it.*

I was here. I was doing it.

But as I walked out onto the gorgeous set, which had been designed to look like a high-end cosmetics counter or medi-spa, I felt like such a fraud. Our whole message was about being confident and transforming yourself into your most authentic self. Our tagline was "Let the Real You Shine Through." And now, here I was, wondering how on earth to shine at this moment, while feeling anything but confident and authentic.

I have to go out there and talk about being strong enough not to let anything destroy your confidence, I thought. I was on shaky ground. I felt embarrassed and weak.

"Let the real you shine through," I kept saying to myself over and over again.

So who is the real you at this moment? Well, she's not someone who crumbles, that's who. You'd better find her, right now, be-cause that's who needs to go out there.

That was enough to make me feel just a little bit better, a little bit more like my core self, who was not defined or de-stroyed by the bad things that might happen in my job or marriage. And yes, I went out there, and I did it. We taped for nearly twelve hours, and I held it together the whole time. Okay, I snuck in a few crying jags in between takes, but no one outside of my loyal little family ever knew.

I learned a really important lesson during that process. The shoot was actually *better* because of what I was going through. Because it made me realize that the product wasn't *really* about confidence alone. It was about women feeling vulnerable and getting past it. And so all of this was an interesting bit of ser-endipity. Although I don't have a birthmark, scar, or rosacea, like many of our customers, I had a mark on me that day (and some dark under-eye circles, which Sheer Cover took care of). I could really relate to all the women out there who feel insecure, undesirable, or weak because of their appearance. My vulner-ability in that moment made our connection that much deeper and more genuine, and it definitely shone through.

I still have the fuchsia wrap dress I wore on camera that day. It hangs in a dry-cleaning bag in the back of my closet. I suppose, in true NLP fashion, I'm keeping it in case I ever really need a full emotional transformation like that again. And we all know I probably will. That's just the nature of life.

The infomercial was a hit, and the product was success-ful, but the marriage was over. I didn't get on that flight, and although Steve kept contacting me all night, asking me where I was and trying to coax me back, I was done. I'm not sure we ever totally recover from something like that, but we do heal, and we move forward.

Steve and I did. We have long since forgiven each other for the pain we caused each other. I see him often these days, with our children, but without resentment or anger. I credit my current husband (who gets along well with Steve) with helping me heal and forgive, and also for shining a light on my blind spot. It's all so adult and *Modern Family*! Seriously, my ex and I have both arrived at better places, for which I'm grateful. But I had to be brought that low in order to find the inner strength that was always there to claim my worthiness.

Of course, nothing will ever be the same again after something crumbles. It's a marriage ending. It's somebody you love getting a terrible diagnosis. It's whatever dark shadow creeps into your sunny little world. Life won't ever go back to what it was, but it can be put back together. And even better. Now I know this to be true. I tell my kids we're still pieces of the same puzzle, we just fit differently.

After enough of these moments, I've learned to compartmentalize in times of personal tragedy, or a crisis of confidence, but to still face whatever is there and own it. Strong people feel the fear, worry, and pain, just like everybody else, but they push through and do what has to be done to make it to the other side, no matter what. Back then, I was just talking myself into the possibility of resilience, and praying that I would get through this challenging part of my journey. Now I know that it is only within the journey—especially the challenging parts—that we become strong. As Carl Sandburg put it so well, "Life is like an onion. You peel if off one layer at a time, and sometimes you weep."

With the type of work I do, I didn't have the option of going off to be by myself until I felt better. I had to keep going out there and connecting with people during this whole awful mess and that responsibility was actually doing a great service to me, and to those whose hearts I wanted to touch. My job wasn't just the thing I loved so much that it could distract me, and give me tools that helped me cope. It also showed me that the pain is actually the link. It's the connection to the core of your humanity, which is at the core of all humanity.

CHANGE IS THE ONLY CONSTANT

I was living my dream, and I didn't want it to ever end.

I loved hosting my own show. After all those years of paying my dues, I could finally make the hires, call the shots, book the guests, run the format, and even more important, create the kind of work environment I'd always craved. My former writer Joe Ferraro, now a TV executive at Bravo, says, "You can either choose creativity or fear. You can't have both." At the *Leeza* show we chose to be creative. I hope I supported all of my colleagues to be themselves and contribute their own unique magic to the mix. It's really affirming to hear many of my former employees say they treasured our work environment, too, because they've found that the kind of sanctuary we created on the job is rare. Sure, it was also tough, demanding, tiring, and competitive, but I tried to make sure everyone was seen through a lens of respect. I was proud and I was happy. The juice for me to do the show always came from our guests and their stories.

All cylinders were firing in my life at this time, but, of course, change came for me as it does for everyone. In short order, my divorce was finalized, my show was canceled, and for the first time in my life, I faced the prospect of rebuilding without the two women who had always been my compass.

When my beloved granny died of complications from Alzheimer's, my mother had already been diagnosed with the same devastating disease. At Granny's funeral, I watched my mother look into the face of the mother she had just lost. It was impossible for me to imagine what that must have been like for her, to know where she was heading. I stood back and looked at the woman who gave birth to me, realizing we were in similar moments of transition. Granny was gone, and my mother was no longer a daughter who could physically show love to her mother as she always had. I was no longer a daughter in the same way, either. My mother was gone, too. Although my mother was still living, she was losing more of herself to her disease, and my real role now was as her caregiver.

I didn't know what to do. The music in my life had stopped. It was deafeningly silent. I felt like I had no one to turn to for help or advice. For a time I just did what I had to do. I grieved, I cried, and I tried to help my family take care of Mom. And then I got a call from a reporter at *People* magazine, asking me to comment on my mother's Alzheimer's disease. My family and I hadn't known anyone was aware of it. This was many years before the omnipresent social media, and there was little understanding of how devastating the disease really is, both to the person who's diagnosed and their loved ones. Even now there is still so much polarization and stigmatization, but it was worse then. I told the reporter that I would have to consult my family before saying anything. I felt guilty that, because I was a public figure, I had caused our privacy to be invaded at the worst possible time. Ironically, being "outed" was the best thing that could have happened to us. My mother, who was in the initial stages of her disease, didn't flinch.

"I don't want us to be ashamed," she said. "Don't hide it."

I turned to my family next, and they were all in agreement. I did the interview with *People,* and a photographer, Erica Berger, came over to my house and shot pictures with Mom, Dad, and me. The one of Mom and me sitting side by side on the hammock with my arms wrapped around her always takes me back to that moment. I wanted to shield her from what lay ahead. To protect her the way she had always protected me. We never know how high we can rise, until we are called, and while I couldn't stop the memories from emptying out of her one by one, I could protect her legacy and her love. I will forever be grateful that, through the kindheartedness of the magazine, the loving soul who took these photos gave us use of those pictures without ever having to pay for the rights. What a generous and very meaningful gesture. Although I hadn't seen her since the shoot at my parents' house that day, twelve years later Erica walked toward me at a speech I was giving in New York, camera around her neck. I recognized her immediately and threw my arms around her in gratitude. I was glad to be able to thank her for her empathy during a very hard time. We had lots of use for those images when we decided we could honor my mother's legacy and our family's journey in a powerful way by creating what we had wished for when we were trying to help my mother. We'd needed resources—information, support, anything except the loneliness and burnout of going it alone. We'd wished we'd had a place where they "get it," so I started Leeza's Place, and then Leeza's Care Connection, and we began connecting caregivers to each other, and to programs and services that could provide the education and support they needed. Ever since then, we've been helping husbands and wives, and sons and daughters, adjust to their new normal as they get recruited into their new caregiver roles, almost always with no training and lots of fear. We've helped them to call on their courage and summon their strength, which in turn gave me more courage and strength, and allowed me to find contentment I hadn't known in a very long time. Finally, the music in my life played once again.

I knew I had to step up and claim what I felt was my calling, but honestly, I was afraid. I was afraid of failing, afraid that if I succeeded I wouldn't be able to sustain it. Afraid I'd never work in TV again.

I ended up being away from TV for four years—the longest I'd been without a TV job in more than two decades. I didn't really get a lot of support for my decision.

"Stick to the kids' charities you've worked with in the past," one of my agents said. "This new venture is depressing, it's not sexy. It's for old people. It might hurt your marketability."

He was voicing what I knew others might be thinking, but I didn't care.

"That just proves how much it's needed," I said. "And, by the way, you're fired."

You don't find your life's work by doing a survey on what's trendy, popular, or marketable. You do what you are called to do and what you have a passion for. When you're lucky, you get to create change or address a need. When I got in the "caregiving business" many people weren't even familiar with the word. Even now that we have national legislation to support them, family caregivers still aren't valued or recognized enough.

At this point, I faced the question so many caregivers do: "Now what?" My answer was to adjust, adapt, and change. I gave myself the pep talk I hadn't found elsewhere. I told myself successful people don't fear change. They change fear. They use it as an impetus to re-create themselves, even stronger than before. The upside to the downside of losing my mother, memory by memory, was that I could give others support, help, and hope. I was passionate about it, and it kept me feeling close to my mom (even though the disease kept her from participating or even really being aware of it). I knew I was honoring her, and creating her legacy, and I held on to that as a source of solace during dark times.

Plus, my role at Leeza's Care Connection involved another form of storytelling, my life's work. I was actually strengthening my strengths in all new ways. I thought about what Mom said when she was first diagnosed: "Tell the story. You've always been a reporter who told other people's stories. Now tell this story. This is our story. Make it count."

THE SECRET OF RESILIENCE

An optimistic person behaves in a way that expects good outcomes, even when they are in the midst of experiencing anything but. Start doing that. Especially when you're going through challenging or disappointing times. Assume that your circumstances are about to turn around. Believe your boss will be open to giving you a promotion. Trust you can forgive your best friend for stabbing you in the back, even if you can't make her accountable. And then, release it. Have faith that tomorrow can be stronger, safer, more abundant than today, especially if today is looking a little grim, and see where that gets you. These are the habits of content, successful people, but you have to put them into action. If you want to open new doors, you can't do it with the same old ways that allowed the old doors to shut. That's the first rule of resilience.

When things don't add up, start subtracting. Get rid of people, schedules, habits that aren't on the direct path to where you're going. Yes, you may have to keep climbing, even when you can't see the top of the stairs, but that's okay. You're strong. And when you know something is in your way, kick whatever (or whoever) that is to the curb!

CHAPTER FOUR

The New Golden Rule (Empathy)

As they say, "Fail fast and fail hard. And fail often."

In my own life, I've had lots of chances to prove this true. It was my first show that failed to thrive, *Two on the Town*, that propelled me to reach even higher my next time out and seize an opportunity at *Entertainment Tonight*. In order to use this temporary setback as a means of propelling myself even further, it was really important that I could forgive myself for "failing" for no other reason than being on a show that had been canceled. I also had to deal with that unspoken but nagging (misplaced) blame aimed at the producers who I thought pulled the plug too soon. Rather than blaming them, or myself, or entering into a spiral of negative thinking, I put it all in a box called forgiveness and moved on with optimism instead of resentment.

If you want to stay positive, forgiveness is a must. Without it we're likely to be trapped in the past and limit our own potential for growth and enjoyment. I'm sure you know people, as I do, who seem to have a core need to hold on to a sin of the past. Negative people have a problem for every answer, and nothing is more toxic than a sourpuss who is holding a grudge. These are typically the ones who often get spiritually and physically sick, because not forgiving is simply detrimental to health. Through forgiveness comes grace, which goes hand in hand with the kind of bliss that will last you a lifetime, the kind that's not tied to the number on your scale, the amount of money in your bank account, or your marital status, but the kind that comes from deep inside, no matter what's happening on the outside.

Once you've accepted that disappointments are an inevitable part of life, you can master the important part: learning how to forgive yourself and others, so you can move on to other attempts and opportunities. Or as Wayne Dyer puts it, stop thinking in terms of failure at all. His approach is to reprogram your view of your life, so that any outcome in any situation can be seen neutrally, and analyzed accordingly, rather than being viewed through a lens of negativity. The upside is that it's much easier to adjust your behavior with success in mind when you're simply regrouping, not recovering from a perceived loss. And the truth is, everybody responds to positivity, even the grumpiest people out there.

I love the show *Shark Tank*, which recently showcased an empathetic turn, thanks to guest judge Ashton Kutcher. I've long admired Ashton for not only being successful and strong, but also philanthropic and kind. The guy's just got it all going on. I was literally cheering at my TV when shark "Mr. Wonderful" (Kevin O'Leary) attacked a woman seeking funding and Ashton came to her defense.

"Here's the thing, you're belittling people," Ashton said, shutting him down. "And that's not okay."

He was the youngest member of the panel, it wasn't his show, and yet he wasn't going to let another shark badger a contestant. Now, that's empathy in action by a class act. (It also makes for great TV.)

Turns out, compassion and empathy are great for business, too. Research done at Stanford University shows that if businesses can create a happier workplace with less stress, it improves the bottom line. Stress breaks down the immune system, which causes people to miss work. Unhappy workers look for other jobs or are just uncooperative and unproductive at the one they have. Makes sense, right? So if a stress-free workplace where niceness rules operates so well, how come more businesses don't encourage it? Many managers or employers don't want to come off as weak, so they are hesitant to take a compassionate approach, but let's think about this: Is the pope considered weak? How about people like Martin Luther King Jr. and many others who led with compassion and kindness?

If you adopt a policy of caring about others while aiming to be your best, you'll win people over, even if they don't expect you to. During *Celebrity Apprentice,* I had to find a way to put the kind part of myself out front and appear strong and deliberate (qualities which are not mutually exclusive). I started with my view of Donald Trump. I chose to make him less intimidating (to me, at least) by seeing him through the lens of fatherhood, thinking how much he'd accomplished by raising such incredible children, including my girl crush, Ivanka. It worked. I managed to revamp my image of him to be not so much the tough guy who points the finger while firing people, but more a father, to whom I could relate. I saw him as being paternal and encouraging us all. With less stress I could be myself, and be victorious.

At the season finale he said, "Leeza, you led with kindness. I don't see these people in New York. I see brutal, brutal killers. I don't meet people like you."

"Well, I'm happy I could surprise you," I replied.

I went on to remind Trump and the audience to *"never underestimate the power of a woman who knows where she's going and what she wants."*

I stayed calm by visualizing success and staying true to who I am: competitive but collaborative. I wanted to win, but I also wanted much more than that, to learn and grow and fulfill my promise to my mom to tell her story. I would have dishonored her if I'd played it any other way, and I hope my victory is a reminder that you can be nice and still play to win.

Winners aren't islands. It's usually because of how they work with or relate to others that they end up out front. That's especially true for those who've found ways to perpetually reinvent themselves, achieving success in several different arenas, or even after a scandal or setback. From Bill Clinton and Bono to Lady Gaga and Jennifer Lawrence, many of those who have shaped our world in the past few decades have done so by connecting with the people around them, and then finding a way to translate our universal humanity into a song, a performance, or a message. They're kind of like portals for inspiration, recycling their creative energy back to the audience. I've always thought this made sense instinctively, and now science is backing me up. A study that came out of the most recent Alzheimer's convention revealed that the ability to contribute and give back has actual health advantages, making people less likely to develop Alzheimer's disease. Having lost my mom and grandmother to this brutal disease, I find this hopeful. Even if we can't remember why we exist, or even who we are, our essence is tied to making a positive contribution.

Stewart Butterfield has proven himself to be both empathetic and flexible. He is the entrepreneur who founded the photosharing website Flickr and the team messaging app Slack while trying to create something else. His ability to adjust and be flexible landed him on *Time*'s top 100 most influential people, with his businesses recently valued at $2.8 billion. Guys like this know stuff. Butterfield is a philosopher who understands that companies run better when their employees respect each other's time and actively display empathy in the workplace. Yeeessss!! From the very unscientific perspective of my own life, this is what I've been saying all along. Being nice is actually the strongest position you can take, professionally and personally, and it will lead to much better results than the traits celebrated by being a hardass and adopting a *my way or the highway* position. This is why Butterfield says that if you have, "a good background in what it is to be human, and understanding of life, culture, and society, it gives you a good perspective on starting a business."

The challenge now is starting businesses and being in business with those who have the courage to proactively adopt a kinder, more open-minded way of being. I know many of you may not work with or live with those whose personal or corporate values include empathy and courtesy, as Butterfield's do, but every day, more and more successes are being built from the opportunity created by failure, and by being nice and empathetic enough to envision and build what's next. I get that these goals can seem like a reach. After all, I work in the TV business that Hunter S. Thompson said is, "uglier than most things . . . where thieves and pimps run free and good men die like dogs, for no good reason." For years I dealt with many producers and entertainment executives who tried to bully and shame the people around them into doing things their way. But "being powerful is like being a lady, if you have to tell people you are, you aren't." We can thank Margaret Thatcher for that bit of wisdom. It was often a challenge to offer some people nothing but optimism. But the way I saw it, I didn't have any choice. When your work speaks for itself, don't interrupt, right? So I learned to autograph my work with excellence and keep my mouth shut.

SHE DID IT THE HARD WAY

"Well, if this isn't the interview, why are you talking to me?" Bette Davis shut down my small talk while the crew finished setting up the lights on the *ET* soundstage.

She'd swept in, lit cigarette in hand, wearing a hat with plenty of attitude, for our interview about her film *The Whales of August* in 1987. During the beat it took me to recover from her icy remark, I accepted that I wasn't going to win her over. (It didn't surprise me when she died years later and had her mausoleum in Hollywood's Forest Lawn cemetery inscribed, "She did it the hard way.") It was well-known that she'd never liked being interviewed. She didn't need to sell herself or make nice. She was probably only there as part of her contractual obligation, and I doubt she had any idea who I was, or even the name of the show for which we were taping. The best thing I could do was to accept and respect where she was coming from.

"Would you prefer that we don't talk?" I asked.

"Absolutely," she said.

Well, I'm not going to get up and leave, I thought. And so I sat there in uncomfortable silence, basically staring her down and watching her smoke. It seemed like an eternity, although it was only a few minutes. Finally, the crew was ready. I exhaled, shook off her negativity, and centered myself. No matter how unhappy she was about being there, I'd been given this time to interview her, it was my stage (thank you, Ted Koppel, for that sound piece of interviewing advice), and I was going to make the best of it.

I took a deep breath and dove in. I didn't come at her with warm-up questions, or suck-up admiration, because I knew that would have only exasperated her more. I asked her about her technique in the movie, so she could talk about her craft, because I intuited that this was where we needed to go, instead of anything to do with her emotions. Finally, we were done. Before she left, she paused dramatically.

"Young lady, you are very good," she said.

I couldn't help myself when a ginormous grin appeared across my face. I don't think you can be a good journalist unless you're empathetic, and in that instance, empathy meant having the self-awareness to realize: This woman has been around forever. It's very unlikely I'm going to come up with anything unexpected or interesting for her. That's my challenge. She knows it, and I know it. So let me just be respectful, and pleasant, and intelligent, and acknowledge the energy she's giving me, which is that she's a no-nonsense lady.

While it may seem like she didn't want anything from me—that was certainly the message she was giving me, *loud and clear*—I think she wanted what everyone wants: to be seen for who she was. Just like I do, and you do, too. And, yes, I know, sometimes these moments can seem contrived, especially when they happen on soundstages, but I think they're still a profound opportunity to share our humanity with each other. And so I don't ever dismiss the process as worthless or silly, even when I'm faced with someone who has good reason to be jaded.

This approach has real-world applications, too. If you always read the energy in any interaction and calibrate your approach accordingly, whether you're trying to get buy-in from the PTA for a fundraiser you're running at school, asking your boss for a raise, or negotiating with your kids about their chores, you'll be much more likely to succeed. (Maybe you'll even convince someone that your way doesn't have to be the hard way.)

"YOU'RE GONNA DO GREAT"

For every actress with the poise of Bette Davis (well, few humans are that poised), there are many more who are not at all comfortable without a script in front of them. To sit down and be themselves is the hardest thing for them to do. When I interviewed Kim Basinger, it quickly became clear that she was nervous. I was well aware that Kim had a long history of shyness, panic attacks, and agoraphobia. She's talked openly about her challenges but that doesn't necessarily make coping any easier. There was no hiding her discomfort, and I was afraid she might not like how she came off if we rolled tape now. I instinctively switched my focus from what I needed to get from the interview to what I needed to give her at this moment so she could deliver her best. This has been the tool that has powered my career as an interviewer and host, but I can guarantee you that no matter what business you're in, your clients and customers want to know that you understand them.

Because I was trying to understand what this was like for Kim in this moment, I knew I had to do something, and fast. I didn't want her to be unhappy with what we got and regret doing the interview. Although the whole crew was around us doing their jobs, and the camera was rolling, I made a quick decision to intervene on her behalf. I waved my hands to get my crew's attention.

"Hey, guys, can we stop for a minute?" I asked. "I think that light over there needs a scrim. Can you check it out, please? Thanks."

These were seasoned industry pros I was working with, and I think they probably knew what was really going on, so they went to check the "technical problem" and gave us some space.

I knew it might make Kim even more self-conscious if I drew attention to how uncomfortable she was, and so I just chatted with her, which was easy to do, since I genuinely like her, and she is sweet as can be. When she wasn't so focused on the interview anymore, she visibly relaxed. When the crew came back and we started up again, Kim was great. In fact, it was a nice segment. I don't know if Kim ever saw it, but if she did, I hope she feels as if she came off as herself. That's my metric for success. Did the person across from me feel that I presented them accurately?

It's easy for anyone who's ever given birth to empathize with a pregnant woman, even if that pregnant woman is one of the music world's biggest stars. It's bittersweet for me to recall the first time I interviewed Whitney Houston. She was coming to the final stages of her pregnancy with Bobbi Kristina. She was visibly bloated, and I sensed she was nervous about the upcoming birth. Off camera, she opened up to me about her fears, and I proceeded to give her advice and encouragement.

"Whitney, look around this room," I said. "All the guys on our crew had mothers who did this. I mean, think about that. When I was pregnant, I always felt better when I normalized the enormity of the moment of giving birth and just remembered that it's a universal thing."

I looked over at our roughest cameraman, who never smiled.

"See, even Rex's mom did it and think about what a dream little baby Rexie must have been!"

Turning back to Whitney, I didn't see the megastar, only an apprehensive mom-to-be, smiling softly.

"You're gonna do great," I said. "By the time you deliver, you'll be ready. And you'll be so proud."

The crew thought we might never get in front of the cameras, but by the time we did, Whitney was my ally, as she had allowed me to pave the way by connecting with her authentically. Later, my colleague Jeff Collins pointed out how what I did with the stars also carried over to my business-world dealings. "I saw Whitney become your partner that day," he said. "And she invested in creating a great piece of tape for the show."

That's our challenge in business, to make everyone feel invested in a great outcome and to be proud of it when it happens. I do try to make everyone feel that we're in it together (we are) and it felt great to create that experience in partnership with Whitney. It's hard to believe that both Whitney and the daughter she was carrying that day are both now gone. Whitney faced that other universal thing: she died. Only with her death, and her daughter's passing, there was no being "ready." I'm not sure there ever is.

Whitney and Kim both had a sweetness to them, and a fragility that's hard to describe. I'm not certain how people come to be this guarded or shy. I'm sure many arrive with it as their worldview, like my son Troy. But I've also learned how others have adopted this position because of a painful experience in their lives, like seventeen-year-old Valerie Weisler. Now a senior, her high school experience was difficult. As a freshman, her parents had just divorced, rocking her world and causing her to retreat inside. Because she was quiet, classmates called her mute and made fun of her, saying she didn't know how to talk. Well, she does now, as the founder and CEO of the Validation Project, which provides teens what Valerie says they really want: validation. She's received a lot of that herself, getting attention from celebrities and the White House. Thanks to her extreme empathy, she's even let her former bullies work with her in her program, which connects teens worldwide with mentors from major companies like Google and *Seventeen* magazine.

I just love this young woman, and her mom, who raised her kids to understand that their "footprint goes beyond their world." Valerie believes positive affirmation is always a good thing. And I couldn't agree more. "I'm hoping that by showing how powerful being kind is," Valerie said, "[former bullies] won't feel a need to be mean to someone else." She represents the next generation of fierce optimists, and with people like her in charge, I've no doubt we are in good hands.

THE CATER WAITER WITH A HEART OF GOLD

When you grow up in the South, I think you sort of have to enjoy entertaining. This was lucky for me, as it was a major part of my job to attend—and throw—a lot of parties when I was at *ET.* One of the many events I hosted during those years was to honor reporter Jeanne Wolf when she left *ET.* I was thrilled to do it because Jeanne had been important in helping me to master my place at the show. Having sat across from her in the office, I'd studied her clues to success, and I'm not surprised that she's still at it today.

At the end of the night, after most of the guests had left, I helped the caterers put my house back in order. While we were gathering candles (it's not a party without dozens of candles!) I paused to talk with one of the servers, Jeff, in my kitchen. He was an aspiring actor with long Fabio-like hair, and I remembered that during other parties at my house, we'd chatted enough to realize we were both from the South. That night I skipped right past the small talk and found myself getting serious with him.

"What do you want to do with your life?" I asked.

"Well, funny you should ask," he said. "I really want to get into your side of the business. I know you know a lot of famous people, and you travel in all of these circles. I think I would be a good assistant to someone like you."

Well, that was bold, and I liked it. He was smart enough to analyze the situation and come up with this answer, tailor-made for me. "Look, I could help you organize," he continued. "I could cook. I could take care of kids. I could wash cars. I could do errands. I'll learn. I'll do anything."

Was he reading my mind? Had I left a to-do list out somewhere? This guy had paid attention, and despite whatever credentials were on his resume at the time, he went straight to the ways he could help, so I didn't find it even the least bit strange when this waiter with no TV experience said: "I think I could be helpful in your TV business."

"Really?" I said. "Okay, let's set up an appointment. I have this assistant now who really wants to be an editor. I'd like to help her. Give me some time to think about it."

I really liked that Jeff was up for anything and wanted to prove himself. No attitude. Still, I wasn't sure if I really had a place for him.

Jeff was persistent. He had very young, brash energy, and other people in my office who met him at our interview mistook this as arrogance. What I saw was that he was not afraid to own his ideas and to live and die by them, and that he had strong decision-making ability and leadership potential. I knew these to be really valuable traits that are difficult to teach. After considering for a few weeks, I called him.

"Kelly's going to get the editing job," I said. "I'm going to have her teach you her job. While you're learning, I'll pay you out of my pocket. When she leaves, I'll assign you her salary from the studio. This is a trial period. Let's see if you can figure it out."

Jeff was there on a temporary basis until he proved himself, but I knew the best way to empower him was to treat him like he already worked for me. And so I told him what I've always told new assistants and employees.

"The only way you're going to learn this business is if I'm open and allow you to understand how it all works, because knowledge is power, and that's how you're going to be most effective," I said. "I want you to see inside my business world. Whatever comes across this desk, I want you to study it, learn the language, and stay one step ahead of whatever I may ask you to do. This can only work if I can trust you, and I will, until you give me a reason not to."

Not only did he never give me a reason not to trust him, he was incredibly loyal and dedicated. As our working relationship began to grow, I put the ball in his court once again.

"If you want to move up, if you look around and you say, 'Well, I can do that job,' or 'I could handle that responsibility,' just tell me," I said. "If you think there's a way that I could help you to get there, let me know, and I will."

We worked together like this for the next five years. Jeff Collins went from being my assistant to having a credit as a producer on *Leeza,* and was eventually promoted to vice president of Leeza Gibbons Enterprises (LGE). He was so much more than an employee. He was my rock on so many occasions when I needed someone I could be vulnerable with, he was a trusted ally, and he was an inspiration, because his path reminded me of so many essential truths that go into establishing a vibrant, next-level career and life.

What Jeff did so brilliantly, in my kitchen after that party, and during so many days under fire at work at *ET* and LGE, was to demonstrate skills that are so much more crucial than being a tech wizard or doing a specific task. He showed himself to be resourceful, creative, persistent, and good in a room—all skills that were really valuable to me, which I couldn't necessarily have taught him or shown him how to get. All of the employees I've seen move their careers forward with this same kind of flair have had some version of this self-possession. Look to see where you can find a variety of that inside of you and take a similar risk on yourself. Don't be limited by what's on your resume; ask for what you want and believe in your ability to make it happen. It will pay off big-time!

I also encourage you to have the open-mindedness and empathy to give people a chance. That's what I did with Jeff and as I hope I've made clear, Jeff was in no way the only one who benefited from my decision to take a risk on him.

No one has time to figure out how you can help him or her, or where you might fit into their organization. You have to go in, like Jeff did, saying here's what I can do for you, demonstrating you already understand her world, know what she needs and how to give it to her. If someone comes in already adding value, that's irresistible.

It was a privilege to help Jeff get his start, and whenever I visit him today at the production company he now owns, Collins Avenue, I get chill bumps. When I first went to his chic office, populated by lots of millennials and hipsters, I saw hanging, among the edgier references, a poster of me from the *Leeza* show days. He told me it reminds him of where he got his start and serves as a touchstone for how he wants to run his business. Whatever he's doing, it's working. Collins Avenue produces dozens of successful TV shows and Jeff is a force to be reckoned with.

We still see success the same way. I had to smile the first time I went out to the parking lot after visiting Jeff. When I saw the hot little Jaguar in his parking spot, I totally understood what that symbolized to him. I know it was the same as what my little Porsche convertible had represented for me: evidence of making it. Since then, I've loved seeing not only how far he's come, but also how he's done it. He's made a commitment to passing along success. When Jeff went out on his own, he had an entry-level editor who was hungry to learn, and so Jeff kept giving him more and more responsibility, until finally the young man went on to be a very sought-after, well-paid producer. Years later, he stopped by Jeff's office.

"I have something I want to give you," he said to Jeff.

He actually opened an envelope and pulled out food stamps. (Yes, this really happened!)

"This is what was in my pocket when you gave me a start," he said. "Without your faith in me, I didn't know where my next meal was coming from."

Jeff still keeps the food stamps at his office as a reminder of the power we sometimes forget we have to change the lives of others. That story says it all. Jeff has a great life. Not because of his success, or the money he makes, or because he drives a snazzy car. Jeff has the life that Winston Churchill referred to when he said, "We make a living by what we get. We make a life by what we give." Do that and you'll have a good meaningful life, and good, loyal friends, and everything else will take care of itself.

WHO KNEW?

One day my assistant handed me a letter that had been left on an audience seat after the show taping. It simply said "Leeza" on the envelope. Inside was a letter, written in painstakingly neat handwriting, from a twenty-year-old girl from England named Holly. Her letter told a heartbreaking story of suffering and abuse. But Holly had seen me on the air in England and felt with absolute certainty that I could help her create a new life in America and finally come to terms with the shadows that followed her everywhere. And so she'd crossed the ocean to meet me.

Of course, everyone on my staff said I couldn't possibly get involved because it was too dangerous. "She might be unstable, and no matter what you do, it probably won't be enough," they told me. "You're not qualified to help her." They were definitely right about that. There were many talk show hosts on the air who were therapists and interventionists, and who *were* qualified to help her, but she hadn't reached out to them. She had arrived in a country where she had never been, with no money and no plan, except to find me. Maybe I wasn't qualified and it was risky, but I could find people who could help her, and I wanted to be that link. I sensed a gentleness through her writing, and I couldn't help but want to step up and try to connect her to the right people.

A couple of weeks later, I got that chance. As I always did

before taking the mic, I walked up the aisle to greet the audience. Standing by a seat on the left side of the crowd was a girl with short hair and glasses who looked like Harry Potter. Somehow I knew it was Holly. I walked straight up to her.

"Hi, I'm Leeza," I said. "Are you Holly?"

She looked timid and fragile, but she smiled sweetly.

"Yes," she said.

I was doing back-to-back shows and radio in between at the time, not to mention having a two-month-old baby backstage, so that day I only made contact.

Several weeks went by. It was the last taping before Christmas and Holly was sitting in the front row. I had no idea that she was running a desperate inner dialogue: *If Leeza and I don't get to speak today I'm going to leave the studio and kill myself.*

It was nearing the end of the taping, and I was standing by the teleprompter about to start the next segment when there was an unexpected break due to a technical difficulty. I saw Holly staring at me and went over to ask her how she was doing.

"Not good," she said.

I let her know we could talk after the show.

Little did I know, in that moment, that I had changed the course of this young girl's life, and she would open my heart in ways I never expected. I did provide the link for Holly to get help, and for years she dedicated herself to her reinvention and recovery like her life depended on it. It did. She enrolled at UCLA, and on her graduation day I sat in the audience like a proud big sister along with the therapist I'd arranged for her to see. We all cried tears of amazement.

Well, eighteen years later, Holly is one of my best friends. I've seen her fight for her mental health and happiness. And how, in her new life in Los Angeles, I've seen her offer support to so many others who are struggling. But, as with all of us, hers is a life in progress.

Eight years ago, we were driving to Marmalade in Sherman Oaks for lunch. I was in the car with Holly and her dad, who was visiting from England, soon after she first came out to him. I'd known she was gay only for a little while, but as far as I was concerned, we had reason to rejoice that she finally felt comfortable being her true self with us. Her dad didn't take it quite so well.

"So, Leeza, Holly tells me she's gay now?" he said. "What do you think of that?"

"Well, I haven't known your daughter as long as you have, but I'm really proud of her for claiming what has to be a really hard truth about herself. I hope you'll come to see it that way."

It took time, but her dad did come to see it exactly that way. He's a good person who eventually rose past his fears into not only acceptance but also celebration of his daughter. He was able to acknowledge Holly for building an incredible life, especially given the extreme distress of her early years. Now she is a writer, has a great job, and she's in a wonderful relationship with a new girlfriend. Her dad (as well as the rest of her family) is supportive and loving of her, and she's truly happy. It's all a tribute to Holly, and how she didn't give up, even when everything was difficult in her life. The way I try to do things (on a good day) is to work hard and care more. Well, Holly worked harder and cared more than anyone else on the receiving end of everything in her life, and it really paid off.

To me, Holly's story is a testament to the fact that everyone deserves a chance and that we don't have to remain the person we were yesterday. We are so quick to judge and marginalize those who are living in circumstances that, for whatever reason are difficult for us to relate to. And yet, people do recover. And they have so much to offer if we only give them the chance to let them show us their true selves.

Holly and I were just together at my son Nate's homecoming football game.

"Can you believe it?" she said. "It was eighteen years ago today that I came to America."

I paused and sat with that for a moment, glancing down the field to where the team had just come out of its huddle to play the next down. Nate was just a baby when Holly and I met. Now he's a high school senior, wearing number 70 on the offensive line. As he got into position, I smiled and looked up at Holly.

"Who knew?" I said.

What on earth could propel Holly to travel to another country where she'd never been, to seek out a talk show host she'd never met, at a studio she didn't even know how to find? Why did she think I could help her claim who she was meant to be? I don't know why it happened, but I had a run-in with fate that day at Studio 26. I never saw it coming.

Holly's story never became an episode of the *Leeza* show. But there are plenty of examples where talk shows demonstrate that even if you can't change people's minds, you can change their hearts, and that's everything.

I know that sounds like a lofty goal, but it happens. Steve Harvey does it all the time. It's the quality I love about him the most. To me he's a great example, not only of reinventing yourself and becoming the person you've always really wanted to be, but of what you can do with a work ethic and positivity. He is an optimist. He sees the doughnut and not the hole. He's used his faith in himself to create a virtual one-man media empire. Remember, this is a man who was homeless for three years, actually living out of his Ford Tempo, but optimists like Steve never assume a bad situation will last forever. Neither did Holly.

CRACK THE WHIP

I'd been as green as fresh-picked okra when I'd first arrived in New York City all those years ago. And I'd never even heard of the legendary musical comedy *La Cage aux Folles* when I was sent to report on a version being staged in the city at the time. I only cobbled together a story with the help of a sweet, funny soul from Georgia who was one of the show's publicists. Troy was the first (openly) gay person I'd ever become friends with and he meant so much that my middle son is named after him. I'd been raised to believe in equal rights for all, and so gay rights made as much natural sense to me as civil rights, women's rights, and any other movement in which the disenfranchised just wanted to be treated with equality.

So, years later, when I first heard through Keith, our makeup artist, about Jon and Michael Galluccio, a couple from New Jersey who were among the first in the country to spearhead the cause of same-sex marriage, I knew I had to have them on the show. At the time, the courts did not allow same sex couples to adopt children, and this couple had been fostering a child they now wanted to adopt. During my years on the air, I had tremendous support from Paramount and was left alone to speak out responsibly as I saw fit. I felt so fortunate to have that trust as we produced an episode with Jon and Michael called "What Makes a Family."

These two men, Father and Daddy, had faced insane criticism and near-impossible obstacles to adopt a crack baby (addicted to heroin, cocaine, and alcohol) that no one else wanted, overcoming enormous obstacles to make it happen. After fostering little Adam for a couple of years, the state said gay couples couldn't adopt. Their challenge of the ruling is what helped change the law. I knew exactly how I felt on the topic: How could a couple be condemned for wanting nothing more than to offer their love and support to a baby, especially one that had been rejected by so many? But the show was rocky. Plenty of audience members were stone-cold against them. I was incredibly proud of our positive coverage. Jon and Michael were measured but passionate, and through them we inspired some audience members to become more sympathetic to their point of view. This was very early in the debate over gay marriage. People were less educated, and many had yet to make up their mind on the subject, or even begin to take it seriously as an issue worth considering.

I soon learned there's often a cost for putting yourself out there. Some viewers and religious groups boycotted our show, and I personally received vicious hate mail. I was even called the Antichrist! If social media had existed at the time, I would have been annihilated. I can't imagine how hard it must have been at that time for Jon and Michael. As far as I was concerned, though, this reaction was just more reason to hold my ground and continue to do our part to educate a wider swath of the public about these issues and allow them to challenge their thoughts.

I couldn't have been more proud when I learned that I'd be receiving an award on behalf of our show at the 2001 GLAAD Awards, given by the Gay & Lesbian Alliance Against Defamation to honor media portraying gays and lesbians, and their causes, in a positive light. My assistant Joe and his partner, Joe, were both active in GLAAD, and I looked to them for help with my acceptance speech. I've always loved and respected "the Joes" more than just about anyone else, and I knew they would help me find the right tone for my remarks.

It was a tense time. Bill Clinton was president but the Republicans had just taken over Congress, and our country had entered a decidedly conservative period. Dr. Laura Schlesinger was a huge force on radio and had signed a deal with Paramount for her own TV show. I was concerned that she might use this new platform to have greater reach to spread her message of intolerance against gays. (In 1999 she'd called being gay a "biological error.") The studio was taping test shows with Dr. Laura and using my dressing rooms and stage. I was happy for Dr. Laura or anyone to make use of my stage and facilities, and she had always been professional with me. Still, I couldn't quite shake the feeling, which was also growing in the entertainment industry, that she might use her platform to perpetuate some negative stereotypes about gays. I knew I needed to take a stand. When the GLAAD awards came along, I knew this was my moment.

I have to tell you, it was one of the most exciting nights of my life. I hit the stage, dressed sweetly in an off-the-shoulder lilac dress, but outfitted like a warrior with a black leather whip in hand. That's right. The whip was the Joes' idea, and it was masterful. When I cracked my whip, the audience went wild. Now that I had dramatically gotten their attention, I had my chance to say some things that had been on my mind and in my heart. Although I'd prepared my words carefully, they genuinely came from my deepest truth as I began my acceptance speech on behalf of the *Leeza* show.

"It is not true that Dr. Laura asked me to 'teach' her some basic things about talk shows," I joked, delivering these words with a half smile to set the right sarcastic tone when I talked about Dr. Laura using my stage for her test shows. "Dr. Laura certainly doesn't need me to tell her how to do a show. She doesn't need me to know the difference between a gaffer and a grip."

I dropped the smirk here and continued in all earnestness:

"But she could use some coaching on the difference between the Bible and the Bill of Rights." (I cracked the whip loudly!) "The Bill of Rights and the Constitution—those documents which are supposed to guarantee rights for all Americans but apparently not for gays and lesbians who every day are losing their jobs, their homes, their health insurance, and their children because of who they are. We can tax them and take money out of their paychecks, but we can't protect them from hate crimes and we can't provide freedoms, like the right to have a family?"

When I finished my remarks and heard the roar of the crowd, which had already risen to give me a standing ovation, I was stunned. I was in a rare and wonderful position in our culture that allowed me to comment on and maybe even influence people's views, and in this instance at least, I felt good about how I'd made use of that platform. I'd taken on another Paramount "talent" because it was the right thing to do. Dr. Laura has never been anything other than kind and respectful to me, but we see things very differently, and sometimes you have to stand and deliver. She would no doubt have done the same.

I wondered if there would be backlash from the studio. There wasn't. But even if there had been, I would have done it all over again. Dr. Laura's show was ultimately taken off the air, unable to withstand the heat (and bailing sponsors) she garnered through her comments. Even though she apologized, protests and low ratings ultimately delivered the ax. Almost a dozen years later she told Larry King that she thought same-sex relationships could be a beautiful and healthy thing, but she still opposed gay marriage.

Being nice doesn't mean you don't have a backbone. Sometimes it means cracking a whip when something you care about is on the line. And if you've behaved with integrity all along, your "go along to get along" good-girl reputation may even make people more likely to listen up when you do stand tall and use your voice.

FAKE EYELASHES AND A TIARA

When my sister Cammy's marriage fell apart, I wanted her to have a soft place to land. No questions asked. I thought a change of scenery would do her good. I invited her to stay with me for a while, so she could create a plan for her new life. When she showed up with two suitcases in hand, neither of us thought this would lead to L.A. becoming her new home. And for a while, her new address was my address. I wouldn't have had it any other way. No matter that we had a very full house that included our kids, our two dogs, turtles, hamsters, our cat, and now her cat. *That cat.* Every time I came into her bedroom, her cat Alex hissed at me from under the bed. So I didn't go into her room.

It was like we were living together in Mom and Dad's house again. Coffee together in the morning, silly movies at night, and her occasional tarot card readings. Before I knew it, months had passed, and I was becoming the overbearing mom, and she was like the millennial who might never move out. Never short on friends, it was clear that Cammy was embracing her newfound freedom, and my house was becoming party central with a revolving door of characters who had all been charmed by my sister.

I had been prepping myself to have a talk with Cam about moving out when she returned from a trip; what she called her "Priscilla, Queen of the Desert Tour" with news that I never could have seen coming. Cam had become friends with a guy who was her "soul mate." They went everywhere together, referring to themselves as "Will and Grace," since he was gay, she was straight, and they were both up for any adventure. They used to joke that at some point down the road, if neither of them was in a relationship, they would have a baby together. *Very cute,* I thought. Until she told me she was pregnant with his child. There was no way I had thought she was serious. But she was, and I could see she was happy. Cammy wanted nothing more than a house with a picket fence and a baby. Of course, she'd always thought a husband or a life mate would go with her dream. As it turned out, "Will" left "Grace" to fend for herself, and that's where I came in. My well-rehearsed "it's time to go" speech would have to wait. For now, there was a baby to be born, and I took a deep breath and readied myself to face the music.

The music, at least at the baby shower I threw for Cam a few months later, was Rick James, "Super Freak" (at Cam's request). The baby's father wasn't there, but just about every other gay man in our zip code was. All the guests were wrapped in feather boas, waving scarves along the stone path in my yard as a very pregnant Cam waddled her way inside to open gifts. It was insane, and ridiculous, and insanely ridiculous fun. It was pure Cammy.

But when we weren't going to doctors' appointments and getting ready for the baby, I was still shell-shocked and concerned that Cam wasn't facing the reality of what life as a single mom would be like. Oh, I know there are plenty of Mama Warriors out there who do it, but all of this was weighing heavily on me. The baby daddy wasn't stepping up, my parents were three thousand miles away, trying to come to terms with what was happening, and I wanted to make sure my little sister had her best shot at a healthy pregnancy and delivery. So Alex the cat stayed under the bed, Cammy's belly got bigger, and we all pitched in to get ready for D-Day.

When it was time for her to give birth, I was her birthing partner in the delivery room, just like I'd envisioned. *Great! I get to be like the Baby Daddy.* Only it wasn't *quite* like what I'd pictured. It was Cammy's vision of reality. At the same time, in my usual control enthusiast way, I was trying to run the show according to what I knew about giving birth.

"You need to have a focal point for your contractions," I said.

"Fine, I want a tiara," she said.

"To focus on?" I asked.

"This is my pregnancy," she said.

"Okay, great, I'll get the tiara."

Now, of course, I'd carefully packed my little bag for the hospital with everything she might need during delivery: tennis balls for when her back hurt, spray mist for her face, and that sort of thing. But I did not have a tiara. So I got one for her. Along with her other request: false eyelashes. Now, I knew from giving birth that many of the details you planned for so carefully in the calm before the storm fall by the wayside when the chaos of birth ensues. And so I figured there was no way she'd think to want false eyelashes on once her contractions started.

Again, I hadn't counted on how uniquely fabulous my sister's take on everything was. As I bent over her hospital bed, she glared up at me from beneath her tiara.

"I am not going to have the baby," she said, "until you put the false eyelashes on me."

"Cammy, you've never been more beautiful. Honey, let's just focus on getting your baby here safely."

"I want the false eyelashes."

"My God, all right, fine," I said, putting on her false eyelashes as ordered, panicked that my misapplication of said false eyelashes would ruin everything.

The doctor wanted to give Cammy a cesarean—needed to give her a cesarean—for her own well-being and that of the baby—but she wasn't having it.

"You know, Cam," I said, "the doctor says it's the only way you're going to get this kid out that's going to be safe for the baby."

"Well, I don't want a scar," she'd said.

I'd had my third baby, Nathan, by cesarean, so I was well versed on the topic.

"Cam, it's not a bad scar," I said. "Remember, I had a C-section, and it's okay."

"Show me the scar," she said.

I looked at the emergency team all around us, eager to get on with their jobs.

"Show you the scar?"

"Show me the scar or I'm not going to do it."

Here we were at a point in her labor where things were getting dramatic—the baby was in duress—and my sister wanted to preapprove the scar!

"The scar is so little that you'll still be able to wear your bikini," I said, trying to be reassuring, foolishly thinking she'd let me off the hook.

"Take your pants down and let me see it," she barked.

Glancing around at the doctors beginning to scrub in for surgery, I unbuttoned my pants and showed her. She looked at me and nodded.

"All right, that's fine," she said. "That's not so bad."

Finally, she had the C-section. Her son, Blake, was born, and he was healthy and beautiful. I got to go with the dads to do the first bath, and then went back to her hospital room with Baby Blake and his perfect baby smell. He was swaddled and sleepy as I softly rocked him. Soon, a nurse wheeled Cammy through the doorway to recovery.

She sat up and gave me a look. I knew she wasn't feeling

great and waited for what she'd have to say about the C-section I'd talked her into having.

"Peyton, let go of my child!" she shrieked, à la *The Hand That Rocks the Cradle*.

I laughed so hard. That's my Silly Sister.

Blake had more love than any kid on the planet. And it was so easy to lavish it on him. Cam started rewriting the next chapter in her life, and we all took the next step toward normalcy.

Everything was more fun with Cammy, even heartbreak. Most of the time, I know I come off as being more than capable of picking myself up, dusting off, and moving on. But that doesn't mean, of course, that I didn't break down and grieve, and cry, and act like a victim or a martyr from time to time. Sure, I've tended to push past these eruptions quickly. I mean, honestly, sometimes I just don't like the idea of things being so out of control, and feeling the pressure of being a rock for my kids and my staff, so I wasn't usually eager to talk to many people about the times I faced my shadow sides and didn't like the view. Cammy has always been there for me. She's the one I can let in when I'm really broken, and she talked to me for hours and hours (and hours and hours) during my divorce. She even tried to knock some sense into me, as I do for her when she needs it (not that either us ever thinks we do).

For years Cammy was one of the only people I ever felt comfortable being vulnerable with. And it was through our relationship that I finally realized that being able to allow people to see who we are and let them do things for us is as important as our generosity toward them.

I think we all have a need to be our own version of significant. But for years I wanted to do everything for everyone, at work and in my family life, without realizing that I was getting cheated, and I was gypping them, too. If you keep doing things for others, it can actually be detrimental for them personally, and for your relationship with them. It was hard for me to work on developing my ability to delegate and share responsibility. It was hard for me even to admit I needed help. But for some reason, with Cammy I could be imperfect and in need. And then, slowly, my ability to have vulnerable moments expanded from there. With my siblings, my staff, and my kids, I've come to understand that people work with you better, and have better feelings for you, when you allow *them* to be significant. Whether it's my brother taking the lead to care for our dad, or letting someone at work prepare research for me so I can do something else I might be better at, these are important moments I wouldn't have been comfortable allowing to happen before. I now know that letting people show up and contribute creates better outcomes both in the short term and the long run.

When things are really out of control, reaching a breaking point, or even just when there's friction, I often try to get enough perspective to remind myself that the person who seems so unreasonable is somebody trying really hard to matter, to be significant, which allows me see them with greater empathy and kindness. Often this actually causes the interaction to improve a heck of a lot better than continuing to battle it out, and it sure feels a lot better, too. Now I can even realize when I'm the one trying so desperately to matter that I wedge my way in so that I can feel that I have something to contribute.

This philosophy is actually what allowed me to work well with Geraldo on *Celebrity Apprentice.* You've gotta give it to Geraldo. This man is a trailblazer and has been fearless in his approach to covering the events of the day. From his Peabody Award–winning, hard-hitting news reports about abuse of the mentally disabled, to getting his nose broken on his talk show, and his aggressive, theatrical, and controversial appearances on Fox News and elsewhere, he is always one hundred percent Geraldo. Everyone thought he was so tough on *Celebrity Apprentice,* and so full of ego, that he was impossible to deal with. And they wanted to know how I handled him. The truth was, I got him. I understood him. And I really wanted to hear everything he had to say. Like anyone else, he got defensive—and a little loud—when he felt like he wasn't being valued or heard. But when he was given the space to be Geraldo, he was able to be cooperative and thoughtful and all those other positive qualities he doesn't generally get credit for having. I think that's a big part of how I won on *Celebrity Apprentice,* by respecting my competitors enough to let them to stay in their zone and continue to strengthen their strengths, at the same time I strengthened mine.

Get fluent in your own abilities and strengths. That will give you the most reliable base and the steadiest platform to offer your validation to others. You don't have to agree with people to be respectful of them, and if you remain an incurable optimist, the contagion inherent in that choice is likely to sway them over to your side.

Look, life is messy. Relationships are complicated. And being true to someone doesn't always mean agreeing with them, or even doing what they want you to do. But if we really care about having authentic relationships that help us to grow as people, we have to allow others (and ourselves) to be the complex, difficult works in progress that we are.

THE SECRET OF EMPATHY

Learning how to practice empathy can give you a richer, more fulfilling life, and it can also help you get ahead in business, get the promotion, make more money, or manage your team (which may be your family or your group of best friends).

Question your point of view. How you see things determines how you engage with the world. It forms your values. But what if they were different? Can you step into an opposite view long enough to actually consider it? The biggest part of empathy is listening and being fully present. So if your brother tells you he got a girl pregnant, or if your son tells you he's leaving his high-paying job, you can be present with your eyes, your body facing them, without rushing to the next thought that you are just dying to say. Those are called attending behaviors. Even your face alone says if you're listening carefully.

When you're in charge, or the boss, are you letting others offer something and really listening to their idea, opinion, or complaint? Engaging as a listener is one of the greatest things you can do for another person. Try repeating what you have just been told. If your employee is telling you that he is too tired to focus during late hours and he is making mistakes because of it, you want to make sure you heard it right and let him know that you're listening, so you can say, "I hear that you are exhausted when the day is long, and you're not able to do your best work when you're so tired."

Empathy comes from being curious about how others feel, so ask real questions that allow you to connect. When people feel close to you, they trust you. When they trust you, they are loyal to you. Practice asking people about what they struggle with, what they're afraid of, how they cope with a challenge. If they open up to you, ask if you can help with whatever they've revealed. You may not agree with the choices that got someone in a tough situation, but you can empathize with how difficult it must be to be there.

Finally, get into the habit of seeking to understand yourself, and others, rather than blaming outside people or circumstances for anything that's causing you discontent in your life. It's often when we want to dominate, be "right," or judge ourselves and others that we get defeated. And sometimes, when we look more closely at a conflict, we see that the person we're having tension with is actually exhibiting the exact same annoying or exasperating habits we're prone to ourselves. Note to self: empathy does not mean solving the other's problem, taking over their situation, or leaping into hero mode. For me, that's when it's helpful to have my husband around to say, "Get over yourself." Find the person who can do this for you in your life.

When you can be patient and present when you have nothing, and when you can be humble and helpful when you have everything, you are on the road to where empathy lives.

CHAPTER FIVE

Playing the Long Game (Loyalty)

I've always had a small group of friends. I think being in friendship with someone requires time, energy, and effort. I try to make sure those I let into my life are really getting the best from me, and I know being a friend means being there, in lots of ways. I take it seriously. Seriously enough that most of the friendships in my life have lasted for decades and have survived all sorts of moves, marriages, and hairstyles. I've also been careful to assemble a talented, devoted team and then stay loyal to them. Many of my employees and colleagues have become some of my dearest friends, which I think points to our mutual respect. They are true blue. They'd have to be to join me, year after year, in dressing up in a bustier, thigh-high boots, and a spiky blond wig to perform musical parodies for the staff on special occasions. Such memorable office performances where we delivered award-worthy portrayals of naughty elves and snowflakes with attitude were every bit as meaningful as those staff retreats where employees play games designed to teach them how to communicate! Vulnerability, trust, and shared experiences inspire loyalty.

Loyalty is good for business. To encourage their employees to be more loyal and more productive, some of the most successful companies out there are finding that it pays to be kinder, more considerate, and more empathetic to their staff. First create the happy, and the rest will come. Companies from the *Huffington Post* and Google to Procter & Gamble have created nap rooms and started offering "EnergyPods" to urge employees to rejuvenate themselves at work. Clearly, they've found that shifting their focus to making sure their employees are content means greater productivity, or else they wouldn't invest in these novelties.

Pro-employee policies go way beyond on-the-clock power naps, too. Netflix earned extensive media attention and praise for its decision to let employees take as much vacation time as they want. That's pretty amazing. And isn't it interesting that this approach relies on the goodness and honesty of people not to exploit a policy like that?

In good times, and especially in bad, the loyalty you've shown to others will come back to you a thousandfold. The science supports this; whether you're talking about our relationships, our business success, or just our overall happiness quotient, loyalty matters. Not moving on to greener pastures and looking out for number one. People who get ahead don't have a dog-eat-dog take on winning. They are loyal, making sacrifices for the team or to strengthen relationships. Customers and clients who trust the products or services they use build loyalty over time. Trust and loyalty go hand in hand. This is the currency of business and relationships. If you can say, "I've got your back," and you know it's reciprocated, you're ahead in every game.

ALL IN THE FAMILY

"I don't worry about you because I know you have Maria," Mom often said in my early years in Los Angeles. And it was true. You have your biological family and your logical family. Maria and I aren't connected by blood, but we have the same heart.

When I bought my first home in the Los Feliz neighborhood of Los Angeles in October 1984, the previous owner asked me to keep on her housekeeper, Maria. Well, at the time I was never home, and I'd never had anyone help me with my domestic duties, so I didn't really feel like I needed a housekeeper, but I hated for her to lose work because the house was sold, so I decided to give her a couple of half days of work every week.

As I settled into my house, and my life there became bigger and messier, the half days became full days, and then it became five days a week. Having Maria around was like having your mom look out for you. She watched (and loved) my dogs when

I was away, even staying at the house so their routines wouldn't be disturbed. Bless her. When I got married, Maria's daughter was my flower girl. Our children grew up together, and when my flower girl was ready to get married herself, I helped celebrate her wedding.

Maria has been a constant in my home during every transition and upset it's possible to undergo, until she became family to me as well. She's like my mom, and a grandmom to my children. Even though she speaks broken English, and my Spanish is *muy malo,* we've never relied on words that much. Maria knows everything about me there is to know, and she's been through it all with me. Like me, she's had relationships that didn't work out, and she's raised children on her own. She's an amazing, beautiful soul, and she has more quiet strength than most people I know.

So, yes, she's worked with me for many years, but it's not really been about that. She's given me loyalty, friendship, kindness, and care, often at moments when I most needed it and wouldn't have been able to ask for it from anyone else. We understand each other.

Now that my kids are grown, I'm back to not really needing a housekeeper anymore. A few years ago, after thirty years of us working together, I told Maria that I thought it would be best for her to retire and enjoy more free time with her family. She's always had energy to spare and was still able to do everything she ever could, but it seemed like the right move. I wanted her to have a wonderful retirement and enjoy her grandkids. When I met Maria, she was forty. Now she was seventy-two. It was time. She agreed and stopped coming to work. For a few weeks. Then she called me and said, "I'd rather be at your house."

I laughed, knowing just what she meant.

"Come on back then," I said.

She's back to doing half days at my house again, and I get it. She's like me. We know how to work. And we know the value of family. I couldn't love her more.

NAUGHTY ELVES CAN BE LOYAL ELVES

A little laughter therapy can go a long way toward keeping you sane. Case in point: the Joes, Jeff, and, for a time, Vincent and Paul from Leeza Gibbons Enterprises used to write these hysterical lyrics set to classics and pop tunes. Add some high camp, a shameless lead host (that would be me), hot backup singers and dancers, and all you have to do is sit back and feel the crazy. One time someone on our staff was having a birthday or something (it really didn't matter) it was reason enough for me to burst out of my office dressed like Tina Turner—black spiky wig, short skirt, high heels—and belt out a special birthday song that my assistants and I wrote just for the occasion, along with a whole choreographed dance number to go along with it.

My inner circle was fearless and limitless, especially around the holidays, when they not only helped me write and perform a special holiday show (this is where the naughty snowflakes and elves came in), but also came over to my house and spent hours and hours helping me wrap Christmas presents while I made these big, fancy bows and did handwritten notes. I loved it all.

I tried to never miss an opportunity to say thank you to everyone who made my world run smoothly, by looking for the perfect gifts, for my family, friends, and employees, but also the agents, producers, lawyers, accountants, and the executives at Paramount (yes, even during the lawsuit years). They knocked down the doors of opportunity for me and kept them open wide. They were allowing me to live the life of my dreams. I always wanted them to know that my love and appreciation were true. As I have posted on many sticky notes: Gratitude is the foundation upon which abundance is built, so assignment number one is: be grateful and show it.

WALK YOUR GREAT WALL

Talk about timing. I signed my divorce papers the day before I was due to join Olivia Newton-John on the Great Wall of China, walking to raise money and awareness for her Olivia Newton-John Cancer and Wellness Centre, which was not yet a reality in 2008.

I'd always admired Olivia for many things, and on top of the list is her goodness and grace. I first met her during my time at *ET,* when I was sent to interview her at her home in Malibu. We did one of those beautiful walk-and-talk interviews, with the ocean behind us. I was immediately struck by the fact that she was real—the same person I'd always admired from afar, and I admired her even more up close. We genuinely liked each other, and although I had interviewed her and seen her at events over the years, we were never really close. Still, my list of those I've drawn inspiration from over the years wouldn't be complete without her. And so, when she first asked me to walk the Great Wall of China with her, my response was: *What? Walk the Great Wall for how long?? Weeks of being with people I don't know, in a place I've never been, where conditions will be tough. And no hair and makeup? Perfect!*

I needed to reset my life and shift the focus off my disappointment and myself, and this was just the way to do it. Many cancer survivors were walking with us and I was energized by their stories. I felt empowered by the entire experience and made lifelong friends, but the most incredible aspect was how I clicked with Olivia.

She had also been in a transition period, but unlike me, she'd already graduated to the rebuilding stage. A breast cancer survivor for years, she'd just married her second husband, John Easterling, who was never without a great story, and always the first one to dive into the unidentifiable food we were given along the way in China. Monkey belly wasn't bad, till he told me what it was! John adored Olivia in a steady, consistent way that always made it seem like he could read her mind. She was glowing with happiness. From where I was standing, amid the rubble of my divorce, seeing how she'd fought through everything so elegantly and come out on the other side so gracefully was incredibly inspiring. Not to mention that, when I worked at Paramount, I had always loved her store, Koala Blue, on Melrose Avenue. It was *the* hot spot and I used to roam for hours wondering if she'd personally guided each colorful choice. She had. I gave her major props for being such a strong businesswoman, so talented, so real, and so nice.

During the walk, every morning before we went out for the day's trek, all of us on the hike held hands and sang her song "Magic," which set the mood perfectly. I'd heard the song hundreds of time before but now it was *my* song: "*You have to believe we are magic. / Nothing can stand in our way.*"

When we were through singing, we all believed that something magical was guiding us and that nothing could stand in our way. We needed the encouragement, too. Walking many of the individual sections of the wall was physically exhausting, and we often stayed in glorified tents with makeshift bathrooms, and sometimes only sheets for privacy. There was nothing glamorous about the experience, which was the whole significance of it. We were all very aware of the power of our journey and what it could achieve.

Partway through our trip, Olivia and I were talking one night before bed. Our discussion about life brought to mind my recent setbacks.

"I'm feeling so guilty that I couldn't make my marriage work," I said. "And so despondent. How am I ever going to attract the right person? Apparently I'm not putting the right stuff out there, and that's why it hasn't happened."

"Just be with it," she said, offering me her sweet smile. "And yet, know that it will happen for you."

"I'm trying, but I just can't convince myself of that right now," I said with a sigh.

"Don't be so hard on yourself," she said. "Try not to blame or judge."

I could have heard the same words from another person and dismissed it as empty pep talk. But hearing it from Olivia was different because she had lived it, too, and because I genuinely had so much respect for her, for her strength and wisdom. I thought about how new love had happened for her, against all odds, and that helped me to have enough faith to hold open the possibility for myself and try really hard not to shut down. And then I had a "pinch yourself" moment. *Is this really happening?* Here I was, getting life coaching from a woman who'd long been on my inspiration list, someone after whom I'd modeled my own behavior and life. Not only that, but when I was a reporter and host in Dallas, her album *Physical* was released and I (like many others) had my hair chopped off, just like hers, and I acquired a wardrobe of headbands so I could look as cool as she did. Of course, I missed the mark, causing *Fashion Dallas* to write that it was time for me to drop the look!

Since then it has been an incredible honor to become and be her friend. The walk was a success, and Olivia kept her eyes on the prize, opening the Olivia Newton-John Cancer and Wellness Centre in Melbourne, Australia. Years later, I was there for the dedication of the center, where she's been able to help people to focus on the wellness aspect of cancer because that's how she overcame hers. She is every bit the superwoman I've always admired, but she's also got her own vulnerabilities and insecurities, just like me, just like all of us. I really think it's her softness, as much as it is her strength, that's helped her to survive so many personal and professional ups and downs. She's more of a role model for me than ever.

In 2009, we wanted to produce a fundraising event for our foundation, and that meant finding some celebrity support. Of course, as usual, I overthought and overproduced everything, deciding it should be a six-hour live event *on Oscar night,* with pretaped packages and roving reporters covering every aspect, and also be a podcast about making a difference that could be seen around the world. And, of course, who better than Olivia to deliver that message? That night she was totally there for me and gave an incredible performance.

When I did *Celebrity Apprentice,* once again there was Olivia showing up in the biggest way possible. The good news about the show was that I'd made it to the finals. The bad news was that it was my anniversary weekend, and my mind was on anything but. Steven came from L.A. to New York to take me out for a romantic dinner. As usual, he had planned everything perfectly, but all I could think of, or talk about, or breathe was *Celebrity Apprentice.* I had to get up early the next morning and get on Trump's plane to Florida to produce our final event, and I was tied up in knots. Steven very sweetly ended dinner early, but I had worked myself up into a real state by the time we got back to Trump Tower, dismissing all of his positive encouragement and focusing only on how overwhelmed and exhausted I was. My confidence was shaken.

The challenge for the show was a triple whammy! We had

to fly to Orlando, where we were to produce, write, and edit a commercial about Universal, and deliver a showcase live event where the commercial would be screened back in New York City. *And* it was a fundraiser. We had two days.

"I have to find someone to perform for my showcase," I said. "I don't know anyone in New York, or even east coast–based."

"I think you should call Olivia," he said.

"I can't call Olivia," I said. "She'd have to be here the next day. She's in Malibu now. I can't do that."

"It's the right move," he said again.

I hate imposing on people, especially friends who have already done so much, and I will go to almost any lengths to avoid it, but this was important. Olivia was *the* perfect score. I had to get it done, and I knew Steven was right. I made the call.

"Olivia, I'm doing *Celebrity Apprentice,*" I said. "And we have to produce a live event in New York, and—"

"Where do I need to be?" she said before I could even ask.

"Really?" I said. "I mean you'd have to be here tomorrow."

"You were always there for me," she said. "You were there for me with my cancer center. I want to be there for you for your foundation. Of course I'm coming."

I was overwhelmed by her loyalty, and it helped me regain my confidence. She had to take planes, trains, and a Big Wheel to get there, but of course, she did, and it made all the difference. We won the challenge. Olivia was my not-so-secret weapon and my good-luck charm. (Plus, I learned to face my fear of asking anyone for money. Now I can pretty much ask anything without apology. I've learned I'm not responsible for their part of the conversation, and they always have the option to say no, which I would respect.) Thank you, Olivia. I honestly love you.

FIND YOUR JIMINY CRICKET

Sometimes the perfect employee—and friend—is already in your life. It's just a matter of calling him or her to you. During the early years of Leeza Gibbons Enterprises, my assistant was Joe Lupariello, one of "the Joes" named earlier, and he was yet another master of intelligence, kindness, and optimism that I've been so lucky to have in my inner circle over the decades. Joe has been like my Jiminy Cricket, always gently helping me reset my resolve. He was the middle child of nine kids, and so, when I hired him, I knew there wasn't much that would fluster him. I actually had the nerve to ask him, during our interview, if he would object to being asked to make coffee and keep an eye on my kids while we were taping.

"Well, I don't really know how to make coffee," he said. "But I'll learn, and I don't mind doing it."

From that moment, I loved him and started calling him "Java Joe." It stuck for the longest time. It was a good thing, too, because his boyfriend also happened to be named Joe. Joe and Joe are known throughout Hollywood simply as "the Joes." After he had worked with me for a while, Java Joe told me that his Joe was doing a one-man show in Hollywood. I wanted to go to support both of them.

From the first scene, I knew there was something special about this Joe, too. Java had always said that he was loyal and kind, and an all-around great partner. And now, from seeing his work, I knew he was smart, inventive, and hilarious. I was still staffing my company, and I definitely needed more people like that. A few weeks later I called him.

"I'm with this production company at Paramount, and I'm doing these radio shows," I said. "I thought you were really creative, and I would love for you to come in, be part of the team, take a stab at writing for me. What do you think?"

"Yes, yes, yes," he said.

As I later learned, Joe punched the time clock as a waiter for the last time the very next day, and he was so excited about his sudden reversal of fortune that he took a picture of himself clocking out, just to prove he was on the way up. Joe was incredibly loyal and hardworking. He used to send in little notes when I was recording the shows he'd written, which earned him the nickname "Memo Joe." I'd be in the middle of an interview, and the note would come flying in with things like this: "Don't forget to ask her about the color yellow. It reminds her of her mom." Or, "Get him to sing. It's hysterical." From fact-checking to helping me recover from blunders, he was like a living Post-it note. The Joes became the glue that kept me together . . . or at least put me back together when I'd cracked. I loved them then, and I love them even more now.

I have a tendency to trust my instincts and give people a chance to perform. When Memo came on board, he instantly impressed me. Joe possessed that attitude of "Why not me? Put me in, Coach, and let me show you what I can do." I've always found that blend of determination and optimism very attractive, and Joe delivered on both promises. Even though he didn't have as much specific experience as others on my staff, he was always very positive and vocal in meetings, and he came with great ideas. Perfect, since my attitude has always been I want to hear from everyone, and I value everyone's contribution.

I don't care if an idea is fully baked, or if it comes from a CEO or an intern. As long as it has a kernel of potential, I'm all for giving it a try. This was the perfect environment for Joe, and he was soon thriving. Not to mention his integral contribution to helping me release my inner drag queen—and naughty elf—at all those holiday parties. We were frequent guests in their home, and my favorite visits happened at Halloween. One year, Leksy was dressed as the Tejano singer Selena (although she looked like a mini Cher to me; I suppose I was just jealous of her hair). Anyway, the Joes understand performers in training and got her to take the stage in their living room that night, and she's never forgotten it. For a kid who was attracted to audiences, she never failed to be given the perfect stage by the Joes. Java lived up to his promise of being a great kid-wrangler and often had my son Troy on his shoulders as he went about his day.

Java and Memo both have sterling reputations, earned over time, as they've continued to grow in their businesses. Java is now a real estate broker, and he tackles that business the same way he did when he ran LGE: always overdelivering, with modest confidence and plenty of optimism. Memo has one of Hollywood's top jobs as a TV executive at Bravo. When I see him now, it's almost as if he still can't quite believe where his life has taken him. But I can see that it's just the way he designed it. He gives his employees the same playground for developing their ideas and talents that I once tried to give him. With the Joes, you'll always find the door open, and they never miss an opportunity to take a chance on those they believe in and help them on their path. Loyalty doesn't come any stronger than that.

YOU'RE MY BEST FRIEND, AND YOU'RE FIRED

Work can be the common ground upon which bridges are built and burned. I found the love of my life after hiring him as a consultant. I fell in love with Steven watching him interact with the world through our work, which gave me a 360-degree view of what he believed in, how he handled situations, and how he kept pushing forward, no matter what. Those were all qualities I admired enough to want him as a manager (and ultimately husband).

When *Leeza* was in need of a producer, I excitedly called my former *Two on the Town* producer turned best friend, Andrea, to see if she could pack her bags and come out to Los Angeles for the job. Although she was a born-and-bred New Yorker, she barely asked what I had in mind and jumped at the chance to put the band back together.

I was thrilled to have my best friend in the same city with

me for the first time in more than a decade, but it soon became clear that our working relationship was much more nuanced this time around. Now that we were working on a show that was a new format for me, and it had my name on it, this felt like a high-risk proposition. Andrea believed in me, and she knew that I could do it. I've always thought she could produce anything, so I believed she was the best person to launch this new adventure with, especially since we were dealing with the expectations of the VIPs at Paramount, and she knew her way around that executive world. She was juggling several other ongoing career opportunities and was often stretched thin, but I'd seen her pull a rabbit out of her hat again and again, and I knew she could now.

As her friend, I wanted her to have the fullest, most rewarding life possible, but as her colleague, I needed my show to come first. It felt complicated. At the end of the first year, I sensed that she wasn't really into it, and I'd heard that she was phoning it in. Andrea was called in for a meeting with one of the executives at Paramount who oversaw my show, and was told they would not be renewing her contract. The next thing I knew, she came to me for answers. Of course she did. She was my dear friend, it was my show, and this news had to feel like a slap.

"Leeza, did you know they weren't going to pick me up?"

"Well, they made it clear this is their decision, and I didn't have any control over it," I said. "But, yes, I did know."

"Well, how could you not tell me?" she said. "How could

you not prepare me? How could you let me go in there and be blindsided?"

She was right. I had gotten so caught up in my work drama that I'd failed to do the right thing. I just didn't pay enough attention or anticipate this moment.

"I'm so sorry," I said, not sharing that they'd told me she would be happy with the decision. That the show was never a good fit for her, and she had too many other things going on. I didn't say to her that I had zero power (or so I thought) to force a staff member on a show where they weren't wanted. None of that mattered.

At the time, I was in way over my head and was barely treading water. She had never given up her apartment in Manhattan, and so I'd assumed she wasn't that invested in the job or in her new life in Los Angeles and would be glad for the chance to return home. It wasn't until years later that I understood just how hurt Andrea had been and how much of a problem it had caused for her in terms of our friendship. Ultimately, she realized I really didn't have control over the decision to let her go, and that the job meant nothing to her compared to our relationship. She chose to move forward, and by the time I knew how upset she'd been, she'd already forgiven me.

Now, with more than three decades of close friendship between us, we can reflect on that moment with total neutrality and see how some of the executives in charge on our show had a tendency to cut loose any producer who'd grown too close to me. Maybe they needed to feel as if they had more control over me. It was like being in reaction and recovery mode all the time. Not a good way to stay grounded.

Was I guilty of classic confrontation avoidance? Probably. I was definitely guilty of making assumptions, which is never a good move. Sometimes staying neutral really is the best approach. But other times, to avoid getting into gear when you feel compromised or conflicted is denying your voice. You may not always have the power to change an outcome, but you have to go on the record with your opinions, beliefs, convictions, and desires. In my situation with Andrea, I knew it was inevitable and probably right for her to leave the show, but I also know that she didn't feel like I had her back. I wish I had called her and told her what was up and not assumed that it was her desired outcome. Now I never assume anyone knows where I'm coming from or that I know what he or she thinks or wants.

I can see now how much significance this moment had, and how much it taught me about the importance of having integrity in all areas of my life, all the time, especially when we're being run so fast and spread so thin. I'd say it's nearly impossible to have the kind of friendship that's worth maintaining over many decades without having at least a few moments that need to be forgiven—on both sides. Nelson Mandela said to not forgive is like drinking the poison and expecting someone else to die. The grudge or blame doesn't hurt the other person. It's toxic to you. When you forgive someone it's not something you do for them . . . it's a gift to yourself. I'm so grateful to Andrea for being one of my forever friends, and for the gift of her forgiveness.

ADVOCATE FOR YOURSELF

It's not about always having the right answer. Or even having an answer at all. It's about admitting when you don't know something while being confident that you know how to get the answer, and being honest about the fact that sometimes you mess up along the way, despite your best intentions. I think this rawness has created a situation where I still have good relationships with the people I've worked with, no matter what's happened between us professionally over the years. The Boston University School of Management found that in a sales job, you're always better off telling the truth, even when you're asked a question that stumps you, and your truth is responding, "I don't know." They call these the most powerful three words in sales, and in many cases, using them can seal the deal, because it inspires trust and credibility. When those who work with you and for you (or live with you, like your children) have the opportunity to see that you don't think you know all the answers, and yet you're still confident as their leader, I think that allows them to really trust you, too. And to be loyal to you, the company, and its mission. A paranoid boss never admits ignorance or claims wrongdoing. Somebody started the false idea that you lose credibility and power if you admit to messing up. If you play it that way, anyone who blows the whistle gets punished and everyone is afraid. How does it help to admit when you're wrong? Well, it shows that you are serious about being honest and accountable. And it allows others to do the same, creating a culture that addresses mistakes without blame. That way, things get fixed and growth is encouraged. Isn't that what you want from your team, and for your team?

We all want to achieve, grow, succeed; to gain respect, money, and freedom. Personally, though, I don't think any of those things are worth it unless you can be proud of how you got there. Winning isn't everything. Competing well, pushing hard, focusing with fierce optimism and empathy, being flexible and forgiving, and earning respect on the way to a win . . . *that's* everything as far as I'm concerned.

With my foundation, we recently messed up by not communicating a change early enough to the people who would be affected the most by it. I felt bad about that, and as a make-good gesture, I hosted a little wine and cheese night to apologize for our (unintentional) mistake and hear their ideas about how we could do better. I needed to ask the right questions. The members of our team really seemed to appreciate the admission of our mistake and being included in making it better, and I felt even more connected to them and how much they contribute. The fact that they openly received the apology showed great respect.

It's a sign of a generous person when they are respectful. That's a crucial quality for successful people: they have to be generous in spirit, they have to be generous with their time; they have to be generous with crediting other people for their ideas and be able to relinquish control when they know it's better for the project or the group that they step back. My friend John

Redmann, who was one of my associate producers at *Leeza,* has these qualities, as I was lucky enough to watch him shine.

John was good at his job and everyone knew it. His shows were inventive and full of his young energy. Even though he was in his mid-twenties and was very much a junior producer in the business at the time, he was focused and persistent. And he wasn't going to sit by and get passed over.

John knew I loved him and would give him my support, so he approached our executive producer to bump him up from associate to full producer. He was told there were not enough spots on the show for another producer, and besides, he didn't have enough experience to command the title.

"I believe my shows are better than those of some producers you've had," he said. "If you can tell me that's not true, I'll drop it, but I think my record speaks for itself."

There it was, that special mix I've always admired so much: confident without being cocky. He was advocating for himself without being disrespectful.

He did become a producer in no time and proceeded to pitch me shows that were spontaneous and fun and helped me to be relatable. Roger Ailes would be so proud! John always made me feel that he would protect me and not make me look foolish, which is pretty much the perfect quality to have in a producer (and a friend), and since I believed him, I always went for it.

Winning is what John's good at, but he's always been fun, nice, and fair on his way to the top. John has learned to survive—and thrive—under the toughest situations at many of the best shows. From strong women like Rosie and Tyra to stars such as

Tony Danza and Wayne Brady, John has produced for them all. He makes everyone better and has the Emmys to prove it. Now he is the executive producer at *The Talk,* where he's faced some difficult times and strong personalities. Through it all, he's held his ground while never raising his voice. He recently told me that his sense of the importance of respecting and investing in his staff's development came from me. Hearing that sure makes me feel great, but honestly, I know John was born with it. Most winners are.

RESPECTFUL BUT BOUNDARIED

"How should I handle The Donald?" I asked my friend and former *America Now* cohost Bill Rancic, before *Celebrity Apprentice.* Bill was on the first *Apprentice,* before Mark Burnett shot new life into the show in 2008 by making it *Celebrity Apprentice.*

Unlike the stars, in the beginning the apprentices really *did* go to work for Donald, and Bill had spent a year under his wing. In the years I've known Bill, he has never said an unflattering word about his former boss. Bill stayed true to form now.

"You're gonna be great," he said. "You'll show him that you're strong, and smart, and you're not afraid to work hard."

I also call it like I see it. And so, when I'm asked about my experience on the show, I answer the unending Trump questions with honesty: "Yes, that's his real hair."

And: "He's always been nice to me."

Seriously, everyone asks me how I feel about Donald Trump. So here it goes. I was so thankful for all the opportunities I'd been given that I wanted to send Donald Trump a personal thank-you that would express my deep gratitude. So I took a photo of us from the celebration party, with his thumb up like he always does, and I put it in a frame, which I had engraved with this:

"Nice girls finish first when nice guys inspire them."

My experience with Trump was exactly that—he was a nice guy.

I know, the frame might not have landed a spot on his desk anywhere, but he did send me a very nice handwritten thank-you note, saying he was proud of me. (Guess I'm not the only person who believes in good manners.) Now, I know there are many of you out there bristling at the fact that I used "good manners" and "Trump" in the same sentence, but as I've been saying all along, everything in life comes down to relationship and how you see things. As Wayne Dyer says, "When you change the way you look at things, the things you look at change."

Over the course of the show I changed the way I saw Donald Trump. I chose to see him as someone who could help me, and as the head of his family. I viewed him as a dad first, seeing him in the boardroom with his exceptional children, Ivanka, Don Jr., and Eric, who all possess a tremendously strong work ethic, beautiful manners, and exemplary decorum. Even though they are the offspring of a man who's commanded the spotlight for years, they more than held their own with him while being totally respectful to the patriarch whose name had both opened doors and made things harder for them.

Throughout the season on *Celebrity Apprentice* I saw Donald be demanding and tough with the contestants because he expected us to be able to support and defend our actions. No surprise there. After all, this is a man who doesn't back down from anything. He doesn't care for weakness and is quick to ignore or discount those who he thinks don't have brainpower. But having said that, at least during my season he was genuinely interested in each contestant, and even when they heard that sledgehammer phrase, "You're fired," Trump wanted to make sure they were okay. Like a dad would do.

After I won *Celebrity Apprentice* I was amazed at the immediate shift in opportunities available to me. It was like my fairy godfather, Donald Trump, had waved his magic wand and changed my life. For a homegrown charity like ours, getting a prime-time platform to share our message was seismic. I had started my work with family caregivers in 2002, but so many people said to me after the show, "I never knew you had a foundation. This is great." That's the Trump factor in action.

Getting a chance to earn over seven hundred thousand dollars for Leeza's Care Connection was also a game changer. I had barely packed my bags at Trump Tower in New York when I headed for my hometown of Irmo, South Carolina, to put my winnings to work, gathering support for Leeza's Care Connection and securing a landmark house in my old neighborhood to be our home-base oasis for family caregivers. This will be our crown jewel, where we offer our free services to those who suddenly have to answer the question "Now what?" when someone they love gets a chronic disease or illness. It was my dream come true to offer support to my neighbors and friends from my childhood. My dad, sister, brother, and sister-in-law still live in the area, and I'm so happy to wrap them up in our mission to honor Mom's legacy in this way. Without Trump, it wouldn't have happened.

Before Donald Trump became a presidential candidate, I called and asked if he could help me to pull off a surprise for a senior citizen in Georgia. She was working with a charity I love called Second Wind Dreams, which is basically like Make-A-Wish for seniors. They grant wishes, large and small, to seniors who feel they are running out of time. This time it was Helen Warren, a former beauty queen, who won a local pageant in North Carolina seventy years ago. Now she lives in a senior living community in Georgia, but dreams die hard, and her wish was to be able to feel like a beauty queen again in her eighty-eighth year.

I didn't want to overreach, but I asked Trump if the Miss Universe Organization, which produces the Miss USA contest as well, could make Helen an Honorary Miss USA, complete with sash and crown. I really wanted that moment both for her, and for the students at Pope High School who discovered her dream and reached out to Second Wind Dreams on her behalf. Donald not only came through but also sent a video message, which was played the night of the event. I was so happy and so inspired that Donald helped grant this wish. He had absolutely nothing to gain from it. He did it just to be nice.

Donald has earned my respect because of actions like these over the years, even though we differ on many of our political views. As his bid for the White House progressed, this has become a complicated duality for me. Most of us will find ourselves in similar situations at some point, where we want to be respectful of someone while standing up for our own beliefs.

For me the situation occurred not long before Donald announced his intention to run for president. That's when he called me. Now, it's not like we're buddy-buddies and talk on the phone every week (I don't *really* work for him—that was just TV), and so I knew something was up. And then it occurred to me that I'm from South Carolina, which is an important state for the Republicans.

"I'm going to announce," he said.

Trump had flirted with this decision for so long that, like most people, I assumed he would ultimately go for it. But still, I wasn't quite prepared for what came next.

"I'm going to do this event in South Carolina," he continued. "My team said to me, 'Well, you have to get Leeza's support because she's important to the state and she's their homegrown darling. Can you get her endorsement?' And I said, 'Well, I think so. Yeah.' So I'm calling you."

"To seek my endorsement?" I said.

"Well, yeah," he said. "I mean, I said I can do that. You can do that for me, can't you? You like me."

"You know I like you, and I will always find ways to be supportive," I said. "Why don't you have your campaign strategist call me, and we'll talk about it?"

I then told him I would always be grateful to him (I am), before wishing him luck and saying goodbye.

At this point, I was thinking to myself I'd likely be a liability to him politically. My state has a Republican governor, and our two U.S. senators are Republicans as well. I have been quiet about my political views, so maybe his team assumed that I was a Republican, too, and didn't know that I'm registered as a Democrat. Shortly after my conversation with Donald, his strategist called me and asked me to appear with Trump at a campaign event in South Carolina. I thanked him for the consideration as I politely told him that I'm not a Republican and don't share the same positions on some of the key issues as many in the party, since I'm pro-choice, and I've been publicly supporting gay marriage for several decades.

He agreed it wouldn't be a good move for me to appear at the campaign stop, but I said I meant it when I told Trump I wanted to find ways to be supportive.

"Why don't we find something to do together, surrounding our mutual support for family caregivers?" I suggested.

I knew how vocal Donald had become on this issue, and we were aligned about offering support to spouses of veterans and others who sacrifice so much to care for someone they love with a disease or injury. That offer was met with enthusiasm. We ended the conversation without making any real plans, but I hope I was respectful but boundaried. While I wanted to show gratitude and loyalty to Donald, I also had to be true to myself. I think Donald would see it the same way.

Unlike others, I'm not a bit surprised how Donald has

whipped up support. How you do one thing is how you do everything. His one thing is winning. He is strengthening his strengths by playing it the way he always has, putting his bravado out in front, taking bold action without fear of shaking things up, and refusing to back down. Large and in charge is the only setting he seems to have. Now when so many are feeling screwed over by government, worried about their future security, and cheated out of their American dream, many want a leader to be as angry about that as they are and say the things they dare not say. Donald sure timed it right.

Donald and I are not often politically aligned, but when it comes to loving our families, we are exactly the same. We also share a desire to create change, and in this respect the man has it down. One of the ways he has done it is by giving celebrities a chance to raise big money as they share their message and test their nerve on *Celebrity Apprentice*. He has been the conduit for providing more than $15 million to various charities. Those of us who have been on the receiving end of that are grateful.

TV COMFORT FOOD

I guess I won't be having any New Year's Eve blowouts for the next few years. Along with Mark Steines from Hallmark's *Home and Family* show, I will be hosting the Rose Parade in Pasadena, one of my favorite traditions. It's like TV comfort food. As they celebrate a new year, families still gather to watch the floats and flowers. Mark and I are excited to take over the host chairs, but I've gotta say it's a little daunting to be taking the reins from my dear friend Bob Eubanks and the supersweet Stephanie Edwards. These two have been hosting the parade for thirty-eight and thirty-five years respectively! They finally decided it was time to stay up and party with the rest of America and chose to step down. Our hosting will be different, of course, as we may be taking their seats but no one can take their place. Thankfully, Bob said he would coach me through it! Even so, I will miss them on the air. And I'm sure their viewers will, too. The loyalty they've inspired over the years is an incredible example of the lasting power of being good to people on the way up and always staying optimistic, even when rain clouds appear!

One year, the network decided to have Stephanie report from the streets, rather than sitting next to Bob in the booth as cohost. It was the year Los Angeles had heavy rains on the day of the parade, and Stephanie was out there in the torrential downpour, wearing her stockings and a smile, as she was drenched, hour after hour. She didn't make a scene about being replaced in the anchor booth and was every bit the pro she is known to be, but viewers weren't having it! After years of watching her report on the festivities, she was like family to them, and they protested and complained by the thousands, threatening to never watch again! It wasn't a surprise that the decision was "auto-corrected" very soon, and Stephanie was back on her (dry) perch, making the parade safe for viewers to watch again. I love this example of resiliency and of the power of being nice, and the devotion both qualities can inspire in others.

Bob and I have worked together on live events, like the years we hosted the Hollywood Christmas parade as a team, and there is no one like him. As a broadcaster and host, he is unparalleled and beloved. Well, the man is an icon, after all. With his characteristic low-key humility he told me simply, "You'll do great, slick!" He is a gift.

What a beautiful legacy we have been tapped to protect.

THE SECRET OF LOYALTY

"I'll take fifty percent efficiency to get one hundred percent loyalty."

Those are the words of film producer Samuel Goldwyn. I get his point, but I think he misses something important on this one. Loyalty is not about getting a bunch of yes-men to follow you to the ends of the earth. It's a quality that *not's easily given* because it really *can't* be given . . . *you have to earn it.* To do so takes time and personal investment.

I come from a generation where you're "true to your school," you give your loyalty to your country, and you stay with brands that you trust. Loyalty today is on the endangered qualities list, though, because it requires that two parties have trust, a relationship, and shared experiences, and we're running out of people who can or will take time for that. It's one of the things we all crave most, however, and the connection companies want most with their customers.

A little loyalty can cover a multitude of sins. For example, when employees feel like "We're all in this together," they're likely to stay with a company even if profits take a hit. When there is loyalty in a relationship, we're more likely to overlook the occasional irritability or neglectfulness.

Today, people don't usually offer their loyalty, simply because they feel it's the right thing to do. It's a "you scratch my back, I'll scratch yours" mentality, and that's actually cool, because that kind of reciprocity itself creates more loyalty.

Loyal people don't feel alone. They are part of something, and they know they're getting something out of it. So how do you cultivate it? If you're loyal you *don't "better deal" people.* If you make plans to have dinner with your friend, and your sister offers you concert tickets, a loyal person will keep the dinner plans. If you develop your loyalty to others, you'll also find it will help you to maintain your integrity and keep your word to yourself. Let's say you're the only one on the board who is voting against a popular issue. If you have loyalty, you'll *hold your position,* instead of flipping.

Here's why I think it's so important. Loyalty reflects how we feel about ourselves; what we're worthy of receiving, and what we're capable of giving. A fair-weather friend who's fun is one thing; a loyal friend is a treasure.

Offering your employer your skills is one thing, delivering your loyalty means more. People without character can't give loyalty or receive it. Avoid them like the plague. And certainly don't *be* them.

CHAPTER SIX

No Regrets
(Forgiveness)

I don't really remember much about being a toddler, which is a good thing, I suppose, because it was the first time our family had a cross burned in our yard. We were living in Cheraw, South Carolina, where Dad's career was on the rise as a young school superintendent who had made more than a few enemies by supporting desegregation. Mom was at home with my brother and me when the doorbell rang. She was holding me in her arms when she opened the door and found no one there. Opening wider, she saw the cross, in full blaze, just a few feet away. Daddy had weighed in on a local issue on the side of racial equality, and this was just a warning.

Growing up in the South in the 1960s meant living through turbulent times, as the nation tried to find solid ground regarding race relations. I realize, in some respects, we still are, but this was one of the most active moments for the Ku Klux Klan, which was bombing houses, burning crosses, and forcing people to jump to their deaths from bridges. My dad confronted this shameful time with characteristic passion. The same purposeful energy he drew on as kid, growing up on a farm in Puddin Swamp near Turbeville, South Carolina, and attending a one-room schoolhouse. Daddy has always been a proponent of civil rights and was summoned to the White House to discuss the barriers of hatred and terror between black and white. One of my favorite pictures, hanging in his office, shows him shaking hands with President Lyndon Johnson at the White House.

As a little girl, I recall heated dinner table conversations about Kennedy and Johnson and their potential impact on history. Dad was the vice president of the Urban League in Columbia and was well-known for his support not only of school desegregation but also of the Voting Rights Act of 1965, protecting the rights of African Americans to vote, as well as women.

I always loved to go to work with Daddy because it was a space so alive with passion and debate. He always seemed to be in the center of the storms of the day, with the best vantage point to see all sides and yet remain calm. Back then, he smoked a pipe, and it added to his aura of thoughtfulness. Never without the right words, in his tweed jacket, with alligator buttons and suede patches on the elbows, he was like an academic activist.

Nothing so frightening ever happened to our family again, or at least not that I was aware of, until I was in high school.

At this point, we were in Columbia, where Daddy was the executive secretary of the South Carolina Education Association. We lived in a suburb with lots of white neighbors. I don't recall any of the nice houses set back from the road, with azaleas and dogwoods in the yard, being occupied by black families. Well, our family had planned a gathering in our home, and several of Dad's African American friends and associates had been invited. Ever the politician, he went door-to-door to give the neighbors a heads-up to avoid a scene. Just a few cool reactions, but most seemed to have no issue at all with his choice of guests.

Cut to the day before the party. When I got home from school, a small cross was in flames by the walkway that led to the front door. The antics of kids, probably.

I've always thought supporting the rights of others is among the most fundamental things we can do as citizens of this country. I've never had to think twice about speaking up for the disenfranchised. My values were formed from watching my father see something wrong in society, speak up against it, and then be a part of the change to correct it. That optimistic belief system is what propelled me on my talk show to stand for same-sex marriage and to offer up stories that could possibly help mitigate the hatred that comes from ignorance.

We can all lack knowledge or sensitivity if we don't understand an issue. I've remained in a place of hope about the hatred born of ignorance that has scarred the soul of our country. The people who put those crosses in our yards can be forgiven for their ignorance, but because I'm not willing to forget, I can also use that experience as fuel for staying resolute in my determination to do more.

FORGIVE LONG AND PROSPER

"I'm very certain that I can do the job as well as Dixie Whatley," I said during a dinner with the studio's executives when *ET* was first courting me to join the show.

If there was a momentary chill at the table, I barely registered it, as I was so laser focused on proving just how much I had to offer the show in the areas where I thought I might find a real foothold. I don't remember how, but the conversation that night had turned to Dixie Whatley, who hosted the weekend show at the time. I just knew this was my chance to demonstrate my confidence in stepping up to the plate, and so I did. It wasn't until later that I learned one of the executives I'd been dining with was dating Dixie and so had probably not responded as I'd hoped to my comparison.

What I had hoped would be a potentially career-making position at *ET* dwindled to little more than a reporter's job, shrinking my dreams with it. The tension of the overall contract negotiations and the increasing unlikelihood of anchor work is what made me initially have my agent turn down the first offer I received. I guess I'll never know if my overzealousness that night had anything to do with what my offer looked like. It may have been totally irrelevant. (At least the offer didn't come with a mandate for me to attend diplomacy class!)

It all worked out in the end, and I did in fact receive a career-making opportunity from *ET*. I had no barrels aimed at Dixie, of course; I was just trying to appear capable. I'm not sure if that put me on shaky ground, but there was nothing gracious about it. Even when I was able to breathe a sigh of relief and set about *really* proving myself, I knew this was an important moment from which to learn. Moving forward, when I wanted to impress upon others that I thought I had a lot to offer, I did it without comparing myself to anyone else. And as a way of acknowledging the forgiveness I received in this moment for my naïve social gaffe, I always make a mental note to be understanding when those I work with—especially younger staffers who don't have an abundance of experience or perspective—say something regrettable (within reason, of course). We've all done it. I like to extend the same generosity I've been lucky enough to receive.

Of course, even our desire to do better doesn't always prevent us from making stupid mistakes, and I hadn't been at *ET* long when I made a big one. At the time I was beginning this exciting new chapter in my career, I was also in the final throes of a volatile relationship with a boyfriend I'd been with for several years. Well, I wanted things to work out with this guy, and so I took a spontaneous Vegas trip with him. I didn't bother to check, or really even think much about, how it might affect any assignments I may have had at *ET*. Now, to put this in perspective, I don't think I've *ever* missed an assignment, or a test, or a day of work in my entire life, except for when I was busy having a baby. But I was reckless in that way we are when we're trying to hold on to something that clearly isn't working.

I blew it. I hadn't checked in with the assignment desk to see that they had in fact scheduled me on a last-minute interview. To make matters even worse, I really loved my boss, Jack Riley, and had great respect for him, and I hated letting him down. He came from a news background where not checking in with the assignment desk was tantamount to professional suicide. Jack was such a great, honorable producer, and one of the reasons I loved my job. I wanted him to like me, and even more than that, I wanted to earn his respect. So when I got a call directly from him in the wake of my momentary lack of judgment, I was mortified and humiliated. I was sure they were going to fire me, and I knew they would have been well within their rights to do so. I couldn't believe it when he generously gave me another chance. After I apologized and expressed my regret and embarrassment, I vowed to make it up to him, and I did.

So there was another learning opportunity, born of my screw-up. But you don't have to teach me any lesson twice. I never again allowed selfish or spontaneous decisions in my personal life to blur my professional responsibilities. My kids, of course, always came first, and I never apologized for that, but I doubled my efforts to be a team player after this, realizing that one person's choices can affect the outcome for everyone. This moment is why I always give people second chances and try to understand that we all have our own personal priorities and private turmoil. Of course, I expect my employees to deliver, but when they can't I try to forgive and let them prove themselves, just as Jack let me do. Now I know from personal experience how forgiveness can lead to better, more loyal relationships in the long run.

In fact, once we master the art of forgiveness, and self-forgiveness, it allows us to achieve even more by striving even higher, with full acceptance of the fact that sometimes we're just going to fall on our faces. There are so many reasons why I'm a big fan of Sara Blakely and her billion-dollar Spanx empire. Here's one of the reasons why I think she's got a lot of things figured out. During her 2012 speech at the National Association of Professional Women's second annual National Networking Conference, Sara described how when she was a girl, her father asked her every evening what she'd failed at that day. If she had nothing to report, he grew disappointed, because that meant she hadn't made any big enough attempts. Fast-forward three decades to her speech, when she attributed her ingrained comfort with the inevitability of temporary setbacks as the secret to the eventual triumph of Spanx. "Not being afraid to fail is a key part of the success of Spanx," she said, describing the two years of being told "No" she had to overcome in order to push through and achieve the Yes of success. You can bet she had to forgive herself more than a few times along the way.

YOU CAN'T OWN A COLOR

Back in the day, when I was at *ET,* it was the height of '80s tackiness. Well, at least that's how I see it now. Crazy, glow-in-the-dark, neon colors with shoulder pads were "totally tubular." Big earrings, big hair, a pair of jellies, and a headband; I was in heaven. Subtlety was not a hallmark of the time and there was certainly no place for it in my wardrobe.

My biggest fashion faux pas were saved for the biggest awards shows, like the Oscars, where, at the last minute, I chose to wear "headgear" with a perfectly nice Oscar de la Renta gown. It was a hat with a veil (which looked silly enough), but I had it perched on my head at such an angle that it looked like either a big bow or a satellite dish!

Anjelica Houston saw me on the red carpet as I proudly posed for pictures.

"Hey, Leeza, nice hat!" she yelled, which encouraged more paparazzi photos.

One of those pictures made its way to the fashion pages here in the United States and down under, prompting a week's worth of interviews in which I playfully defended my choice. No such thing as bad publicity, right?

I supposed, then, it wasn't a bad thing that I wasn't exactly given free rein when it came to what I wore on the air. I was the new kid on the block, as I was well aware, and I respected my place in the pecking order. I looked at Mary Hart and saw confidence, beauty, and brains all wrapped in a friendly package. And not the kind of woman who would ever wear such a silly hat! We both got our wardrobe from a store called Lillie Rubin (which can't be blamed for my headpiece). Our talented wardrobe stylist/designer, Matt Van Dyne, was on the scene, making selections for us. We both loved Matt and still do.

There was never any question that Mary truly owned the town (and our business). But could someone really *own* a color? At *ET* maybe they could, if that someone was Mary Hart and the color was red. From the time I arrived on the Paramount lot, I'd always heard red had been designated for Mary, and not for me. Our dressing rooms were next to each other, and as Matt later told me, one day Matt said she asked about a red suit, with a houndstooth pattern and black collar, that she saw hanging on a rolling rack.

"That's for Leeza," he said.

"It's red," she said.

"You own the color?" he said.

"You know what I mean," she replied, without attitude or animosity.

Mary and I laughed about this recently and she told me that no, she never banned red from my wardrobe but she was insistent that we have separate, distinct styles. Smart girl. Look, Mary Hart was a brand long before people started talking in those terms, because she knew what worked for her. Red was on the list. You bet I was taking notes. Name it and claim it; that's the way to own your life. So while red was not the property of Mary Hart, and though there was never an official edict from her banning me from the color, because I'd heard the legend that she had so many times, I'm still a bit phobic about red to this day!

It was really important to me to earn Mary's respect, so I tried to act cool around her, no matter what. She was always lovely to me. In fact, that's how she is with most everyone. It's just her way. Over lattes recently, I was able to thank her for paving the way for so many of us, and to fess up about having been intimidated by her decades ago. I was shocked to hear her tell me that she actually used to feel threatened by me. This was a good moment for both of us, I think, because it allowed us to share stories about the way we'd been positioned against each other, and also to see how much we'd had in common, more than anything else.

"Hang on . . . what?" I said when she made her confession.

"Sure," she continued. "I used to think you were a threat to my job, and I was hurt a bit when you got your own talk show, feeling I would have been given that opportunity."

I always thought she had been offered a talk show, along with prime-time specials, a diamond-studded tiara, and a pony, if she'd wanted. I could understand if the studio wanted to keep her strapped to the host desk, though.

"Mary, you were too important to *ET* for them to dare mess with your position and the continuity on the show," I said.

It's true. She anchored that chair on that set for almost thirty years. A small-town girl from South Dakota with confidence to spare, she had parents who believed in her, and she fueled her dreams with hard work. With a lot of life behind us now, I can see how similar we were, including our very real vulnerabilities. Mary told me she never thought she was creating the longest-running show in entertainment history. She was just moving forward. *ET* was a success born of failure for Mary, just like it was for me, too. Mary had been cohosting a show with Regis Philbin that was canceled after four months when *ET* interviewed her about how it felt to get the ax. The next day they hired her. Mary has always been a wholesome beauty, and now in her mid-sixties, she still looks like America's Sweetheart. When I asked why she thought America took such a shine to her, she said she thought it was because her "*optimism was conveyed through TV.*" I couldn't agree more.

I was blessed to have her in the "big" chair while I was at *ET* because she helped me grow up; she made me a better reporter, and anchor. We were colleagues—and competitors, sure—but, remember, I've always been the girl who likes to be pushed, and Mary kept the bar high.

She was already the queen bee of entertainment TV when I started at the show, and I sometimes felt like I had to craft a presence out of whatever was leftover from her image. This wasn't because of anything Mary did. She was just darned good at her job. I was new in Hollywood and unsure of how things were done, but I instinctively knew that my only option was to be myself. In the end, it was a good call (as it always is), and I found my own way to the career—and success—I was supposed to have, on my own terms. And the self-worth follows. Mary, thanks for leading the way.

My favorite recent example of how it's possible to thrive by just being you is Jessica Alba, who founded the Honest Company when she was thirty years old. And now, less than five years later, she has turned it into a $1.7-billion business with five hundred employees, and everyone in Hollywood is raving about how she changed the celebrity model. Here's what she did. She built a business based on something she believed in and cared about: delivering safe and effective consumer products that were easy to get and affordable. She was sick with allergies as a young girl, and she worried about the dangers of chemicals to her own children, so she wanted to offer products that were not potentially toxic. Venture capitalists turned her down over and over. Being an actress, she knew how to take hearing no and barely paid attention to the rejection. The industry may have underestimated this beautiful business tycoon, but she never doubted herself for a minute. To this day she's very hands-on, even straightening signs at her pop-up shop at a mall. When asked if that's something Steve Jobs would have done, she said: "I don't know. I'm doing it my way."

She says her doubters were the driving force behind her success. I get that.

On my own path, I was a hardworking, well-meaning, people-pleasing young woman who was probably a bit too ambitious for her own good; all I wanted was to be taken seriously and to make my mark. When I read Donald Trump write about himself, "I wasn't satisfied just to earn a good living; I wanted to make a statement," I could relate. I hadn't yet learned the *under*statement part of making a statement, or discovered that the strongest statements are often made through silence. Thank goodness my overearnestness didn't usually reveal itself on camera. I hope my southern roots showed through more often: At *ET* I tried to be the lady my mom had raised me to be. Yes, I did have mall hair, but so did most of America. And, yes, I did wear pantyhose (Hanes Barely There) no matter what. But so did most ladies, including the one whose legs were insured for a million dollars apiece: Mary Hart!

Since Mary was America's sophisticated sweetheart, I suppose I was the less refined but approachable girl next door. Or, as the studio executives told Matt when they soon ordered him to change our looks up again: "Mary looks like a politician's wife, and Leeza looks like someone who would steal your husband." Not exactly the look I thought I was going for! That's where Matt did his thing, and I'm ever so grateful he did.

I was devastated when, not too long after, Matt was fired. It was rumored he'd been let go in part for being too close to Mary and me, which the executive producers feared might undermine their influence over us. What a sucky thing. But, as I'd soon come to learn, those kinds of power plays were constant in our world, and you know what? The executives were right in their own way: no one means more to a TV host than the man or woman who makes her look great on the air every day.

THE FIXER MEETS HER MATCH

Life has a way of reminding us who's really the boss, and it's not us.

I should have been on top of the world. My career was taking off, and I'd begun to build a life for myself in Los Angeles that I really enjoyed, settling into the house I'd bought in Los Feliz, going for runs, and walking my dogs in Griffith Park and through the sun-kissed hills of my neighborhood.

My parents were visiting, which normally would have filled me with joy. But something was different this time. Even though we'd spent the week doing the usual touristy stuff— a boat trip to Catalina and dinner overlooking the beach in Santa Monica—by the time they returned to South Carolina, my heart was heavy.

Although my mom and I had always been extremely close, and we'd had a ball when she'd driven cross-country with me the year before, I'd noticed that she'd recently become increasingly paranoid and insecure. That wasn't my mom. She seemed to be attempting to find solace in alcohol, which was only compounding the problem. I'd grown alarmed the night before, at a restaurant, as I watched her drink too much wine with dinner, and then get into the wrong car while I was paying the check. I just knew my mom must have been hurting, and I went into rescue mode.

My fear was that we were all in danger of losing Mom to what looked like alcoholism, so I'd decided to encourage my family to band together to help her. As the middle child, I was always the one who tried to be "the fixer." I felt compelled to straddle both sides in any conflict and try to make everybody happy. And now I was prepared to lead an intervention to get my mom the help she obviously needed. I knew alcoholism was a disease and not a death sentence, and that there were abundant resources available to help her. I wanted to make sure my mother was one of those who had a chance to fight back and win. Since the rest of my family all lived in South Carolina, I organized a phone meeting.

"Mom needs help," I said. "We really can't ignore this anymore. I think we need to take some steps."

Before we could get anywhere with our planning, I heard someone pick up on the line.

"I know what you're doing," Mom said. "I know y'all are planning to send me to that Henry Ford Center."

Despite how tense the moment was—or maybe because of how tense the moment was—I couldn't help myself, and I started chuckling.

"Mom, we're *really* not going to send you to Henry Ford," I said.

In fact, we didn't send my mom to rehab (at the Betty Ford Center) or anywhere. Instead, we held on tight, with lots of love, and tried to maintain as much normalcy as possible, even in the face of her increasingly erratic behavior. It wasn't until five years later, when she was finally diagnosed with Alzheimer's disease at the young age of sixty-two, that we finally understood everything.

Suddenly it all made sense. She'd had a terrible car wreck in her late fifties, after which she'd never really been the same. I've since learned of scientific evidence to suggest that a head trauma can escalate the onset of Alzheimer's symptoms. I think that may have been what happened to my mom. Now that we knew what was really going on with her medically, I understood that if she had been drinking a bit too much, it was likely because she'd been experiencing the first stages of memory loss without comprehending what was happening. Because she was scared, I believe, she started self-medicating with the alcohol to numb her fear. It was still unbearably painful to witness her suffering, but at least we knew what we were up against now and could do our best to support her fully. Name it, claim it, and deal with it. That was Mom's advice on most things, and now we all had to follow it.

Of course, I had already forgiven my mom for all the erratic and challenging behaviors she'd exhibited before we knew their cause. This was my mother, and there was nothing she could do or say that would cause me to abandon my commitment to her. And I'm grateful that she'd forgiven me for lecturing her about her drinking and leading the charge to get the whole family to "gang up on her." Neither of us had understood the situation. In our relationships with others, we often don't have the whole picture or understand the full implications of much that's happening, so holding on to the pain of resentment is counterproductive and toxic. There was nothing easy about the next ten years, as my mom lost more and more of herself to this devastating disease, but the one thing that carried us through was our deep love and devotion to each other as a family. I felt so blessed that, despite the rocky times we'd faced, we took care of each other. It was strength we would need for the even tougher times ahead.

READ THE FINE PRINT

I've always had the philosophy that my business is *my* business. My agents and lawyers can give me great advice, but it's still my responsibility to be informed about everything I'm signing, and to carefully consider every aspect of a deal before entering into it. And now, given the fact that I've been burned, I'm even more careful.

From the beginning I've read every contract I've ever been given, closely. And when I've had a question about why something was a certain way, I always asked for clarification, even if it was sometimes embarrassing to have to admit my ignorance. When I'm done with a contract, it's all marked up with red lines, bubbles and arrows, and inked-in changes. To get there I'll go back and forth, and back and forth, with my agents and attorneys and advisers about every little detail, including the fees and the dates. I know that sometimes the people I'm working with would prefer to get the paperwork off their desks and move on. Fair enough. For them it's one of many deals. But to me it's a big deal, because it's *my* deal. My name and reputation are at risk with each move. I respect both, and I take my word very seriously. I want to make sure I don't agree to anything I'm not comfortable with and can't deliver on. *What's the expectation? What's my commitment? What am I allowed to do outside the agreement?*

These were all things that came into question when Paramount, my home studio, sued me over my infomercial with Tony Robbins. As always, I had been very careful going into this new agreement, and I'd been under the impression that I was all clear to take on this job and sell products. I mean, my contract said I could do *commercials.* Paramount interpreted my contract in a different way. I found myself in the very uncomfortable position of being pitted against an organization—and its individual employees—that I liked very much and still had to work with every day. It was embarrassing, and grueling, and ultimately a big life lesson.

If I'd examined my contracts with a magnifying glass before, now I read them with a microscope. Asking for a few extra days to look over the contract, just to be certain, is never too much, thank you very much. The same could be said of anything important in life. Apply total focus throughout. Don't rush. And don't involve yourself with anyone who wants you to make a decision or finalize an agreement before you're good and ready. You're worth more than that.

The Paramount lawsuit was a big lesson for me in the possibility of genuine resolution and forgiveness. Both sides ended up with what they needed out of the situation. As fraught as that whole period had been, when the case was decided I was quite happy with the outcome, and they were, too. Although we had both fought hard against each other in the courtroom, the conflict never seeped into our working relationship.

Seeing this was possible even in such a high-stakes situation has allowed me to aim for this same kind of resolution in other areas of my life. It's a conscious focus on forgiveness that has released me and the other parties, and for which I'm incredibly grateful. While cutting people out when necessary has always been very difficult for me, forgiving them and moving on has always come naturally. Forgive, be flexible, and move forward. Those are the strategies that have lit my path to winning, not to mention making it possible for me to be able to look at myself in the mirror and have respect for the woman staring back at me.

NEVER SPEAK OF IT AGAIN

Once you've had a tabloid say you fear your husband gave you and your unborn baby AIDS, you tend to be a lot more sympathetic to the fact that there are real people—and their innocent families—struggling to continue their normal lives beneath the shadow of their public embarrassment whenever a scandal erupts. Such compassion is a good thing, because when you've been an entertainment reporter for more than a decade, you're bound to cover more than a few sensational happenings. No matter how salacious or unsavory the scandals I covered were, I always tended to have sympathy for those involved. Particularly because, having had my own marriage get dragged into the tabloids, and sometimes with stories that weren't actually true, I was very aware that the behind-the-scenes reality might be different than the headlines.

Occasionally, a scandal touched me more directly, sometimes for surprising reasons. I was working at *ET* when Gary

Hart, a married Colorado senator and Democratic hopeful in the 1988 presidential election, was publicly outed for his involvement with a young woman named Donna Rice, who'd been seen leaving his Washington, D.C., townhouse and famously photographed with him on the unfortunately named yacht *Monkey Business,* on a trip to Bimini. I was not assigned to cover the story at this point, but I knew Donna, we grew up in the same neighborhood and went to high school and college together. When I saw the reports that painted her as a seductress, I thought how awful it must be for her while the media sharks circled around. Then I got a call at the office. It was Donna Rice. She had not really spoken about the whole affair yet, and she was calling me to get my take on what she should do.

Donna was a year behind me at Irmo High School, where I was a cheerleader, and we both went to the University of South Carolina, where she was a cheerleader. I knew her family and knew she'd been brought up with small-town values. Donna was well aware she was facing a media firing squad, and I could only imagine how devastating it was for her to have made a foolish mistake that landed her in the eye of a hurricane, which she knew was devastating to her family. She told me she was off track at the time and had strayed from her faith.

This situation was new not only for Donna, but also for the media, and there were no precedents. I took my best shot at advising her when I told her: "Go on the record once, do Barbara Walters, come clean with what's true, and then never speak of it again," is the gist of what I told her.

She did do the interview with Barbara Walters, but by then

the vultures were out for blood. She told me she got hundreds of offers. *Time* wanted to put her on the cover. *Playboy* wanted a pictorial. Starting price: one million dollars. Her story shifted the way the mainstream media covered a scandal. She was being chased, and stalked, and couldn't go home to South Carolina and risk her family being hounded. At *ET* we covered the ongoing story, of course. One particular day I was on set with Mary after one of our packages ran, and she and I had some "host chat" about the situation, during which I was not quick to paint Donna as a vixen. Donna later told me, "You really stood up for me on air at a time when it mattered. I was so grateful to hear your supportive comments."

The scandal died down soon after Hart withdrew from the presidential race, but up until then, Donna said she realized that she had to walk with faith and just keep going. Amazingly (and to her credit), Donna has never talked about what happened between them, while always maintaining that their relationship was not sexual. She gave an interview to a Christian magazine about the strength she got from returning to the flock, but she took her grandmother's advice about the interviews: "Don't talk. Whatever happens with his career, you'll be blamed."

Donna and I remained friends, and I was impressed with how she admitted her mistake and went about the hard work of forgiving herself and Gary Hart. She didn't make excuses. She gracefully reinvented herself in later years, getting married to a good guy named Jack Hughes, and creating the nonprofit organization Enough Is Enough, dedicated to issues related to child pornography and Internet safety.

LEAD BY EXAMPLE

Cue the tension. *Leeza* had launched strong, with great ratings, but a few years in, the ratings slumped, and we all knew we needed to make some changes. For those in charge, this meant bringing in a new executive producer. She came from the world of conflict television, where dubious booking tactics and the practice of misleading guests were often a common by-product of getting the show on the air and keeping it competitive. I got the feeling that for us to be competitive, I would soon be asked to loosen up and ratchet up. Producers from some of the other shows were paying guests, sending gifts, making promises, and doing anything they could to put together cutthroat episodes that would kill in the ratings. I knew it looked as if we were at a disadvantage because we didn't go there, but still, I believed in the integrity of our approach and stood my ground.

This new woman was brought in to "fix" the show, and there were problems from the start. During one of our tapings, she stormed out of the control booth onto the stage and stomped out to where I was with our segment producer, as our live audience sat a few feet away, taking in the spectacle. She was glaring, hands on her hips, gesticulating and yelling about everything that she thought had gone wrong. As I recall, f-words were flying.

I tried to defuse the drama of the moment by nodding and tried to distract the attention away from the fury-fest. I was so embarrassed and upset. Was she really having what my mom would call a full-on hissy fit, right here in front of everyone? I've always really respected the audience, Dick Clark–style. I would never in a million years have embarrassed her, or any of my colleagues, in front of our live audience. And I wasn't going to do so now, even though her behavior would put her in strong contention as a guest on a segment called "My Boss Is Insane." I managed to hold on to my manners long enough to work through the production issue to the point where she returned to the booth. But the incident lingered in my mind long after we wrapped shooting for the day.

The question was what to do about her attitude and behavior. I didn't want to come off as someone who was whining because she couldn't take the heat. I just couldn't shake how she'd spoken to our staff and me in front of the audience. I could have forgiven her for the greater good of the show if I thought her toughness was just an act or a technique to keep people on their toes. Then I might have been willing to see where she took it. But it became increasingly clear it wasn't. I continued to notice that she was being unnecessarily tough on my staff, whom I really loved. These people cared and worked their butts off, spending an extraordinary amount of time to produce the best show possible. It was my job to protect them, and that's what I intended to do.

I decided to send her a letter, allowing it to stay between the two of us and allowing her time to take in the words and think. When I sat down to write it, as upset as I was, I chose to give her the benefit of the doubt. *This is not who she really is, or who she's going to be going forward,* I thought. *She's expected to come in and do something big, and so she's scared.* I consciously framed my words from that point of view.

In my letter, I made sure she knew how hard the staff worked for us, how much they did, and how much they cared. I reminded her that they loved to be recognized for their dedication to the show. I was hoping to passively suggest a different way for her to get the best out of my team, thinking maybe she just hadn't thought to approach it that way.

I suppose someone that brash is immune to impassioned pleas of any kind. It was as if I'd never sent the letter at all. Her negative, destructive behavior didn't go unnoticed by the execs. But it took a while. That was a very difficult time for me because those one hundred and thirty employees, that was my family, and that was our life. I kept thinking that because I couldn't bring her around and make her "nicer," I had failed everyone. She broke my heart.

Thankfully, I didn't have to storm into anyone's office and demand that she leave. She was removed by the powers that be when her negative approach failed to get the results they'd desired. Chalk this one up as a victory for the nice guys. As it played out, this was another moment when I was glad that I didn't let myself get pulled into the swamp of negativity and conflict she was dumping on the show. Although it took me a while, I was able to forgive her for berating my staff and undermining me. I had to assume that she had never felt the kind of safety and support that we all gave each other on the staff, and she was operating under some misguided notion that because her neck was on the line, she had to be tough.

The thing is, I can be tough, too. I care about the outcome of everything I do, and I'm willing to fight to make sure it's great. But that doesn't mean being a bully or compromising my belief system to get there, so I won't berate or be argumentative or dismissive. I've always believed you're not responsible for how other people act. You're only responsible for how you respond. People will bring their energy to their jobs—mostly, they're bringing their childhood—but how you deal with it is up to you.

FORGIVENESS CAN BE FIERCE

Transitions are tricky.

Happy Days was about to end its legendary run at Paramount around the same time I hit the air on *ET*. As my tenure at Paramount drew to a close, the world was a very different place. And now, everything was about to change.

I'd been approached about becoming an anchor at the nationally syndicated newsmagazine *Extra* in 2000, and it seemed to be the right offer at the right time. My talk show was wrapping up. I was closing the door on sixteen years at *ET* and leaving my home base in Hollywood at Paramount to go "over the hill" to Warner Bros. in the Valley and join the Telepictures family. I'd gone through four presidents while I was at the lot, and I don't mean studio heads. From my first day, when Ronald Reagan was in office, through George H. W. Bush and Clinton, to my last day, eight weeks before George W. Bush was elected.

I knew it was all winding down, and I guess I should have been ready, but despite all my rhetoric about embracing change, it was still hard. When I took the job at *ET*, I was a childless single woman. When I took my name off the door outside the entrance to our stage, I had married and divorced. I'd given birth to three kids who grew up knowing that *Cheers* was taped next to Mommy's stage, but not having any idea that for naptime at the lot's preschool, they were bunking next to the kids of some of the biggest stars in the world. When she was in kindergarten, my daughter used to sit right out of camera sight on *ET*, by the desk with the lights in it, meant to illuminate the ladies' legs. When he was little, Nate came out and greeted the audience before I taped episodes of the *Leeza* show, like he was running for office.

Those days while I was at *ET*, I'd always liked *Extra*, which at that time was seen as being edgier, because it covered some sensational stories I wasn't sure I could be comfortable with. I wanted the job, but in order to take it I needed to be certain it was a fit, and that they'd be open to hearing about where my lines in the sand were.

For whatever reason, *Extra*'s offer included an ultimatum that the talks had to be completed by midnight on a given day, and that if they weren't, they were walking away. With this pressure on us, the conversations between my reps and their reps grew nasty during a series of phone calls that became increasingly personal. By the day of our deadline, the situation had devolved into a war of egos between reps on both sides of the deal. On the final day, several calls happened, with one side or the other hanging up on each other every time.

As the evening wore on, one of the key players, Jim Paratore, the president of Warner Bros. Telepictures Productions, said he was no longer available that night. There was one more call around nine o'clock, which also ended with a hang-up. The deadline loomed. I thought this kind of childish behavior was ridiculous, but regardless, it's often where negotiations end up and I didn't know how to get things back on track, or if it was even possible to do so.

I paced by my desk, questioning my moves and looking for a solution I'd somehow overlooked, when my friend and VP of Leeza Gibbons Enterprises, Jiminy Cricket himself, Joe Lupariello, approached my desk. I had some walls up that were new to me. My marriage was shaky, my mother had been diagnosed with Alzheimer's, and I was about to leave a studio that had been such a home for me that, even after our show ended, my car just headed in that direction no matter where I was going. I wasn't feeling much like myself.

"It's done," I said to Joe as he was wrapping up the office. "I don't know what to do to make it better."

"I'm sorry, Leeza," he said.

"I'm just going home," I told him and began the short drive to my house with my head full of questions.

I was in my car when Joe called me.

"Do you *really* want this deal?" he asked.

"Yeah," I said. "I think it would be the right move for me."

"Why don't you just give Jim a call then, and let him know that?" Joe said. "And that, yes, there are minor points, but you guys can work through them."

I paused for a long moment, and then I smiled. It was a supremely simple idea that was absolutely brilliant, and an approach I hadn't thought of in the midst of the drama (and ego) of the high-stakes talks I'd been embroiled in all day.

So I called Jim myself—no middlemen, no subterfuge—and we were able to put the deal together, just like that. In order to make that call in the spirit of harmony that was required, I'd had to release any frustration I'd had, or any false sense I'd had that we were adversaries. Instead I focused on the fact that, really, we both wanted the same thing: for us to find a mutually beneficial way for me to join his show and be part of making it even more successful.

For years after that, I would take the same tactic: start by remembering that business (and life) is all about relationships. And then, break down a situation to its elemental parts and take direct action with those involved to achieve the best possible outcome for *all*. The key element, though, is to engage your optimism and be fiercely committed to that. "Things work out best for those who make the best of how things work out." Thanks again, Coach John Wooden, for advice I use almost daily.

I always think that in a negotiation it's best to make sure the other side knows they will get what they need. That's different than saying their demands will be granted. But when they feel their basic needs are met, they tend to be more open to giving you what you need. Having said that, don't give without getting. I like to be the side to give something up first, just to set the right tone, but it has to be reciprocal. Some people feel you need to get the other side to fight for a concession, so they feel better or stronger than they would, "getting it for free." Not me, not as long as I stand firm on the fact that my concessions come with a string: one for me, one for you. I'll start.

While trying to negotiate, it's definitely a time to engage your empathy and not take things personally. That's what Joe reminded me of when dealing with Jim. If you can see the pressure the other side is feeling, then you can understand how to get them to give in to what you want. You know your own pressure points, but you don't want to get trapped by focusing on just your side of the deal. Instead, listen intently and get the other side to answer as many questions as you can. When either side starts getting personal, by calling names and slamming down phones, you both lose. Being willing to walk away is a vital part of the game, but doing it in a crass way is never necessary. Being nice and treating people with respect and fairness are really the power positions. And slow your roll. Being in a hurry means being sloppy, and seeming weak, and almost always hurts your deal. Jim and his team were shrewd enough to impose a hard deadline (whether it was artificial or not) and it did just what they hoped. I started spinning and rethinking my positions. Negotiations can get heated, but when you sign on the dotted line and shake hands, you are on the same team. Don't go back to the table until you can offer more and get more. Shut up, be grateful, and deliver!

So, I took the job at *Extra*, I was on the payroll, I had a parking place, a hair and makeup team, and a positive attitude, but all of that wasn't enough when I was set to interview Cher.

Her publicists pulled the interview I was scheduled to do with her for *Extra* because they weren't sure it was a good venue for her. Well, I wasn't having it. I called back and pressed for an answer as to why.

"The show has a reputation for being sensational and too tabloidy," they said.

"That's just not the case," I said. "And besides, that's not my reputation. I'm asking you to trust me, and to have faith that we will be responsible and respectful."

They did, and we were.

Once I commit to something, I'm committed. I think you have to be all in or get the heck out. Play hard for the team that signed you.

I made lots of memories and friends while I was at *Extra*. It was an important stop in my journey because I was very vulnerable at the time. I felt raw and a bit wounded by life, so I was looking for a situation where I felt protected and safe, and I had lots of requests and boundaries to try to make that happen.

Well, looking back now, I know that it's not your employer's role to make you feel safe when you're a reporter whose job is to risk feeling uncomfortable at times, in order to deliver the story. For example, I didn't want to cover celebrity divorces when kids were involved who might be hurt. I didn't want to work the red carpet. Because I felt as if I needed protection, I tried to protect others. It made perfect sense at the time. I had walls up because I felt as if I'd run away from the home where I'd been for so long (Paramount), and I didn't have my true north (my mom) to help me see things clearly anymore. The studio honored the requests that were reasonable, and out of appreciation I tried hard to add value to the show. It worked. At least for a little while. I loved my colleagues and my producer, but my focus was on following the pain that was leading me to make a difference for other families like mine, who were facing the helplessness of Alzheimer's disease. Change was calling me, but all I knew was television. I'm grateful to Lisa Gregorisch and the others for giving me a venue where I could use my belief in myself to keep growing my career. That base helped me to rebuild my confidence and get back onto much sturdier ground. Once I could steady myself, I could dare to move forward and be willing to introduce myself to the person I needed to become to open the door labeled *Change*.

OTHER NO-NOS

You've got to know your audience. In 2004, I did a speech at a jewelry convention in Arizona. Trying to relate my words to the news of the day, I mentioned Janet Jackson's recent nip-slip wardrobe malfunction during the Super Bowl halftime show, and because I was going for comic effect, I made a joke about nipple rings that didn't go over. It was really a lame attempt to tie in how the jewelry industry could capitalize on the trending faux pas. I can see now that I was ridiculously wrong, but I didn't know the room, and so I didn't see right away what I'd done.

Well, my agent received a call from the client, who said that I had not delivered what they wanted and they didn't want to pay. I was horrified. I can't stand that feeling of disappointing anyone, so I cold-called the client back, apologizing, and then I did my best to make it up to her by offering to do another speech for free *that they could approve ahead of time.* While she didn't want my makeup speech, she was open to hearing my apology for not being sensitive enough. I was embarrassed and I really did feel bad about it, but I had delivered what I was contracted to do and I had put in the time to do so, which I felt should still warrant payment. In the end, I think we both felt resolved and heard and I did get paid. I think she turned around because I didn't get defensive or try to tell her why I said what I did. Instead I tried to correct the situation (which I think surprised her). Again, forgiving yourself, admitting you made a mistake, and owning the moment can all go far, and definitely much further than digging in your heels and attempting to defend a questionable position just because you're embarrassed and don't want to admit it.

Don't be that person who is always bringing up another problem or reason why something went wrong. Whiners aren't usually winners. Instead, focus on solutions by taking action. This doesn't happen by standing on the platform at the top of the trapeze bar, thinking about jumping. Take the leap. Reach out. Grab the next bar.

THE SECRET OF FORGIVENESS

There is no time limit on adopting forgiveness as a point of view and I'm asking you to trust that if you take this step, it could be a game-changer for everything that comes after.

If you hold grudges and can't forgive, that's like letting someone be a squatter in your head. Don't give them this emotional space! Chances are the person you can't forgive might not even have a passing thought about the thing that is eating you up.

Usually, healing comes before forgiveness, but what if you can't heal, and you can't gain the compassion you need to understand that people who hurt you do it because they have been hurt themselves? Do this. Decide right now that when you're "wronged," or when someone does something you don't agree with, you will be fluid, like water. Soften over all the hard edges and flow wherever you find obstacles or closed doors. It's easy to be mad at someone for lying to you. It's easy to blame a colleague for trying to trip you up. It's next to impossible to forgive a spouse for cheating. But the price you pay for hanging on to these feelings is limiting *you*. It's really your thoughts that are hurting you more than anything that happened. Those grudges are way past their expiration date, and you're the one they're really harming, so throw them out. If you can't get there, forgive yourself for not being able to let them go and try again tomorrow.

CHAPTER SEVEN

No Whining, Just Winning (Optimism)

When I was a late-blooming sixth grader who had yet to develop breasts like my female classmates, my mom had the perfect, positive outlook and an ingenious solution.

"Yours are coming," she said.

"Really?" I asked, doubtfully looking down at my flat chest.

"Yes, really," she said, grinning. "And besides, what God's forgotten, we'll stuff with cotton."

Genius, right?

I always knew I'd have my parents' love and support no matter what, and that they would catch me when I fell. I have to tell you, though, when I was in the tenth grade, I had an experience that might have had me questioning that a little bit.

My dad has always been my hero for so many reasons. He is the one who showed me that if you want to lead and be successful, you have to risk being unpopular. You have to stand up and face down your fear. I had plenty of fear when I stumped for Daddy in front of a crowd of several hundred when he was running for State Superintendent of South Carolina. It was the spring of 1974, and being a seventeen-year-old on the campaign trail seemed like the coolest thing ever.

Our whole family was involved, wearing our little straw hats with a ribbon announcing GIBBONS above the brim. Daddy and my brother had gone to some other town in South Carolina, leaving Mom and me to take on an important venue in Bamberg County. I found all this very exciting and was strangely confident when my turn came to take the stage (a patch of grass under a huge oak tree). It was spring, and I was wearing a peachy little sundress along with a bronze tan I'd acquired from a preseason sunny day, on which I'd used my cocoa butter and Sun-In to get ready for the summer season at Myrtle Beach. I was chewing on the inside of my bottom lip (a habit I still have when I'm anxious) when Dad's opponent approached me.

"Well, isn't this sweet?" he said, with his thick southern accent. "You are the cutest thing to show up and go out there to speak for your dad."

Suddenly I felt a pinch on my bottom.

What?

Had this man actually reached under my dress and pinched me? The organizer of the event then walked up to us and said it was my turn to speak. I walked away without saying anything to the lecherous man, but as I took my place, I heard myself, in a calm southern voice, say to the crowd: "I was going to tell you about why my dad is best qualified to lead our state, but instead I think I'll talk about his opponent."

I didn't dare glance over in that direction, so I just plowed ahead.

"Do you really want to vote for someone who just reached under my skirt and pinched my behind?"

If there were gasps, I didn't hear them. All I could think about as I went to find my mother in the crowd was: *Oh no. I'm not so sure Daddy will be okay with this.*

"You tell 'em, darlin'," Mom said, beaming as we bolted from the venue.

When Daddy found out, he wasn't mad. In fact, he said he was proud of me for having been able to shift my focus to what really mattered. It was a big moment for a teenage girl. My parents' support allowed me to believe that any problems I encountered would be temporary, or if not, I would be able to recover and regroup soon enough. This ingrained optimism and ability to reset very quickly was incredibly helpful during the rocky moments in my life.

As I grew older, I began to analyze the power of optimism and the mechanism of how it works, and it's not just a way of thinking. It's a skill that can be strengthened, just like a muscle, through frequent use. The successful people I've interviewed say it is the key to building and maintaining their success and attaining their next set of goals. If you're running your companies, or leading your teams or your family, with servant leadership—wanting everyone to win and get their needs met—you're smart. That's optimism at its most effective, and you can see it spreading when others want to sit next to you and work with you. They want what you have!

Simply put, I believe optimism is the secret to the good life and that it can spread like an airborne virus to infect us all with a better way to approach tough times. When we add positive experiences to our emotional bank accounts, we build up reserves, like credit on account. So, during times like many are facing right now—times of feeling cheated, disenfranchised, hopeless, or insecure—you can debit that account. They say you can't "save up" on your sleep, but thankfully, you *can* save surplus optimism. Imagine if enough people had enough deposits in their emotional banks to feel they could weather any storm. How much fear could we eliminate?

Optimism pays. Think about this study of law school students conducted by Suzanne Segerstrom, the author of *Breaking Murphy's Law: How Optimists Get What They Want from Life—and Pessimists Can, Too.* She found that, for each point of optimism a person had, on a scale of one to five, they ended up earning an additional $35,000 a year. Good reason to keep the faith, baby.

More support for how optimism creates dividends is found in the book *Unfinished Business: Women Men Work Family,* in which author Anne-Marie Slaughter says that happy workers are 12 percent more productive than their disgruntled peers. And productive workers are successful workers. That feeds the bottom line. It's all connected, and it all adds up to greater abundance and quality of life.

SUPREME OPTIMISM

When I was in elementary school, we lived in a trilevel house that I was certain was a mansion. It's understandable when you consider that, as a preschooler, we lived in Washington, D.C., in a little apartment with a tiny bedroom for Mom and Dad and a Murphy bed in the living room for my brother and me. Actually it was the living room *and* the den *and* the kitchen. My mother could stand in one spot to make dinner and make the bed.

I was as happy as could be when Mom took us on walks through the zoo, which was a staple for us, since money was scarce and the zoo was free. For a treat, she gave my brother and me each an ice-cream cone. That's it, just the cone. No ice cream. We didn't even know we were missing anything. By that example, Mom taught us to focus on what we have and not what we don't have. And we had perfectly good cones! My aunt Wayne later found this circumstance so upsetting that she sent Mom 25 cents a week, with strict instructions that she was to use it to buy us ice cream. Through such windfalls, I developed a solid belief that good things happened to me, and that if something was bad, we'd figure out a way to get through it.

Of course, there are times when even the staunchest optimist should probably hang up her jumpsuit. By the time our family moved into that trilevel house, I was unstoppable! Right next door to us lived a soldier named Frankie. He had served in Vietnam and had a hot car he washed in the driveway with his shirt off! It was just him in his army fatigue pants and the sound of Tom Jones singing "What's New Pussycat?" on the radio. Dreamy.

My friend Suzette Hawkins and I had just gone to the dime-store to get the outfits that we were certain would change our fate. They were polyester, hot-pink jumpsuits with spaghetti straps and a row of ruffles across the chest that made us look stacked! Bell-bottom legs with a matching flounce. I worshipped Diana Ross and just knew if I could look and sing like her, Frankie would fall desperately in love with me. I practiced my dance moves to "Stop! In the Name of Love" a million times.

Frankie must have been, I don't know, like twenty years old, or so. I figured he'd wait for me, and I never quit believing . . . at least until third grade started, and I finally gave up.

My point is my optimism carried me through most things. Until the next thing came along. And you know what? That's a winning formula.

OPTIMISM COMES FIRST

I was lucky enough to have an optimistic outlook ingrained in me from an early age in small ways that really count. Not that it's always easy, no matter how many blessings we're delivered, and I've had plenty. No matter how much I achieved, I've often felt like one big epic fail. As is typical, the advice I gave to others on my shows, and in the articles I penned for women's magazines, was easy to dish out but much more difficult to follow myself. I really did believe it was possible for me to have it all. I had to buy into this fantasy because I was on the top of the balance beam, and I didn't dare to look down.

During this "I am woman, hear me roar," phase of my life, I was all in. Jeff was my assistant at the time, and he was skeptical. As he recently told me, when he heard me describing my Norman Rockwell life to the press (gushing about making time for everything), he listened incredulously, really hoping it was true. Because otherwise, I was setting myself up for a big fall.

Well, Jeff was right to worry. But he didn't know then what he knows now. I am always going to put the best face on everything, and if there is a way to at least try to make something true, I'm on it! I still think dreams always come a couple of sizes too large and that's how we work our way into them. Pessimism is exhausting and a big old energy suck, so choose to be deliberately optimistic. Of all the things I couldn't control, my way of thinking was the exception. I'm glad I dared to set the bar so high, though, in terms of what I expected from my life. In many ways, it was my belief in possibility that got me through the long, hectic days I was living at that time. Also, I think that being so busy finally forced me to rely on others, even though, as I've already admitted, it took me a long time to get there.

Our business can steal your soul; it can deplete and depress you, without regard for (or because of) how hard you're working. When I feel out of step, I look to the women I admire who always seem confident and hopeful, like Diane Sawyer, Maria

Shriver, or ABC News anchor Robin Roberts. They've got the world on an optimism string. So which came first, the confidence or the optimism? Always the optimism. That's the thing that causes us to believe we have it in us to make things better. It thrusts us forward and that leads to confidence. I always think about how Robin's mother told her to "make her mess her message." She has shared her optimism generously and shown how it's helped her through her breast cancer diagnosis, bone marrow transplant, and grief. When you're a person who sees the bright side, you are always attracted to others who see it your way.

When my marriage to my sons' father was ending, even though I felt wounded and betrayed, and he had his own list of grievances, the real thing I could never overcome in that relationship was that he just couldn't find a way to accommodate my optimism. He usually thought it was naïveté. And I could never make room for what I saw as his pessimism, or what he called his realism. We were fundamentally different people, with fundamentally different spirits and ways of experiencing the world, and that was the deal breaker. Years later, as we both look on with pride at the fine young people our children are becoming, I can see we're both much happier being who we were meant to be, in our own lanes.

Years ago, I saw an episode of *Oprah* about someone in a coma, and it really stayed with me. The medical expert on the show reported that, even while in a coma, people have awareness of the energy and intentions that others are bringing to the room. I took that to heart. Wherever you are, whatever you're doing, somebody is receiving your energy. I know that's what happens during televised Dallas Cowboys games, which Steven has watched religiously with his father since 1981. As an eleven-year-old boy, when they first started this tradition, Steven would never have imagined that, one day, his dad would not be jumping up when their team scored, cheering at the screen with him, but sitting silently with a blank stare that I know all too well. Steven's father has Lewy body dementia and can't say "I love you" anymore, or even lock eyes with his son to show that he's aware of his presence. But that's the thing. He *is* aware of Steven's presence, his love, his heart, and his intention to deliver something uplifting to his dad.

I was backstage at an event for ACT Today! recently, ready to go onstage to help drum up support for treatment options for children with autism, when I met a young man with autism who I was supposed to introduce as one of the performers. I could tell he was blind, but I couldn't tell he was a brilliant singer. And then, his mother helped him onstage, where he sang "Lean on Me." We were all spellbound. How could this blind kid with autism connect so brilliantly with an audience that he couldn't see? I asked his mom if he always came alive like that with a crowd.

"Yes," she said. "His blindness and autism are just inconveniences. My son is on a path of purpose, and he knows it."

That was my moment to receive inspiration from someone I will probably never see again but whose optimism ignited mine. I left feeling renewed as a mother, and more certain as a storyteller that such optimism is no small thing. It's the *only* thing.

But moments of adversity are exactly when we have the most hope of turning things around. Everybody wants to be a diamond, but nobody wants to get cut. But you know what they say, diamonds are polished under pressure. And so are we.

We have the power within us. I've been given extraordinary opportunities to help others through my career, but you don't have to be a therapist or a politician or a TV personality to see that someone is hurting and take a step toward them. Don't just ask them to let you know if you can do anything to help. Do something. There is always *something* you can do. They'll tell you if it's wrong, but at least try. It's in the trying that we change the world. I've learned this through working with caregivers in our communities at Leeza's Care Connection. If your friend or neighbor's family is facing something really difficult, tell them you're making two casseroles, and you're going to bring one by. And while you're there, grab their dry cleaning and drop it off for them. Walk the dog. Rake the leaves. Don't wait to be asked. People who are feeling that overwhelmed aren't going to ask for help. One of my favorite pieces of advice I got from my mom: "Show up. Do your best. Let go of the rest." That's the easiest way to apply an optimistic outlook every day.

NEXT TIME, TRY TEQUILA

It may seem ridiculous, but among the many professional challenges I've faced over the years, none has proven as difficult as pouring myself into a minuscule spandex outfit and letting my-self be whirled across the studio on season four of *Dancing with the Stars.* Now, I'm well aware that, if this is the worst thing I ever face, I will be very lucky indeed, but that doesn't mean it was any less difficult for me.

I knew the experience was going to be extremely chal-lenging, and it was only due to the pressure from my friends, employees, and family that I even said yes.

"You're being a hypocrite," my daughter said. "You're al-ways telling us everything you want is on the other side of fear, so how can you not say yes?"

Busted.

I had a temporary leave from sanity and committed to do-ing the show, but I knew right away things weren't clicking. The problem was, I tried to approach this new trial with my same old tricks. When the other contestants were interviewed going into each episode, they talked about how much the grueling schedule was hurting them. Not me. I was in my little bubble, or at least trying to pretend I was, and I always answered with "Oh, I'm learning a lot. Everything's great."

In reality, everything was far from great.

For once my optimism and focus on working harder and doing more were not going to save me. It wasn't just that I did a terrible tango and I failed at foxtrot, but I was so funda-mentally stretched by the whole thing that my carefully con-structed image of myself soon began to crumble—in front of the cameras, no less—which felt like being emotionally na-ked in front of the world. Of course, these are the experiences where the real lessons are. In this case, greater self-knowledge, and even deeper and more lasting optimism, were waiting for me, along with the body glitter and spray tan. I just didn't know it yet.

During the course of the episodes I lasted through, I learned lessons that continue to serve me well to this day. Before I even had my ballroom shoes, I called my therapist and said, "I'm not coming in for a while. I'll be working out my control and intimacy issues on air in front of twenty million people."

And that's exactly what I did. So, here's what I learned along the way:

Ask for help. We are not alone in life's adventures, and yet we invariably try to handle things by ourselves. Not me, not this time. Knowing how hard it was going to be, I put out an APB and gathered up a team of Ballroom Buddies, ranging from my life coach and nutritional guru to my Pilates instructor and circle of goddess girlfriends.

Put your trust in others. Okay, let's be real about the costumes on *Dancing with the Stars*. This is an environment where more is more, and too much is never enough. Body glitter, Swarovski crystals as eye shadow, spray tans as natural as the color of Play-Doh, and eyelashes so long they can cross two counties. When I first met with the show's hair, makeup, and wardrobe teams, I was petrified.

"I'm the oldest woman on the show," I said. "You have to protect me."

The contestants don't get approval over their costumes or music during the show, so you really are at the mercy of the glam squad, which actually turned out to be a good thing, once I learned to trust and have a little faith.

Each week, Kirsten from wardrobe sewed a butterfly into my outfit, reminding me that I was undergoing a transformation. I loved that. And I've held on to that way of looking at life since the show. The way I see it, we all get to decide in life when we are ready to break free of our cocoons and spread our wings. No one is in charge of our transformations except us. Your best life shows up when you do.

They'd told me that once I got into it, I would be ready to show skin, take some chances, and turn up the sizzle. *Not likely*, I thought, clinging to the idea that I was entering my fifth decade and I should dress appropriately. For my first dance I looked like a nun or something, pretty much all covered up. Who knew? They were right. Week four, I walked out onstage to dance the paso doble in a rocker-chick meets *Beyond Thunder Dome* getup. It was bare in the middle and open in the back, just a halter and miniskirt, really. My hair was about four stories wide and twelve stories high. Hair that high was very close to God, and so I guess you could say I was very spiritual as I danced (badly) to Bon Jovi's "You Give Love a Bad Name." Like Patty Hearst, I had become my captors!

Be coachable. As important as it is to be strong and focused, the most successful people are often the ones who are the most teachable. Having virtually no dance experience, I had to be open to my professional partner, Tony Dovolani, a wonderful man who nevertheless pushed me to the breaking point again and again. Many days I felt like a second grader being scolded because she hadn't memorized her math facts. Letting go of any and all defensiveness and opening up to the answers he offered was essential in this dance drama. With only four days to learn each routine, we had no time to develop a safe, mutually respectful relationship. And so I had to strengthen myself to receive coaching as it was given, and do my own emotional cheerleading, at home alone in the bath, where no one could see me cry.

Fake it until you make it. The judges kept telling me to loosen up and let go, in order to put more Latin heat into my mambo.

"Find your tramp," Judge Bruno Tonioli said.

Well, I tried my best to shake and gyrate my hips, but my inner tramp remained elusive. I resorted to having a henna "Tramp" tattoo applied to see if it would help me to channel my trashy side, but the best I could get from the judges was "Elegant but stiff." Hmm . . . too much of a lady to sell the sizzle? I had to reset this image I had of myself, so I could reset it for them.

Undaunted, I played Latin music in my car nonstop, convinced the judges had it wrong. *I am sexy and sassy,* I thought. *And besides, this is my birthday dance.* On the very day of the live mambo, I celebrated my fiftieth birthday. I share the day with my mother, who was also born on March 26, and who was then trapped in the silent mausoleum of her Alzheimer's disease, although she would have had no trouble tramping it up in her younger days. I danced my booty off in honor of that courageous woman and for all those who felt that they had no reason to dance. I felt proud of my performance; even if the judges scoffed, their scores were irrelevant to me that night.

But you know what? Being judged is not always a bad thing. The dancing judges kept telling me that I was stiff. I was not taking enough chances. I was playing it too safe. Yes! That was so true. Forget the dancing; in my life I had become way too analytical, way too concerned about how things worked and how I might best control them.

I finally decided to really listen to what the judges were telling me, with no defensiveness, just looking for the greater gift in their words.

"You're relying on Tony too much."

Do I do that in life? Am I giving away my power to other people too often?

"You need to loosen up."

Wow, that one hurt because I knew it to be accurate. It wasn't about my hips and my arms. It was about my worldview, which had become too heavy and fear based in the wake of my recent divorce and my mother's Alzheimer's diagnosis. Listening to the judges gave me wonderful insights into what I needed to work on in my life.

Get real. I've always been very conflict-averse, and I hadn't yet learned to work through this fear, as I'm trying to do now. I think if I'd been willing to be more realistic about the situation and what it really required—having a combative relationship with my partner, Tony—it would have worked better for both of us. There was no way I was going to confront Tony, so I did what I always do, which is to take it on myself to fix everything. I determined to try harder, be more coachable, to get my nutritionist to ramp up our work together.

Still it wasn't enough. My assistant at the time, Bobby, finally pulled Tony aside, since I clearly wasn't going to.

"Leeza doesn't deal well with this kind of negative input," he said. "You're not going to get the best out of her if you continue to beat her down. That's not how she thrives."

Of course, Tony didn't have time to figure out how the heck I was going to do well. His job was to teach me to dance, and to get me out there every week, using what he knew how to do, and that was it. And so we struggled along, show to show. Sure, we got by, but if I'd gotten honest with myself, it could have gone much better.

When my friends Zaidee and Terri came to Los Angeles to see me dance, Z was very frustrated by my lack of progress.

"You've got to try harder," she said.

"I *am* trying, Z!"

"Well, you need a strategy," she replied, looking like she was about to reveal all.

"Great, but I'm all out of ideas. Why don't *you* come up with a strategy?"

"Oh, I've got one," she said. "TEQUILA!"

I would have seriously gone there if I had to confront another week on the show.

My paso doble proved fatal. After I did the press line on the night I was voted off, I hopped into a car provided by the show to go home, change, and go to Jimmy Kimmel's studio in Hollywood to tape an appearance. As we pulled up at my house, I quickly realized I had no keys, which meant no way of getting into my house. Going into crisis management mode, I made my way to the back of the house, where I maneuvered myself through the doggie door still wearing my hot little leather mini. If I had shimmied that well on the show, I might not have been voted off! As it was, I couldn't have known then how well this lesson in trying to preserve my grace, class, and positivity under pressure would serve me when I had to figure out how to handle myself during my *Celebrity Apprentice* experience a few years later.

I learned that my mambo was miserable and my paso was pathetic, but I also learned how much I could take and how much I had to give. I learned to let go of outcomes and just listen for the music to tell me where to go next. I learned I couldn't always lead, that I had to rely on someone else to make a move, and then I could react and respond. It softened my rough edges, while it toughened my spirit. It gave me my butterfly wings and a new take on optimism.

COUNT YOUR BLESSINGS, NOT YOUR STRETCH MARKS

When my husband, Steven, and I first met, I was fifty-one and he was thirty-eight. Yes, that's thirteen years younger than me. I didn't consider him a romantic prospect. I knew he was a great guy, so I set him up with friends who were great girls. Girls in their early thirties who made sense for him. At first, I couldn't get past the age difference, which was a nonissue for him, until ultimately I believed him when he said he could take care of himself in our relationship, and he didn't need me to worry about him. It was just that those numbers, and everything they represented, loomed large in mind. When we first started dating, I used to wish that I'd known Steven when I was younger, so that we could have had more time together, and so I could have had more of life's special moments with him, like having a child together. Back then it was hard for me accept the compliments he gave me and simply be grateful for them.

"You're so beautiful," he would tell me.

"Thanks, but if we'd been together when we were thirty . . ." I said.

"Well, then you would have been arrested," he teased me.

"You know what I mean," I said.

"I just want to look at what we have, and not what we don't have," he said.

He didn't just say it once. He said it again and again. When I became obsessed with the fact that he'd be missing out if he chose to be with me instead of a younger woman who could give him a child. When I became worried about the future and how he might feel about our age difference then.

Finally, he wore me down, and I started to listen to him.

"I can see that this is something important to you, but will you agree to table the discussion about children for a year?" he said.

I did.

"I'm still good," he tells me every year.

That man is a good negotiator. (And, as I'd later find out, a great husband.)

I realized that we'd needed to have the years of experience, and all of the relationships that hadn't worked out, in order to create the people we are now, who fell in love and are building an incredible life together. And, finally, I admitted how perfect our relationship is, exactly as it is now.

Initially we'd both said that we were never going to get married again. I mean, we were adamant about it. Getting married again? Well, that would just be ridiculous. And then, we felt so strongly that there was nothing for us to do but get married. Because we're both very traditional, we believe the highest honor, and the greatest gift, we could give each other was to commit through marriage. We had no higher vessel in which to hold our love and to represent how we felt. And so that's what we offered to each other. At our wedding, Troy and Leksy became ordained ministers so they could perform the ceremony. Nate handled the rings. No one was there but the five of us at midnight on the rooftop of the Montage hotel in Beverly Hills, where we'd had our first date.

We asked Leksy to sing "Bless the Broken Road," popularized by Rascal Flatts. She'd never heard the song but it was just like her to nail it. We echoed every word with the emotions in our hearts, because it really is how we feel about each other: *"This much I know is true / That God blessed the broken road /*

That led me straight to you." Each relationship that ended, and the lessons we had learned about ourselves through them, prepared us for each other.

If I'm going to accept the blessings of the experiences that brought me to Steven, I also have to accept the years it took for me to live and process them. I guess you could say I'm counting my blessings and not my stretch marks. I have learned from him: why should I focus on my wrinkles or my flaws, when he's really not? And so now I can just accept compliments from him and be grateful for all of it. I'm certainly not going to argue with him if he thinks I'm the sexiest woman he knows! Bless him! Every woman deserves the same.

I know it might seem like a disconnect for someone who likes to be in charge as much as I am and is as career focused as I am to be married to my manager and president of our company, but I finally feel that the pieces fit, and that really hasn't meant being married to my work. There's a very fluid language to our professional collaboration, and we use our differences to our advantage. Steven and I don't keep the same office hours. He's a creature of habit, and he likes to have a place to go work every day. I really can create my workspace wherever I need it to be. So I don't work at our office much. This gives us both the space we need to flourish.

Not that our working life has always been totally seamless. There was some bickering early on that only happened in the evenings. When I don't have any physical reserves, I can retreat and resort to sweeping things under the rug, while Steven is intent on hammering out every detail of everything that went wrong and what we can do better next time. So we came up with a plan that works well. If I'm too mentally drained or physically exhausted to get to a consensus, understanding, or even a truce, I have a go-to solution.

"I think it's probably best if we talk about this tomorrow," I say.

That's when Steven knows it's not going to get us where we need to go, so we agree to put a pin in it until we can both recharge and replenish.

Because we touch base so often during the day, when we come together at night we're never on different wavelengths professionally. And that makes it easier for us to transition into being on the same current personally, at the end of the day.

And, thank heavens, just at the moment when I'm finally able to take help from others, I have someone there to help me. When we travel, we're sometimes out for two or three weeks at a time, and together around the clock. But we still have enough space—and closeness—within our relationship to make it work for both of us. We've both sort of self-assigned our own duties. As the president of our company he's in charge of bookings and appointments, travel logistics, communications, encouragement, travel-size toiletries, and cash. I make the coffee and ask a million questions. I'm not even kidding!

Truth be told, he shoulders almost all of the details, which changes everything for me. I've always had the pressure of making sure that the kids were okay, and making sure that *everything* was okay, on top of making sure my work was okay. Now Steven makes sure everything's okay, and I just focus on the work. When he's working in a similar capacity, I do the same for him. That's been really, really nice.

We've both learned so much that contributes to our current happiness. He's learned along the way that he'd rather be happy than right. And I've learned if he's going to do all of these things for me, I'm certainly not going to tell him how to do them.

The best way to prepare for the future is to be totally present now. That's what I try to do in all areas of my life, but especially in my marriage with Steven. He and I are very aware that what we have together is not a birthright. There is no guarantee you're going to find someone that you love, care about, and respect, who feels the same way about you and has your best interests at heart. That's the stuff of dreams. I have a little dish in my kitchen that says, "Sometimes right in the middle of an ordinary life, love gives you a miracle." Steven is mine. Having been in unhappy relationships, both of us feel very blessed to have found each other, and just when we were ready, too.

IF I WIN, YOU TAKE IT

One of the best side effects of optimism is that it can help you to take chances, even when all signs would suggest it would be better not to. In 2010 I was approached about hosting a show, *My Generation*. It was devoted to all of those topics that are really juicy and sexy for me: how to live your best life, how to reinvent yourself, how to create abundance, how to give back. But I knew from experience that it can be hard to create opportunities to market shows on topics like this. The show was being created in partnership by the AARP and Maryland Public Television, which was worlds away from my prior experience, having lots of easy successes with syndicated network shows that were distributed widely. This show was on PBS and that really appealed to me, even though I knew it could be tough to shift it into high gear. Still, it was right in the pocket of the content I most wanted and loved. I was falling all over myself with enthusiasm about doing it.

Steven got involved, in his role as my manager, and started asking the pivotal questions.

"Does this show really have legs?" he asked. "Can it sustain itself? What are the chances for its success?"

We tried to get involved under the hood as much as we could, suggesting a new title that wasn't also the name of a daytime soap opera that had just begun airing, and that wouldn't automatically exclude anyone and everyone who wasn't in "my generation." But that wasn't happening, and so I simply threw myself into doing the best hosting job I possibly could, while growing increasingly frustrated by the lack of growth in the show. Here we were, making content I was extremely proud of, and I loved the producers and crew, but just not enough people were seeing it.

Because our team delivered some fantastic stories, I stayed optimistic. And then, in 2013, I was nominated for a Daytime Emmy. As a producer, I'd seen our show take home plenty of awards, and I was always proud to have my name along with our team on the victory list, but my nominations as an individual had failed to capture me an Emmy of my very own.

This was the same year my friend Suzanne Somers had been nominated in the same category. She called me and we got all giddy talking about it

"Look," she said. "I think you're going to win, but if I win, will you accept the award for me?"

Suzanne knows I'd do anything for her, but *what*?

"Alan and I are not certain we are going to be able to make it," she said. "I have a live performance, and I'm not sure it will be over on time. Would you do it?"

"Of course!" I said. "What do you want me to say on your behalf?"

"Well, you don't need to worry because I really think you'll win, but if not, just say whatever comes to mind."

My buddy David Michaels, who is the senior executive director of the Daytime Emmy Awards and Events, called me about the request.

"We've never had this happen before," he said. "But would you do it?"

"Yes, of course, and if I win, I'd like Hillary Clinton to accept my award!" I joked.

The night of the awards, as I waited for our category to come up (it was almost last), I was focused so much on what I might say for Suzanne that I didn't have any thoughts about what I would do if they actually announced *my* name.

They did. I kissed my husband and walked up to accept

with a big smile and a lot of gratitude. This was pretty cool! As I stood there, I realized that my dream of having the golden statuette with my name on it had come true, but it really wasn't about me. As clichéd as this sounds, I really believed that I shared this award with everyone who'd worked so hard on *My Generation*. TV is not a solo sport and if time had allowed me to call them up onto the stage with me, I would have. As I posed for pictures with the Golden Girl, in my turquoise dress and fluffy hair (old dreams die hard!), I got it. This wasn't a show that I generated or controlled. In spite of my frustration that I "wasn't enough," or that the show wasn't growing fast enough, this was my way to get my first personal Emmy! You never know when just doing your best will actually lead to big rewards (as well as the ultimate reward of just knowing you were doing your best the whole time).

SUPREME OPTIMIST ALERT

Nobody can work a pair of pom-poms like Betty White. Not to mention, if there's one celebrity who's synonymous with Fierce Optimism, it's her. She's smart, pretty, funny, and she works more and tries more than most people half her age. (Betty is ninety-four!) And so her life is the perfect representation of what happens when you really do try harder than anybody else and you're nicer to others along the way. You get to be Betty White. You get to find yourself in the golden years of a *long* career, still be in it, and have every single person you've worked with applaud you and admire the way you have maintained your work ethic and integrity. A 2011 poll by Reuters and the French global marketing research firm Ipsos found that Americans think of Betty White as the most popular and trusted celebrity out there.

I've known Betty for years, having interviewed her for *ET* and had her as a guest on *Leeza,* not to mention the many occasions on which we'd run into each other socially. I'd always admired her. And then, a few years ago, I had even more reasons to put Betty on the top of my "Women Who Always Win" list. My husband created a charity, the Beverly Hills Athletic Alumni Association, at his alma mater, Beverly Hills High School, to raise money for its athletics department. Every year they organize a fundraiser and this year I agreed to host. I mean, I was sleeping with the organizer; what else could I do? That night Betty White was being honored as one of the school's distinguished alumni and everyone was over the moon about it. She'd been very gracious about saying yes, but we decided to press our luck. We checked in with her agent, Jeff Witjas, who happens to be Steven's mentor from their days together back at the William Morris Agency, and hinted about how great it would be if Betty sang the school's fight song during her acceptance speech. In the most gracious way possible, he mentioned that her production schedule was brutal, and she gets invited to everything every night of the week. I got the hint. Maybe we were lucky just to have Betty White at all! The last thing we wanted to do was push Betty, so maybe she should just accept the award, and that would be enough.

Fast-forward to the night of the event, which was being held at the Beverly Hilton. Partway through dinner, we lost electrical power. As in all the lights and ovens went out. Everything. They didn't have a backup generator. And so that meant not only did we have no lights, we had no microphones. And we'd yet to announce any winners. We were able to light some candles as we scrambled for a solution. Someone brought a megahorn to the stage, and I did the introductions that way. However, the team had made video packages to celebrate our honorees, and they were not going to roll. So we rearranged our lineup so that the awards with the video packages were at the end now, and we vamped enough to keep things going until finally, over an hour later, the power returned.

At this point, the event had gone on for an eternity. Betty was the last award of the night, and no one had left, because they all wanted to see her. Meanwhile, it was getting later and later, and she had to be on the set of *Hot in Cleveland* bright and early the next morning. I kept sneaking glances at her from my post backstage, and there she was, seemingly carefree. Whereas the majority of Hollywood stars would have had their people give us their apologies while making their getaway, she stuck it out, showing so much class and respect.

Finally, we got to Betty. She burst onto the stage as though it was five in the afternoon, just so vibrant and fresh and happy to be there. Flirting with the guys onstage behind her. She was incredible. So incredible, in fact, that it seemed to just beg for pom-poms.

"Wow, wouldn't this be a great moment . . ." I said, pausing dramatically. "How many of you guys can remember the fight song? I bet you Betty White remembers it all."

I made sure to set up the moment in such a way that she could get out of it if she *really* didn't want to do it. But she took the ball (and a pair of pom-poms I'd strategically stashed in the podium earlier in the night) and she slayed the song and got everybody on their feet. Betty White rules! She's such a pro. To me, that was just one more example of what a really beautiful person she is, and how making an optimistic, generous spirit the hallmark of your personality can only lead to the best stuff that life has to offer.

I saw Betty recently and asked her, "What are we gonna do for your one hundredth birthday?" She didn't pause before saying, "Oh, I can't make it . . . I'm working."

OPTIMISTS ONLY NEED APPLY

When I was project manager the first time on *Celebrity Apprentice,* Trump asked me who our weakest link on the team was.

"We don't have weak links on our team," I replied with sincerity. "We have shining stars. Some shine more brightly than others." On *Celebrity Apprentice,* and throughout my work life, I chose where to focus and what to emphasize. You have

that same choice. Choosing to focus on how other people oper-
ate, how they feel, what they want from you is not a soft, weak
quality. It's a smart strategy for earning respect and claiming
gratifying victories that are built on allowing others to perform
at their best by showing them how to get there. Vince Lom-
bardi said, "Winning is a habit." So, if you really want to have
an edge at work, develop the habit of consistently seeing things
from the perspective of your colleagues.

As I learned from my experience on *Celebrity Apprentice*,
pressure really does turn us into extreme versions of who we
are. When I won, I received a lot of attention for having managed to be nice and come out on top without ever having had
to compete with any of the backbiting and sabotage that can
make the show so fun to watch, but that's just not the person I know how to be. Really, I think the quality that helped
me the most on the show was my optimism. Believe me, I got
down. I got *low* down, but my optimism allowed me to always
bounce back in time for the next day of taping.

I was glad I had spoken with Holly Robinson Peete and
Marilu Henner, my friends and former contestants on the show,
before I left for New York to begin taping, so I didn't put too
much weight on the fact that during the first week I was *miserable.* They told me it was such a different world, and so disorient-
ing, that in the beginning I would probably pray to be fired! I was
alone in New York City, thousands of miles from my husband,
kids, friends, and anything that resembled normal or regular. I
was facing some pretty tough behavior on a daily basis, and I was
trying to look for land mines and analyze the competition.

I played it cool on the show, but every night I called home to talk to Steven and unload. Bless him; he probably just put his phone on mute and let me rant. I couldn't help but vent sometimes, about whatever mean thing somebody had done that day. I don't mess with mean. I can usually drop the drama and cut the crazy. But this was an overload of all of that!

"You have no idea what it's like, honey," I said to Steven during one of our calls. "It seems like most of the contestants have people to support them, their assistants, or publicists, or hair and makeup. I'm here by myself. I didn't even have time to pack the right clothes."

It was award-winning whining, which he usually calls me on, but I think he felt bad for me!

None of this mattered, of course, because during the tasks, you're on your own, and it wouldn't help if you had an entire staff of Mensa members and Angelina Jolie's glam squad waiting in the wings! We couldn't even use our own phones, much less our own posse.

I think this was a defense mechanism, because I wanted to be as good as everyone else, and I was feeling insecure. I was a last-minute addition to the cast, and I just wanted him to acknowledge that I had my work cut out for me because of this. I also wasn't at the top of my physical game during taping (I'm sure it was all stress related), but I barely had time to get my doctor on the phone to address the problem. When I did, I was told: "You really should just get some rest." *Right, that's helpful. I'm averaging four hours a night. Do you think I should up that to four and a half?*

I reminded myself not to get tripped up playing this game and turned my attitude around, so I could strategize the best approach for outlasting the other contestants and winning big for my foundation. Because I was able to unload with Steven, I was able to recharge and keep going. (Baby, thanks for the safe place to land.)

By the next morning, that frustration was always gone. Normally I woke up to find that the negativity had evaporated in my sleep. But if it hadn't, I made a conscious effort to put it aside and focus on the new day. Marilu and Holly were right when they said that after that first week or two, I'd be chomping at the bit for the next assignment and totally ready to get in my lane and run.

Running my own race always means a return to old-school values and wisdom. Simple stuff that fits into any business at any time, like asking yourself: *Am I keeping my cool and staying level-headed?* When the finale of *Celebrity Apprentice* aired, I had to smile when I heard an announcer describe the standoff between Geraldo and me like this: "Level-headed Leeza versus Hurricane Geraldo." I have big respect for my friend and colleague Geraldo, but operating with hurricane-like force in business (or life) would drive me insane. Meanwhile, it's perfect for him. (It makes sense, in retrospect, that his team was actually called Vortex, and mine was Infinity.) I'm comfortable letting others gather up as much steam as they want. Some define that forcefulness as passion, but for me it's a distraction.

There are always going to be drama kings and queens in the workplace. Don't get sucked into their storm. Learn what you can from their outbursts of energy. Listen before you react and don't provide commentary as a way to feel you belong or fit in. Use old-school wisdom to keep your wits about you and think before you speak. I'd rather be the master of my silence than a prisoner of my words.

Who knew a reality show would turn out to be one of the most rewarding moments of my professional life? I got to draw attention to my foundation, and raise money for the work we do, and I also got a chance to show that you can win on reality TV, and in real life, by playing it your way, with your own rules. All you have to do is know where you're going, what you want, and what you're willing to do—and not do—to get there.

For me, it meant I could lead like a lady with my optimism out front and use that to outlast the competition. The truth is, more than 75 percent of success comes from being optimistic. It's all about how your brain processes complications. Successful people see stress as a challenge to figure out, not a potential threat to take them down, and they know how to get others to support them, also by being positive, not threatening. It's not a secret formula. It's the basics.

REARVIEW WISDOM

We all hit the wall. I get comments from people constantly about how lost they feel in their personal and professional lives. To that I often say that the first step toward finding your way is to actually take a look around at where you are. Do you need to get out of the passing lane and downshift long enough to test-drive some new attitudes? By this I mean, don't get sucked into the grueling details of whatever is bringing you down, and the negativity of the other people who are involved. Instead, choose optimism and integrity, and see what this new positive outlook can do for the situation. Then, if that doesn't work, ask yourself what your next step needs to be in order to make your life better. Maybe you need to stop achieving and start receiving?

Sure, there were times along the way when I've felt negative, depressed, stressed, or defeated (remember the time I used Coke cans as ice packs for my tear-swollen eyes?). These moments have always been my cue to open up my window on the world—or my WOW factor, as I call it—and see things another way. How you see your life is everything.

My window on the world (W-O-W) has always been what some would call my pie-in-the-sky positivity. If I'm ever intolerant, or negative, I say to myself, "Oh WOW." And that reminds me: *Raise your window, girl, because you're not seeing it right.*

Reframe. Regroup. Redo.

Research shows that optimism has a genuine effect on your ultimate success or failure in business. Since optimists can see a bright future, they have more resilience to face the potholes in their path.

Create a force field of like-minded people around you. If you get a loop of positivity encircling you, you'll be less tempted to abandon course and go back to the nitpicky stuff, so choose people whose dispositions are upbeat. I know compelling arguments are made to support those who have pessimistic points of view, saying that this type of negative thinking, and more optimistic thinking, are both used to motivate performance. Okay, so if they are both strategies for coping in an uncertain world, I'm still going to go with the Blue Skies team when I consider the scientific connection between optimists and good health. Being healthier, less depressed, and better able to cope with disease and recover from surgery is enough for me. Not only that, but research shows that an optimistic outlook early in life can deliver better health and a lower rate of death during follow-up periods for the next fifteen to forty years. I'll try to jump down off the soapbox now, but even after I do, no one can argue the benefits of feeling hopeful.

I know very few people—if anyone—who can put things in the rearview mirror faster than I can, or who can *not* hold on to a grudge like I can. I always joke that it's one of my few talents. (That, and falling asleep on a plane from liftoff to touchdown!) Instead of letting myself indulge in negativity, I've always just stayed focused on what I've needed to do, and done it. Over the years, that's worked out pretty well. The power to create a better set point is all yours, and it always has been.

KNOW WHEN TO LEAVE THE STAGE

I once overhead Steven talking with a colleague on the phone, saying I don't have a rewind button: "Leeza never tells me, 'I need to do another talk show or host a morning show.' If those things come, fine, but she's not interested in going back and is always looking for what comes next."

He's right. Instead of just going for the obvious next step, out of some need to be in the comfort of where I've been and what I know—just to prove I still can—I've decided to remove all limits. This is one of the things I love about Richard Branson. From the risks he takes in business to his risky attempts to break world records, he's always asking: *What interests me? What excites me? What do I want to do?*

As for me, I've said to Steven, "I think it'd be great fun to do a game show. Or voice an animated movie. Or produce live events. Or go to med school."

I've got a long list of "Maybe I could."

The goal isn't necessarily to be back on the top of the same mountain, when the view from the top will always be the same. The goal is to do things that I'm passionate about, and things that are challenging and rewarding.

The one aspect of my former jobs that I really do miss, though, is live audiences. I miss that special reciprocal relationship. And that's why I've started doing speaking engagements. I love the shot in the arm I get from being immersed in the energy of other people who are either giving me something (or not giving me something) back.

Fortunately, I also get that energy through my foundation work. When I go into an empowerment group at one of our centers, or a dance therapy class, or any of the services we offer, just receiving the energy in that room is amazing. When you can stand in a circle, hold hands, and sing, while your husband is dying, or your wife has forgotten your name, that's the ultimate form of optimism. I have such respect for family caregivers.

Whether you are thirty, forty, fifty, sixty, or better, the days and decades ahead are another chance to turn the page and start over, whenever you want. You can declare that today, that *every* day is a new blank page. You can paint, scribble, erase, and create anew, any way your heart desires. But that's hard to do when you love who you used to be.

Believe me, I know that it can be very difficult to relinquish the crown, but it's a must. I think you can learn so much about people from the way they exit a situation, whether it's a job, a stage in life, or a relationship. You can certainly learn a lot about yourself. These are the moments when you *really* get to prove who you are by becoming who you need to be. That's why in interviews about how people made it to the top, I always asked them not about their accomplishments, but about their failures. *That's* where the real lessons are.

When you're handing over the crown, and changing jobs or positions, you have the opportunity for a moment of real self-awareness. There's nothing worse than somebody who's stayed on the stage too long. When your music changes, it's best if you can move forward to the next stage, letting go of who you were before. That takes trust that there's new music playing for you somewhere else. In order to grow and live your best life, you need to find that next new thing.

Along the way, we often get scared. And what happens

when we get scared? We lose the strengths we've gained. And we clutch on to what we have, even if it's honestly not making us happy anymore. We think if we just hold on tighter, we can keep our lives exactly the way they were before, because it feels comfortable and safe. But it's often when things get ripped from our grasp that we can finally let go, in order to open up and receive what's next—maybe even what's better. Trust me, giving up control was a hard one for me. I've always talked a great deal about living fearlessly—and aging fearlessly—but sometimes I'm terrified, just like I'm sure you are sometimes, too.

And it's understandable. Change is hard for most people. Very hard. Remaining optimistic during times of transition, especially those that aren't entirely of our choosing, can be nearly impossible. Whether it's a job or a relationship, most people will hold on for dear life even if the situation is making them miserable. It's like a plane's turbulence. When it gets rocky, we grip the armrest, as if somehow that's going to keep us safe.

I've seen it so many times during my years in Hollywood: the producer who wants just one more movie premiere. That pop star who wants just one more hit. For me, when I left TV to start the foundation, I was tempted to reverse course and go back to what I knew, too. The only way I was able to remain optimistic was to see this transformation as a chance for me to embrace new challenges and successes.

I have an image of an eagle taped on the edge of my computer screen. It reminds me to soar above the clouds of negativity. Here's why. Most birds will try to find cover and get out of the rain, but eagles approach it differently. To escape the turbulence of storms, they simply fly above the clouds. Just think about that, and how your perspective changes everything. You can soar above it all, too. You really can.

Shonda Rhimes, the brilliant writer-producer behind several game-changing megahits like *Scandal* and *Grey's Anatomy*, recently published a book, *Year of Yes*. I thought it was fantastic and right on point. As successful as she's been, she was just as miserable. In the book, she details how she transformed her life as a social introvert by agreeing to do things that were frightening to her. As she says, she did it by practicing "badassery." Gotta love that. I want to challenge you to say yes to a binding contract with yourself to be optimistic. Do it completely, passionately, fiercely. It will make any latent pessimism put its tail between its legs and whimper away.

"Cynicism is a self-imposed blindness, a rejection of the world because we are afraid it will hurt us or disappoint us," according to Stephen Colbert. He reminds us that cynics always say No, but saying Yes is how we grow.

Optimistic people say Yes. They have confidence in the likelihood of successful outcomes. So expand your life, your business, your love, your opportunities, and your bank account by saying yes to all these not-so-secret strategies we've talked about. Cream separates from the rest of the milk and lands at the top. That's where you'll be, too, if you bet on yourself and move away from those who don't believe in your (fiercely optimistic) way of doing things. Any badass will tell you that. Now get out there and Play Nice to Win Big.

THE SECRET OF OPTIMISM

Before Alice got to Wonderland, she had to fall down a deep hole. Maybe you did, too. Maybe you've never reached Wonderland. But just because things didn't necessarily turn out the way you wanted them to before, doesn't mean the next go-round can't be better even than your wildest dreams. The past doesn't equal the present. Sure, you can thank the past for all the great lessons. And then, dismiss it! That's the secret. To optimism, and pretty much everything else. If you can first forgive yourself for having had a negative perspective, you're home free. If you can be realistic without being fatalistic, you win.

Mentally put on a tiara, or a crown, or whatever else you need to remind yourself of who you are and let others know they're dealing with someone who isn't going to be knocked off her optimist's throne. And remember, that crown will fall off if you don't hold your head up high, so shoulders back, especially on the days when to do so is a challenge. The King himself, Elvis Presley, said, "When things go bad, don't go with them."

Engage your optimism, not through positive thinking but through positive feeling. You have to feel yourself being successful, because in the psychology of success, physicists tell us it's your emotional energy that attracts or repels things into your life.

So use your optimist magnet to attract others who think like us!

I hope you'll share your stories about what qualities you've used to strategize for your own success and happiness. I'd love to connect with you, so look for me at LeezaGibbons.com, or @leezagibbons on Instagram and Twitter.

ACKNOWLEDGMENTS

Gratitude is the engine that drives my life, so getting to the end of this book and being able to offer thanks is the greatest victory. Here is an expression of my love for the people who show up for me, instruct and inform me, liberate and challenge me, protect me, love me, let me sleep in, and bring me a latte or a chardonnay.

Steven, I would have been content to let the thoughts on these pages exist other places, *any* place other than a book, if not for you. Your faith in me allows me to believe in myself. I love you more completely every day. Because we dream in the same direction, you often pluck my dreams out of the clouds in my mind and make them real before I can even say, "I wish" or "I want." How could we have created the beautiful life we have without being fiercely committed to our optimism? Thank you for understanding the late nights while I was writing, which often turned into mornings without my head ever touching the pillow beside you.

My three children are the greatest blessings ever given to a mother. Leksy, Troy, and Nate, I am so proud of you and so grateful that I have the gift of being your mom. You keep me laughing, call me on my stuff, encourage me to own my opinions, and allow me to live my truth. You are the foundation for my life, my love, my wishes, and my heart's desire . . . all caught up in your huge hearts and your beautiful smiles. I love you AFNMW.

To Lacy Lynch, my remarkable, soulful, supersmart agent and friend. "Never give up" is tattooed on your heart. Thank you for indulging my insecurities and my impatience, and for bulldozing full speed ahead toward winning with integrity. We make a great team. I fight hard. You fight harder. I'm grateful, Lacy.

I found a perfect home for my message at Dey Street/ HarperCollins. I'm grateful to Lynn Grady for seeing the value in this book and to your team, led by Julia Cheiffetz for guiding the vision. Thank you, Julia, for challenging me and supporting our path to publication with confidence and flexibility. Special thank-yous to Sean Newcott for your incredible, tireless work ethic, and to Beth Silfin and Joseph Poppa for your professionalism and encouragement.

As I was gathering up my stories on voice memos, thumb drives, and Post-it notes, grabbing facts from old journals, and calling friends from the past, it was Sarah Tomlinson who was sitting right across from me, helping me organize it all into something that made sense. Sarah, no one has a better attitude or a better approach to work than you. What a pleasure, thank you.

To my remarkable friends who contributed to the book, I love you for your beautiful support. To Andrea Ambandos, you are rock-steady in my life. Our friendship has grown stronger as we've grown older and my appreciation for you is limitless. For my "Twisted Sister" Julie Kozak, your ability to grow and be real, often in the face of heartbreak and pain, reminds me how important it is to strive for the courage you have. To Jeff Collins, you're always the first person to think I can succeed, whether it's winning *Celebrity Apprentice* or being a great mom. Thank you for your graciousness and generosity that always help me get there. Your kindness is legendary. Joe Lupariello, no one has more personal integrity than you, and along with Joseph Ferraro, you have inspired me with your energy, your love, and your commitment to doing the right thing. Loyalty doesn't come any better than "the Joes." I have so much respect and gratitude for you and couldn't love you more. John Redmann, you're the ultimate nice guy who succeeds in proving the power of positivity every day. Thank you for making the case for optimism so brilliantly. Dean Banowetz, I loved you from the minute you first lit a wish candle in front of me! Thank you for being so helpful no matter what I need. Matt Van Dyne, your friendship is always offered so effortlessly. Thank you for your optics on our time together. I am fortunate to have each of you as such meaningful anchors in my life, and I am thankful for not only what you offered me while writing, but for your love everyday.

To Olivia Newton-John, Mary Hart, Donna Rice, Dixie Whatley, Maria Hernandez, and Holly Tyrer. Thank you for allowing me to share times in your life and mine that, I hope, offer value to readers. The strength you have shown reminds me that women who believe in themselves and who support other women are truly unstoppable.

Steve and Kristi Welker, your "radical resilience" has inspired me from my very first days as a talk show host. I'm grateful for your example of courage and faith.

Bobbee Gableman, thank you for not only starting me on my career path, but also for consistently being there. To Billy Olson, I have always thought you were the coolest. Still do. I enjoyed the walk down *ET*'s memory lane.

Love to John McGill who, along with Mark Hopper, is so dear to me. How great is it to have gone through all the laughter, tears, and shenanigans to arrive at a bulletproof friendship? To Annette Haynie, my first professional friend in Spartanburg, South Carolina, thanks for helping me then, and now, to put things in perspective. To Deb Jenkins, no matter what, you are the one who is counted on to bring the muffins or bring the truth. Thank you.

Thanks to Caroline Greyshock, not only for the beautiful cover and back shot on the book, but for being a really lovely person with a lot of decency. Chelsea Bell, you've been there through it all and kept a smile while always searching for answers and solutions. I'm so grateful for that.

I have been deeply moved while writing this book by two women who have always won by being nice, even when it's not easy. They don't know any other way. Joan Lunden and Kathie Lee Gifford's stories of grace, strength, and optimism reminded me to keep going, and keep trying to do it as lovingly as they do.

I have learned so many of my strategies for success through my partnerships in business and from the people behind those companies. Thank you to Rick Bradley, Bill Guthy, and Greg Renker for twenty-five years at Guthy-Renker Corporation. Gratitude goes to Dr. Adrienne Dense, Senior Helpers, Philips Lifeline, and LA Rocks for living the principles I write about in this book everyday.

To my brother, Carlos; my sister-in-law, Anne Marie; and my sister, Cammy; we've had a rough year after Daddy's heart attack, but thinking we might lose him reminded us that we never truly lose anyone who lives in our hearts. Imagining life without you is impossible. Cam, my "Silly Sister," thank you for showing how powerful we are to become whoever we want to be, at any point. I love you all and the perfect imperfection that we bring to being a family.

Daddy, you've always been my hero. I have always tried to make you (and Mom) proud. More than that, I hope I have shown you how eternally grateful I am that you gave me a road map to follow where the signs along the way are clearly posted: "Try hard, help others, be loyal and grounded, grateful and gracious. Admit your mistakes, learn the lessons, and move on without bitterness or resentment." I learned from you and Mom to be kind and to just be me. You've taught me to be present today while seeing even better things for tomorrow.

To Mark Burnett, Donald Trump, Page Feldman, Eric Van

Wagenen, and the team at *Celebrity Apprentice,* I owe big-time thanks. This book started with you. For me, this was not just about competing on a business reality show, it was a turning point. All of us at Leeza's Care Connection and the families we help are grateful for the money I earned on your show to support caregivers as they take care of someone they love with a chronic illness or disease.

I offer my respect to the amazing competitors during my season of *Celebrity Apprentice:* Jamie Anderson, Johnny Damon, Vivica A. Fox, Brandi Glanville, Kate Gosselin, Gilbert Gottfried, Sig Hansen, Shawn Johnson, Kevin Jonas, Lorenzo Lamas, Kenya Moore, Terrell Owens, Keshia Knight Pulliam, Geraldo Rivera, and Ian Ziering. I learned so much from you, and I loved being on the show together, where we could raise money and awareness for so many charities. I feel blessed that we had the opportunity to show that each of us is best when we stay in our lanes and honor our own journeys.

To Jack Reilly, Marty Haag, and Harvey Cox. Although you are gone, your legacy lives on in so many like me; young hopefuls who fueled our dreams with your example and who climbed on your shoulders to see farther into our futures than we ever could have without your boost up. Thank you to these "bosses," and to all those who allowed me to be on your teams, in your newsrooms, and on the air with you to develop the optimistic strategies I write about in these pages. I'm a lucky girl.

ABOUT THE AUTHOR

Leeza Gibbons, one of the most well-known pop culture icons on the air, has an impressive background in entertainment and news media as well as advocacy for healthcare, wellness, and caregiving. A wife and mother, she's also a businesswoman, Emmy Award–winner, and *New York Times* bestselling author with a star on the Hollywood Walk of Fame. Her diverse career ranges from cohosting *Entertainment Tonight*, to her award-winning talk show, *Leeza*. She cohosted the syndicated TV newsmagazine *America Now* while also hosting the PBS show *My Generation*, for which she won the 2013 Daytime Emmy for Outstanding Lifestyle Host. In the same year her personal growth guide *Take 2* became a *New York Times* bestseller. In 2015, she won NBC's *Celebrity Apprentice*, becoming the second woman ever to take the title. A testament to her entrepreneurial savvy, Leeza recently crossed the one-billion-dollar mark in direct-response sales as a result of her nearly twenty-five years with Guthy-Renker, the longest studio/talent partnership in the history of direct response. Recognized as a social entrepreneur, Leeza is a leading voice for family caregivers. In 2003, to honor her mother's journey with Alzheimer's disease, she created the Leeza Gibbons Memory Foundation and its signature program, Leeza's Care Connection, which provides free support and services to family caregivers. In 2016, Leeza became the spokesperson for Philips Healthcare, a world leader in diagnostics, treatment, and preventative care. She also provides education and support for families facing caregiving challenges as the spokesperson for Senior Helpers. Leeza lives in Los Angeles with her husband, *New York Times* bestselling author Steven Fenton and is mother to daughter Leksy, and sons Troy and Nate.

These are the two men who always encourage me to play nice and win big, my husband and my father.

This kind of love and support means everything. (*Courtesy of the author*)

When you're positive and look only for the best, maybe you get to grow up and be Betty White . . . my favorite optimist! (*Courtesy of the author*)

Loyalty doesn't come any stronger than Olivia Newton-John. She has my gratitude forever. (*Caroline Greyshock photography*)

I've known competitive, loyal, and empathetic Jeff Collins and John Redmann since they started their careers. Their success reminds me that nice guys really do finish first. (*Caroline Greyshock photography*)